Mr. Ding's Chicken Feet

Terrace Books, a division of the University of Wisconsin Press,
takes its name from the Memorial Union Terrace, located at
the University of Wisconsin–Madison. Since its inception in 1907,
the Wisconsin Union has provided a venue for students, faculty, staff,
and alumni to debate art, music, politics, and the issues of the day.
It is a place where theater, music, drama, dance, outdoor activities, and
major speakers are made available to the campus and the community.
To learn more about the Union, visit www.union.wisc.edu.

Mr. Ding's Chicken Feet

On a Slow Boat
from Shanghai to Texas

Gillian Kendall

Terrace Books
A trade imprint of the University of Wisconsin Press

Terrace Books
A trade imprint of the University of Wisconsin Press
1930 Monroe Street
Madison, Wisconsin 53711

www.wisc.edu/wisconsinpress/

3 Henrietta Street
London WC2E 8LU, England

1   3   5   4   2

Printed in the United States of America

Library of Congress Cataloging-in-Publication Data
Kendall, Gillian.
Mr. Ding's chicken feet: on a slow boat from Shanghai
to Texas / Gillian Kendall.
p.   cm.
ISBN 0-299-21944-5 (pbk.: alk. paper)
1. Kendall, Gillian—Travel.
2. Americans—Travel—China—Shanghai.
3. Intercultural communication.
4. English language—Study and teaching—Chinese speakers.
5. Ocean travel.   6. Texas—Biography.
I. Title: Mister Ding's chicken feet.   II. Title.
CT275.K453A3   2006
910.4′5—dc22   2006007361

This book is dedicated to

my mother,

who encourages all adventure and
finds it everywhere.

Contents

Acknowledgments

Although this work is based on real-life events, I have changed names and other identifying details of ships, businesses, and people.

Thanks to my friend Margie Wachtel for reading the manuscript and telling me what was wrong with it, and for doing so with grace and manners that amount to diplomacy.

Thanks to Susan Shanshan Qian for giving me Chinese acupuncture to heal my repetitive stress injury and Pinyin words to heal my translations.

Thanks to Raphael Kadushin and Sheila Moermond at the University of Wisconsin Press for treating me, and this book, so well.

Finally, thanks and love to my partner, Nicole, for respecting a closed door and humoring a writer's moods.

Mr. Ding's Chicken Feet

Prologue
Salary—Generous

My boyfriend and I had just walked into the English Department's grotty "graduate student lounge"—a gray, drafty room with a stained carpet, a hundred mailboxes, and a bulletin board. As I went to check my mail, a flyer caught my attention:

ENGLISH AS A SECOND LANGUAGE (ESL) TEACHER NEEDED

TO ACCOMPANY A CRUISE FROM SHANGHAI, CHINA, TO GALVESTON, TEXAS, AND TO TEACH ESL EN ROUTE TO CHINESE SEAMEN, SHIP'S OFFICERS, AND MECHANICAL ENGINEERS. THE *EXPLORER* LEAVES SHANGHAI JUNE 23, 1991 (APPROX.), AND ARRIVES GALVESTON AUGUST 1, 1991 (APPROX.). ALL EXPENSES PAID (INCLUDING AIRFARE FROM HOUSTON TO SHANGHAI).

SALARY—GENEROUS

Before I'd finished reading it, I had ripped the flyer off the wall. Without looking up, I walked to the phone and dialed the number at the bottom of the page.

3

If there is one thing I'm good at, it's getting jobs. Having them I hate—at the age of thirty-one, I'd been fired twice. If I'm not kicked out, I invariably quit in less than a year. But I love compiling CVs, writing letters of application, and interviewing. Making this phone call felt like stepping on stage.

The contact person—a Mr. Olaf Nicholayssen—had a heavy Scandinavian accent, which relaxed me. I figured he might be self-conscious about his English and thus not too judgmental of other people—at least not teachers of English. In a slow, formal tone he said, "I am glad to hear from you, but—"

"Yes?"

"Well, the ship's crew is all men. I suppose I was not expecting a woman to call."

"I'm pretty comfortable in that kind of situation," I said, fast. "I've worked on Navy ships."

"Oh? You have been in the Navy?"

"Well, no, but I worked for them." I launched into the explanation: the Navy hired civilian teachers to give classes on board its ships. The teachers worked through a contracting college, and the sailors earned undergraduate credits. "Also," I said, "I've taught EFL overseas."

"Sorry, you've taught what?"

"EFL. English as a Foreign Language. It's very similar to ESL—English as a Second Language. I taught in Egypt for seven months and in Germany for almost a year."

"Is that so?" He sounded relieved. "Well, then, I would like to talk to you."

I learned that he was a manager for a large seismic operation that was hiring a ship from China. I had no idea what "seismic" meant, but I didn't ask: I could look that up later. The Chinese vessel and its crew were coming to work in the Gulf of Mexico for a year, assisting large oil companies. There would be only one other American on board during the journey, which would take about six weeks and would have no breaks and no ports of call. The more he spoke, the odder and more interesting the job sounded. Finally, Olaf suggested an interview for that Wednesday, June 3. "But one thing," he said. "Where are you working now?"

"I'm not. I'm a graduate student at the University of Houston, and the term just ended. I won't be teaching again until fall." Hence the impetus for my sudden interest in all things seismic: my checking account held less than three hundred dollars—not enough to cover July's rent. Student loan funds had given out months ago, but I had car payments to make and my half of the rent to pay. "So," I added, before he could change his mind, "I really look forward to meeting you on Wednesday."

As I hung up, my boyfriend, Martin, was craning over me, trying to read the job description. "What's this?" Peering over his little Gandhi glasses, he had the eager look of a scholar, a look I usually adored, but at that moment I resented his curiosity.

I flipped the paper over, so he couldn't see it, and said, "It's mine. I saw it first and you can't have it!" Every greedy impulse possible arose in me: I flashed back to that first Navy ship—the contractors had called to offer me the job, thinking from my application (and my name—then very unusual) that I was a man. Even though I'd had all the qualifications, that ship couldn't take women, and some guy had ended up getting that job. Later I'd sued the employer for sex discrimination and won a good out-of-court settlement, but the injustice still rankled.

"You can't do this." I folded the flyer into a wad and shoved it into my purse, then zipped the bag and crammed it under my arm. "Please, please, don't apply for it."

Martin, with his PhD in literature from Oxford, and his

ingrained, upper-class British accent, and I with my MA in English and years of experience, were both qualified to teach on the Chinese ship. But he'd taught in Japan as a prelude to his visit to America, and I was sure that if he applied, he would get the job and I wouldn't.

Martin grabbed my hands. We wrestled for a second; he was playing, but I hung on to my purse, grimly. Six feet tall, he had four inches' advantage, and he easily twisted behind to tickle me. As I writhed away, he got my bag, and a second later he was reading the flyer. "Gosh!"

"It's mine! You would never, ever have seen that if it weren't for me!"

Martin had to admit that was true—he was so tall he walked around looking at the sky and ceilings most of the time, or else he was hunched over to make sure he wasn't tripping. Consequently, he found a lot of change, but he missed much that happened at eye level. "Well," he conceded, "maybe I wouldn't have seen it if you hadn't, but I can still apply now."

"Martin, if you do, I'll break up with you, I swear. It wouldn't be fair."

"Fair? How fair is it to deny me an interview because you're afraid of the competition?"

"I will never speak to you again," I blithered. "I'll hate you for the rest of my life. I'll—"

"Stop." Martin handed over the flyer. "You wouldn't truly hate me, would you?"

If I said no, he might go for the job knowing he wouldn't suffer any consequences, but if I said yes, he might try for the interview to spite me. So I decided on the truth: "I don't know. I just don't want you to try."

"I knew you wouldn't hate me," he said, relieved. But I think that admission on my part wasn't why he relented and said he wouldn't try for an interview. I think he agreed in spite of, not because of, my manipulative tactics and desperate threats. I think he agreed not to go for the job because he loved me.

Although Martin and I had been struggling—first with whether or not he would come to America to be with me, and then whether or not he'd move into my one-bedroom apartment, and more recently what he'd do if I moved to Iowa to begin a different graduate program—I felt affectionate and secure with him. The security came from having known him for some ten years—we'd met during my junior year abroad, at Oxford, when he'd coached the team I rowed with. I had been the worst rower in the worst boat on the river, but Martin had guided me, and my crew, through the ignominy of repeated defeat and to the relatively calm waters of self-acceptance. I'd never be the kind of athlete he was, but I'd loved him, even back then, as my mentor in all things Oxonian.

A decade later, as I was starting my PhD, Martin was just beginning his two-year trip around the world. But he had aborted his travel plans after he got to Houston. After a few weeks' affair, we'd declared ourselves more or less in love. He'd moved in with his backpack, his Japanese kimono, and his life's savings. That had been the previous September, and he'd been with me for nearly a year. The whole thing surprised me, continually—that we'd become lovers, that I'd let him move in, that we had stayed together despite an eight-year age difference and some difficult, ongoing battles. It amazed me how we could be so happy together most of the time, and yet so unhappy sometimes too.

But that afternoon, when he relented, gave me the flyer back and told me he wouldn't get in the way of my applying for the job, and said he would help me however he could, I felt grateful.

As I was leaving the lounge, guilt got to me, and I put the flyer back up, although in a most inconspicuous place. I stuck it in a

bottom corner of the board, below an army recruiting poster, where
no one would look.

As we walked from my car into our apartment building, my shirt
stuck to my back, and I felt my freshly washed hair turning into
limp, oily strands. It was only 10 a.m., but the day's heat pressed
down the atmosphere, making the smog seem heavier and smellier
than usual. For the first time in my life I had allergies; my nose
dripped with a cold, unpleasant sting. The thought of leaving town
held enormous appeal.

In the apartment, I cranked up the air conditioning and started
preparing for the interview, which would take place in forty-eight
hours. I get charged up about interviews the way some people get
excited by auditions or significant dates. I dug out my summer suit
from the back of the closet and ran it to the cleaners for rush service.
I updated my CV, rephrasing a few job descriptions to emphasize
their nautical nature. I drove to Kinko's and made copies on heavy,
cream-colored stock, and I bought matching stationery and enve-
lopes for the thank-you-for-the-interview letter, which I drafted so
that I could mail it the same day as the interview, so it would be on
the interviewer's desk the following morning. Using precious dollars, I bought a new lipstick and had my hair trimmed.

The next day, I plotted the route and took a practice drive out to
the seismic company, just so that I wouldn't get lost before my interview. The office turned out to be over two hours from where I lived.
It didn't look far on the map, but the route wound through the wilds
of downtown and into the mess of freeways that tangled around
Houston. Traffic oozed, hot and slow, along the four-lane highways,
giving me time to gaze at the dreary businesses no one would ever
need or want to go into: auto-glass replacement shops, billiards-
table manufacturers, aquarium suppliers, hospital-uniform stores,

fertilizer factories, die-maker plants, and other gray, greasy, anonymous buildings. They were interspersed with fast-food chains, all selling the same pseudo-food to the same faceless customers in the same boxy cars. I was going to China and couldn't wait to get away.

As I started and stopped, braking for construction or halting at lights, I considered the possible questions that Olaf might ask me the next day, rehearsing various answers until I found those that seemed right. I imagined what he might be looking for: *a man.* I tried to think of how I could come across as capable and efficient, the kind of woman who wouldn't think twice about being the only woman on board.

In fact, I was thinking a lot about being the only woman on board. I thought it sounded intriguing and challenging—not just the part about being the only female, but being at sea for six weeks, trying to teach English to adults, learning about China. I wanted that job more than I'd ever wanted any other job, or almost anything else. In the days before the interview, my desire for it felt like a romantic obsession—I couldn't sleep, I ate over it, I talked about it endlessly. I called my mother, in New Jersey, and my best friend, in Philadelphia, and several other people around the country, just to obsess about the interview, and to get their prayers, visualizations, or advice.

Martin and I speculated at length about what "generous" (as in "salary—generous") might mean to a Norwegian seismic systems manager. Desperate for money, I would have accepted the job at virtually any wage, but I fantasized that it might pay well, maybe as well as the Navy ships had.

By the time of the actual interview, I was ecstatically prepared. I arrived ten minutes early, and apart from hyperventilating a little in the elevator, I felt confident. My cream-colored suit was pretty but businesslike, and my work pumps added to my height. My briefcase was packed with flattering letters of recommendation, crisp résumés, and several pens, in case I had to sign a contract. I felt eminently hirable.

As the secretary led me into Olaf's office, I almost fell off my heels. Someone who looked like a young Robert Redford was sitting with legs crossed on his mahogany desk, wearing jeans and scuffed cowboy boots. His hair was a fantastic gold, wavy and long by American standards.

He swung his feet down and stood up, coming around the desk to shake hands. He had dark blue eyes, and he was smiling as if we were real friends. "So," he said. "I am very pleased to meet you in person." His accent was even more charming than it had sounded on the phone: he spoke with soft, rounded vowels.

Somewhat breathless, I was glad to sit down, but he was so gorgeous I couldn't help beaming at him. I smiled through the whole interview. When he asked for my CV, and I stood to hand it over, I held my stomach in.

"So—you have done this sort of work before?"

"Oh, yes." Realizing that I was leaning forward too eagerly, I straightened my back and took a breath. "As I mentioned, I've taught English on two Navy vessels, one in the Persian Gulf and one in the Mediterranean. I've spent a total of three months at sea, so far. I'd like the opportunity to use some of my teaching skills for your company."

He pushed his lips into an amused pucker. "But I think that you were teaching Americans, is that correct?"

"Yes, on the Navy ships I taught writing, mostly, although there were some Filipino sailors who needed help with speaking English." This was quite an exaggeration, so I skipped to another subject. "Most of my EFL experience has been in other countries, although I taught in California, and we had a lot of Asian students." The Asian part was true, but they'd been from Japan or Thailand. I'd never had a single student from the People's Republic. "I've learned how to adapt my teaching methods to a variety of different students."

He nodded. "These men would be, well—" He paused, sucking air through his lovely, rounded lips. "They would not be typical for you." He explained that the captain, the first mate, and a few others would have gone to college and might have degrees, perhaps in engineering or electronics. But the rest of the crew would be mechanics and laborers, without much formal education.

"I see. How much English do they speak?"

"I don't know." Olaf looked up at the ceiling, thinking. "I was in Shanghai about a month ago, but we had an interpreter the whole time. I didn't have much time to talk to the men, but it seems to me that one or two of them spoke a little English. But their accents are very bad."

He went on to say that my job would involve tutoring the men who would talk on the ship's radio. The crew had to learn how to speak English well enough to use the radio in the Panama Canal and the Gulf of Mexico. If the Chinese people spoke unintelligibly, other vessels couldn't understand them, and serious accidents could occur. So at least indirectly, lives might depend on the English teacher's skills.

I began to doubt my ability to do the job. Was I getting beyond my qualifications? I'd had no real EFL training, just on-the-job experience. And these men sounded so . . . foreign. I didn't even understand their work. To take the focus off my own skills—or lack of them—I asked, "What will they be doing once the ship gets here?"

"The ship's task is to tow a seismic platform." He placed a stapler on the edge of his desk, to represent the ship, then a box of staples some distance behind it, to indicate the platform. "The platform carries machinery for imaging the ocean floor—basically looking for oil. The platform is almost as big as the ship itself, but it's flat. It's connected to the ship by cables about a mile long."

"You mean it floats a mile behind the ship?" I couldn't imagine such a thing.

"Yes, exactly. That means that when the ship crosses the path of another vessel, the other vessel must be very clear about the location of the cables. They're under water, you see. Invisible. So no other vessel can pass between the ship and the platform, because their propellers would destroy the cables. It would be a very expensive mistake."

I wasn't going to say so, but the whole proposition seemed both expensive and unlikely to me. It seemed incredible that Olaf's company was hiring a ship from China, but it wasn't my place to question their finances. I supposed that the equipment and labor cost less in a communist country, saving enough to compensate for the expense of the voyage.

Olaf held the ends of a pencil between two fingers, playing with it as he continued. "During the journey, the men will be getting the ship ready for operations in the Gulf of Mexico. On the way, they'll be making repairs and changes, as well as working on the computers that control the seismic operations. We're going to send a company representative, an American man, to oversee that part of the trip. But the Chinese will be working—they will not have very much time to study."

I was used to having overbooked students. In the Persian Gulf, the American sailor-students had worked twelve- or fourteen-hour days, seven days a week, on top of which they'd had to stand four-hour watches in the middle of their sleeping time. They came to class haggard and pale, apologizing if they were a few minutes late or if they had to rush out during class for a drill. Still, they had thanked me for offering the classes and told me that they were grateful for the change of pace and intellectual stimulation. "Sometimes, a class can be a good break for people," I said. "It helps them to have something else to think about besides work. How many classes will there be a day?"

"Well, that we don't know. There will be approximately twenty men on board, so perhaps four classes a day? An hour each?"

Small classes sounded delightful, but I was stunned by the crew's size. "Twenty?" Navy tenders had crews of about twelve hundred men and women; my last ship's *laundry* had employed more than twenty people.

"Maybe twenty-one. Let me ask you about remuneration. We are a new company, and quite frankly, I have never hired anyone for such a position before. You didn't indicate on your résumé how much you made on board the other vessels . . . ?"

That question I hadn't prepared for. I hadn't worked for the Navy for some years, but I recalled earning about $800 per course. "Well," I hedged, "that depended on how many courses were being taught. But if I had four at one time, and they lasted six or seven weeks, it'd be about thirty-two hundred dollars." I held my breath, because the figure was high. In fact I had made that much on some cruises, but not on all.

Olaf stopped smiling. He was making notes. "So that was about five hundred a week," he said. "For four classes."

"About that." I was drawing a breath to add that the Navy contract had been quite generous, and that I wasn't necessarily expecting it to be matched, when Olaf interrupted.

"Yes, I think we could manage that. The vessel is going to sail from Shanghai on the twenty-third of this month. The teacher has to leave for China about a week before that—by the seventeenth or so. That's about two weeks off; we don't have very much time to get ready. We'd have to equip the person with everything necessary to teach on board the ship—they will have nothing, not even pencils." He looked at me hopefully, peering from under his golden waves of hair. "If we did offer you the position, would you be able to get things organized?"

"Oh, of course," I said, as if I set up schools on ships every day.

He seemed relieved. "I think that we will be able to—yes, I'm sure that we can. I will have to go through some formalities with my colleagues, but I am sure that we can offer you the position as teacher on board the *Explorer,* for one thousand dollars a week. Plus expenses, of course."

A thousand dollars *a week!* I'd be earning four times what I made as a teaching assistant. In forty-eight hours, I'd gone from expecting financial ruin in Houston to going on an Oriental adventure for the most money I'd ever made in my life. I was euphoric.

But over the next few days, I recognized that I also felt afraid. I'd never been nervous about traveling with the Navy—the tenders on which I'd taught had been huge and stable, like floating villages, with state-of-the art communications and safety systems, including lifeboats as big as apartments. However, the Chinese vessel was going to be small, and the trip was supposed to last six weeks. I'd never been at sea for that long without stopping in port, and I felt irrationally afraid of the ship's sinking. Embarrassed, I told only my mother and Martin about my fears.

"Oh, well," my mother chirped into the phone, ever optimistic. "I wouldn't worry if I were you. Ships are very well-made these days; they hardly ever sink."

"But when they *do,*" I pointed out, "it's always some little Chinese engineering vessel. And you read it and think, 'Well, that's a shame, but at least there weren't many lives lost,' and it doesn't seem very important . . ."

She laughed and told me that I would have a wonderful time. Having served as a Wren in the English navy, she was thrilled that I would be working on a ship again. I could see the trip through her eyes: rounds of parties on sunset-lit decks, being served exotic drinks and Chinese cuisine, surrounded by male admirers. While I doubted her vision, it made me feel better to share it for a few minutes.

When I told Martin about my fears, he, too, minimized them. He was more interested in discussing *his* feelings, particularly his feelings about being abandoned for the summer. Having jettisoned his round-the-world itinerary in order to be with me, he was suddenly and resentfully facing an empty summer.

To appease him, I encouraged him to travel in the other states or Mexico; I suggested that he join a local rowing club and make some friends. I felt guilt way out of proportion to my sin of commission, leaving him for six weeks, because I also had a sin of omission on my conscience: I hadn't committed to staying in Houston for the next year. I was thinking of changing graduate schools, going to a smaller program in Iowa. My indecision made it hard for Martin to plan anything. He was doing short-term programming contract work, not knowing if he should try to get a real job in Texas or keep doing temporary jobs till I moved. If I did move, he didn't know if he could find work in the Midwest.

In time, I convinced myself that my fright about the ship's sinking was just a manifestation of my nervousness about the trip, or guilt about leaving Martin alone in horrible Houston. But as it would turn out, my fears were far from ungrounded.

An English Rat Chases
Her Luggage

In the two weeks between June 3 (when I signed the contract) and the morning of June 18 (when I was to fly out), I had to do at least a thousand things. Olaf hadn't been exaggerating about my needing to prepare *everything* for the on-board classroom. Initially I'd planned just to buy textbooks, but as the days passed, I realized how much work it took to set up a school. Not only head teacher, I became also principal, book supplier, and audio-visual coordinator.

The weeks filled up with driving and shopping. To avoid the morning commuter crush downtown, I'd start each day by going west of the city to stop by the seismic company's offices and to hit remote bookstores. Before the lunchtime traffic snarls, I'd dash to midtown to order an out-of-print text from a specialty bookseller, then load up on educational comics before my midday doctors' appointments, where I got seasickness pills and inoculations. I made rounds to the post office and to the bank, arranging for automatic payments and applying for extensions on credit cards. Several times I had to go to the Chinese consulate—where it was impossible to park—to work on my visa and to the university to get health records and to order copies of my transcripts. After offices closed for the day, I did late shopping at the department stores, travel supply shops, and supermarkets.

I consulted bibliographies to find books for all levels of English students: grammars, dictionaries, dialogs, collections of news articles, writing workbooks, and a few story collections and novels. From a thrift shop I got children's alphabet books for the very beginning students, and in a yuppie travel boutique I discovered a fantastic, illustrated technical dictionary. From the language school where I'd worked earlier, I pirated a few dozen tapes and violated copyright restrictions by photocopying textbooks. Every evening I shuttled forms and documents to the twenty-four-hour Kinko's, where I made zillions of copies and sent and received faxes. At night I'd return home—with sore feet, an aching back, and a throbbing head—to start packing.

The living room of the apartment Martin and I shared disappeared under all the stuff I assembled. Boxes and bags lay everywhere, awaiting shipment. Olaf had said that we were going to mail the materials to China ahead of my flight, so that everything would be waiting on board when I arrived. All I'd have to take, he said, were my personal belongings. I hoped we would even hire someone to package the stuff for mailing, since I didn't have time to box everything up and there were some very awkward things.

For instance, I had procured a lovely, but large, whiteboard. It was about a yard long, but lighter than a chalkboard, so it wouldn't cost too much to mail. Along with the board, I needed a six-week supply of special whiteboard markers. Having taught in Egypt on chalkboards that were so old and dirty you couldn't see the new marks, I knew I'd need to clean the board: that required special erasers, and the erasers required a spray cleanser—altogether they cost about sixty dollars. I had filled more than one large box, just to get a writing surface all my students could see at once.

I also assembled pencils, erasers, and steno pads, as well as folders for the men to keep their notes in. Because the students would need to learn American measurements, I bought rulers, calendars, and measuring cups. From my house I scavenged not only books and tapes, but also knives and forks in case the men wanted to learn to use Western utensils, and photographs of my family and friends, to start conversations. Someone told me that gifts were important in any Chinese business transaction, so I bought a number of small lapel pins, American flags, and chocolates.

Toward the end of each afternoon, I'd try to contact my boss. Olaf inspired me: he always returned my phone calls within a day, he never failed to ask how I was coping, and he spoke politely, even the time he had a cold and was calling me from the office at his first opportunity in the day—at 11 p.m.

When we talked, I'd nervously tell him how much I'd spent that day. I knew he'd reimburse me for all my expenditures, but he hadn't given me a budget. "I'm sorry, but I wasn't able to get enough Chinese-English dictionaries at the secondhand stores. Would it be okay to buy a couple of new ones?"

"How much are they?"

Having priced dozens of books that day, I couldn't remember. "Well, they vary," I hedged. "I think they're going to be about fifteen or twenty bucks apiece."

"Yessss . . ." He drew out the word as he thought. "I think everyone on board ought to have one."

"Really?" My voice was a pleased squeak. Trying to sound less excited, I said, "That'd be very helpful to them, I'm sure. Now, the tape players are going to be more. I can take mine, but I'd like to have a few more available for the students. I went to Radio Shack, and they'll give us a ten percent discount if we buy more than five."

"Yes, I think that we could do that."

As the weeks progressed, I realized that I was no longer constrained by the tightness of an academic budget. Olaf was running the ship as a *business:* my teaching supplies were investments in the business's success, like the ship's navigational equipment. He allowed me complete freedom in selecting my tools; it was a fantastic liberation from the usual begging that teachers had to go through for the most meager supplies. Since I'd be reimbursed later, I loved spending money. Particularly, I loved calling the credit card companies and saying that I needed extensions for "business travel in the Orient." Out of gratitude, I tried to save the company money, while still supplying what students needed.

In the middle of that first week of rushing around, Olaf decided that it'd be helpful if I spoke Chinese. "At least a little," he said—as if I might be able to learn *more* than a little in two weeks. After calling a dozen places to find out where I could get Mandarin instruction, pronto, I went over to Rice University and arranged for private lessons with a senior professor of Asian languages. After that I had to squeeze in a few hours each day to meet with my teacher.

My poor, patient teacher! Invariably, I arrived late for my lessons, shuffling in tired and distracted, full of questions about Chinese etiquette, but too scattered to concentrate on learning the language. Consequently, our time together consisted of her giving me perfect lessons, and pronouncing the dialogs for me, while I ran a tape recorder and tried, very poorly, to imitate the sounds she made.

I did grasp that Chinese has four "tones"—rising or falling or flat inflections—and that to use the wrong tone on any word could ruin a sentence's meaning. For instance, one of my first sentences in

Chinese meant "I am an English teacher." The word for "teacher" in the Pinyin transliteration is *"lao-shi,"* with a flat tone on the second syllable. However, I kept mispronouncing it, with a rising tone; my teacher told me that I was announcing, in good clear Mandarin, "I am an English *rat.*"

Toward the end of my preparations, Olaf had some bad news for me. "I'm sorry," he said, "but there have been some problems with the international mail. Some documents that we have sent to the ship have not arrived. So, our operations manager thinks it more feasible for you to carry everything with you, as excess baggage. Do you think you can do that?" He sounded so hopeful, and he had been so kind, that I couldn't refuse.

"Of course," I said. Looking at the piles of stuff filling my floor space, I couldn't think how I was going to manage the flights to China.

In fact I nearly didn't manage. The first part of the trip was relatively easy: all I had to do was check in, with six huge suitcases and boxes, at 5 a.m. The hardest part was talking Martin into driving me to the airport, but in order to see me off, he agreed.

For all its miseries, Houston Intercontinental does have curbside check-in, and the skycap took pity on me. I must have looked a mess—I'd been up packing all night, I had cried while saying good-bye to Martin, and I hadn't washed my hair for days. My face was broken out, and gray circles lined my eyes. It took me several minutes to locate my ticket, because my purse was so stuffed with receipts and reminders, and then we found out that no one had booked a seat for me. Too stunned to complain, I stood silently as the skycap told me that I'd have to sit for eight hours (from Houston to Hawaii) between four other people in the center aisle. Then he weighed my bags and announced, "This is a hundred and fifty pounds over."

I guess the look on my face touched him, because he winked, made a note on my paperwork, and didn't charge for excess baggage. From the state I was in, he probably thought that I was going to visit a dying friend or something, and that I had enough trouble without being charged another thousand dollars.

I was carrying less than two hundred dollars. My contract said that I'd be paid when the ship got back to Galveston (or, if I bailed out, upon my return to Texas), and I hadn't yet been reimbursed for any of my expenses, since I hadn't found time to prepare the forms. As a result, my main credit card was maxed out. I had acquired a second one to charge hotels and meals, but it had a limit of only two thousand dollars, and if I had to stay in China for any amount of time, waiting for the ship, I was afraid that I'd hit the limit on that one, too. To show my gratitude to the porter, I gave him a precious ten-dollar bill, and we were both happy.

I was so tired that, even though I was seated in the middle of a chattering family, I slept through the Houston-Hawaii flight. Then, flying into Honolulu, we got a stunning view of Oahu's rainbow-sheathed mountains, so by the time we landed I felt pretty good. I was liking my new employer—and my new job—enormously. Olaf had agreed to my leaving Houston a few days early, so I could stay with friends in Hawaii en route to Asia. Although it had meant even more of a panic at the end of my preparations, I was grateful for what amounted to a free vacation.

I had an hour in the Honolulu airport before the hop to Maui, and it wasn't much trouble to find the airport's long-term storage area and stow my luggage. I got a cart and piled everything onto it, making sure the whiteboard was on top, so that the heavy boxes of books wouldn't crack it. I ditched almost everything in storage, keeping just an overnight bag for my layover in Maui. I jumped onto the little inter-island plane in a great mood.

In Maui, my friend Linda took me straight from the airport to her favorite beach, where a stiff southerly wind was beating the waves into watery cliffs. Surfers slid down their sides, and more bright boards dotted the blue just beyond the breaking point, where more of the locals hung out, waiting for a ride.

We swam out pretty far that day, and though the water was choppy, I couldn't have been happier. Floating on my back, with my dear friend paddling nearby and the prospect of an adventure ahead, I gazed at the rainbows. Houston seemed very far behind.

Three days later, at the Honolulu airport, I lost all the magical Maui serenity. Dropping me off in Maui, Linda had worried that I might not have enough time in the Honolulu airport to make my next flight. "It's a big place," she said. "And these inter-island flights run late pretty often."

On the plane to Oahu, I caught my breath and figured out my game plan for the next airport. All I had to do was (1) retrieve my luggage from storage (2) check it in, and (3) get myself to the gate. I was supposed to have an hour to do all that. It seemed simple enough, until I got off the flight—which landed, as Linda had predicted, about ten minutes late.

Stepping out of the gate, I realized that I had no clue where to find the luggage storage. I'd been there, yes, but that had been several days ago. And then I'd arrived on a different airline in a totally different part of the airport. Now I had only fifty minutes to find the stored bags and make my next flight, which was on another airline in a distant terminal. I ran to an information desk to ask for help, but the only person working at it was helping a deaf passenger, giving him complex, written instructions.

I turned in circles, looking for a sign or someone to help. A porter went by, and I buttonholed him. "Can you take me to the place where they keep luggage?"

"Huh?"

"The long-term storage place. Where is it?"

The porter clicked his teeth, looking past me. "I'm United, honey. You got a ticket?"

"Yes, but it's on American." Minutes were ticking by.

"Well, you got an American ticket. I can't help you."

"Where's someone who *can?*" I wailed. The United porter calmly shrugged, wheeling his trolley off to help a legitimate customer.

I ran down a corridor at random, hoping to find a sign or another information booth. But I saw only miles of plastic seats and pebbled ashtrays and loose herds of tourists.

Vaguely, I recalled that the storage area was in a basement, underneath the parking lot. Since I was still on the gate level, I needed to get downstairs. I ran until I found an escalator, but got stuck behind a woman with a baby carriage and two small children. Although I felt like shoving past them, I restrained myself and stood behind, shifting my weight from one foot to the other, for the long, slow ride. Descending, we passed a clock: it was 10:25 a.m., and my flight left at 11. I imagined calling Olaf and telling him I'd blown it even before getting to the job site.

When I finally escaped the escalator in the basement, I ran to the first porter I saw and held out a five-dollar bill. "Listen, I've only got a few minutes. Will you please help me?" The guy shoved back his hat, pocketing the bill although obviously unimpressed.

"I need you to come with me to the long-term storage." I felt like a tape recorder. "I have an eleven o'clock flight."

"No way," he pronounced. "They slow."

"Well, we can *try,*" I said. "Please?"

"How much stuff you got?"

"A lot."

Shaking his head, he went across the hall to get a hand truck from a convoy of porter's vehicles. Someone else asked him something, and several more minutes went by before he came back trundling a flat, four-wheeled cart. I was biting my mouth closed to keep from snapping at him to hurry.

He started off toward a door, with me bustling along next to him, then stopped. "Quicker if we go upstairs first," he said. We had to wait for a special service elevator—another three minutes before it finally arrived, clanking and slow, and the doors opened.

Finally we were moving down the hall I recognized—the long, fluorescent-lit one that led to the baggage storage area. My porter friend was ambling behind me, barely moving. The hallways sloped down, and he wasn't even pushing the cart, just allowing it to wallow ahead of him. "Listen, I'm going to run ahead," I told him. "I'll get the stuff out of the lockers and by the time I've done that, you'll be there and I'll be all ready for you, okay?"

"I hope you got a refundable ticket."

I ran down and skidded into the storage place. Two other customers were waiting, leaning on the counter, but no one was behind the desk. "Is anyone working here?" I said.

One woman—who seemed to be from New York and unaccustomed to slow service—snapped, "I can't tell. I've been here for ten minutes."

"Hello!" I yelled. I didn't call—I bellowed.

"You just have to wait," said a man behind me. He was wearing a suit and a look of resignation. "I do this every week. You have to give them the key, then they go get the stuff. I don't know why we can't just go get it ourselves."

Behind the counter I could see rows of metal lockers. I took the locker key out of my pocket and read the number: 8689. It was twenty-five minutes to flight time. "If that porter comes," I told the man, "tell him to wait for me."

After ducking behind the counter, I started down the rows of lockers. The first aisle—a good thirty feet long—was 7000 numbers. The next was 1000s.

As I turned the next corner, I almost tripped over a dwarf-like man sitting on a stool. He had tools around his feet, and he was working on a lock. He looked at me with some surprise, but since he wasn't in a uniform I gathered that he wasn't an employee of the storage unit. He seemed like a locksmith brought in from outside the airport.

Trying to seem as if I belonged, I said, "You happen to know where the eight-thousands are? They keep this place in a mess."

He snorted. "You're telling me. This damn lock's so rusty I couldn't get it with a blow-torch."

I thrust the key under his nose. "I'm really in a hurry. Do you know where the eight-thousands are?"

He took the key and held a grubby fingernail under the number. "That's not eight-thousand; that's six hundred. Ignore the first digit. They don't have thousands of lockers here; they have hundreds. Six hundreds are right over there."

Two minutes later I had dragged my luggage out of the locker, but I couldn't carry it all. I slung my overnight bag across my chest, grabbed the two most important suitcases, and headed back out, past the counter toward the hallway.

"Hey!" someone yelled behind me. It was a kid maybe twenty years old, red-headed, a little scared-looking.

"It's okay," I said over my shoulder. "I'm not stealing anything. This is my stuff. See, I have the key." I wasn't even looking at him — I was moving toward the door. The porter was there, and as I heaved the bags onto his truck, I said, "Can you go back in there and get the rest of the stuff?" I thrust the key into his hand, and he started off in the right direction while I turned back to the red-haired kid trailing behind me. "I have twenty seconds for this transaction," I said. "I had one big locker for three days; how much do you want?"

"I gotta give you a receipt," he whined. "I hafta ring it up with the codes."

"You ring up whatever you want," I said. "I have a plane to

catch." I could feel the ire of the man and woman behind me, who had been there before me and whose time I was taking up. I pointed to the sign behind the counter. "Five dollars a day? Is there tax?"

"I can't do this," the kid said. He stepped back behind the counter, started dithering with some papers, then picked up the phone. "I should call security."

The porter reemerged, carrying two suitcases with each arm. I threw a ten and a five on the counter and made the man run with me—both of us huffing and pushing the cart—up the incline toward the terminal. It was ten to eleven.

By the time we reached check-in, I wanted to rush the first-class counter and demand that they hold the plane for me. Fortunately, the porter stopped me, saying he could check me in. He rolled the cart to a stand in the middle of the terminal, and took my ticket. "This is at gate 46," he told me. "It's about as far away as you can get from here." He handed me a form, thick with carbons. "Sign here. This says that you are checking in late and you won't hold American responsible if we can't get your luggage on this flight."

"What do you mean?"

"Ma'am, the baggage for that flight is already loaded, probably. The best we can do is get it on the next flight."

"Then what?" I said. "I'm going to China!"

"How long you staying in Tokyo?"

"Just overnight. When's the next flight?"

"We'll get it to you. Just tell the American reps what hotel you're staying at; they'll get it to you tonight."

I signed the form.

As I fumbled for my wallet to tip him, he said softly, "Ma'am, your flight is on time. You know how to *run?*"

I ran. Running has never been my forte. Besides being a little overweight, I'm not very well coordinated. I can and do jog for miles, but at a speed not much faster than walking. I hate running fast even, say, in springtime, alone on a bike path in northern California, when I am well rested. Sprinting exhausted through a crowded, concrete airport, with a leaden carryon strapped across my chest, while looking up and sideways to make out the gate numbers, was my idea of hell. But no matter how tired and breathless I got, I kept running, thinking that it might be that second, or the next one, that made the difference.

After a long time of heavy footfalls and deep panting, I saw the gate ahead of me. I lunged, without air, without much strength, toward it.

But the door to the Jetway was shut. There was a steel bar across it and the uniformed gate agent was walking away.

"*Wait!*" I yelled. I had been doing a lot of yelling that morning.

"Oh, Jeez," he said. "Tokyo?"

"Yes! Please! Please let me get on!"

"All right, all right," he said, and unlocked the door.

Everyone else on the plane was Japanese. The flight was almost as packed as the one from Texas had been, but at the back there was one empty row. I expected it to be nabbed by the occupants of nearby seats after takeoff, but to my surprise none of the passengers moved.

As soon as the seat-belt sign pinged off, I unbuckled my belt, pulled my bag from the overhead rack, and sidled back to the vacant row. There I lifted all the armrests and stretched out luxuriously. The people around me stared. I pulled the blue blanket over my head and smiled, preparing for a long nap. American pushiness had—as usual—triumphed over Oriental obedience.

A few years previously, I had spent twenty-four hours in Iceland, breaking up flights between Germany and New York. Knowing that

I wouldn't get back to Iceland much, I made my time there a condensed vacation: I learned more about that country in a day than I had others where I'd stayed for weeks. I took a tour of the city, bathed in the hot-springs pool with a local, got tipsy with a flight attendant, watched a snowstorm, and ate smoked fish for breakfast.

Ever since then, I've made an effort to enjoy even the briefest of stops in other countries. I've relished six-hour layovers in the Azores and Anchorage by getting out of the airports and hiking around. My first visit to Hawaii, years ago, had been a twenty-four-hour stop between Manila and San Francisco. I hung out all night with the locals in a park on Waikiki, listening to conga drums in the rain. Now I would have a day in Tokyo before my next flight, and I meant to get in as much experience of Japan as possible.

Unfortunately, I was booked at Narita Airport Holiday Inn, a million miles from downtown and from anything remotely interesting. All I could see in any direction were high walls of industrial buildings.

It looked as though my exploration options would be severely limited. However, a sign informed me that the hotel itself offered a "Japan tradition" massage, so after getting into my room and washing up, I called downstairs for an appointment. The clerk said the masseur would be right up.

"Masseur?" I said. "Is it a man?"

"Yes."

"Is there a woman who does massages? A masseuse?"

"No, I'm sorry." She sounded shocked.

"Oh—okay."

After hanging up, I wondered about Japanese massage protocol. Certainly I wouldn't be the first American the guy had worked on, but maybe customs differed in Japan—or at least in the Narita Holiday Inn—from those in the States, where I usually just stripped off and got under a sheet before the masseuse came in. Feeling uncertain, I put on some clean underwear under a dressing gown and stood waiting, getting tenser and more in need of massage.

The masseur who came to my room was a small man—small even for a Japanese person—wearing a perfect white kimono. He looked not unlike the dolls I'd seen robed for martial arts. "Oh, hi, come in," I said. I felt silly in my rose-colored silk gown.

He said something in Japanese.

"I'm sorry," I said. "I don't understand. Do you speak English?"

He said something else in Japanese.

I smiled apologetically.

He smiled apologetically. He gestured for me to lie on the bed.

I did so, lying on my back, eyes closed. Nothing happened. I opened my eyes. The man in white smiled again, and gestured for me to turn over. We were doing plenty of smiling.

I flipped over on my stomach, my face turned to the side. He said something else, and I looked over my shoulder; he was making signs for me to take off the robe.

I reached under myself to untie the belt, then dragged the robe off my shoulders while lying down. It felt awkward, but it was better than scrambling up and getting naked in front of him. When I had the robe halfway off, he folded it over my legs so that just my back was exposed.

He knelt next to me, and I felt how tiny he was—it was like having a cat on the bed. He started with cool, soft strokes above my shoulders, and I thought that it was going to be a pretty wimpy massage.

But after a minute he segued into a series of quick, short strokes, some chopping motions, and some pattering as if he were typing on my skin. I'd never felt anything like it. It was superficial—he barely seemed to connect with any of the muscles beneath the skin—yet I could feel each area he touched begin to loosen and feel warm.

In the next room, a man groaned. It was loud and serious, as if he had dropped something heavy on his toe. Then bedsprings creaked: I imagined the hurt person lying down to recover.

My masseur moved down my arms, tapping and rubbing, leaving each bit of me renewed and invigorated. I relaxed, no longer worried about protocol or nudity, just enjoying the sensations.

Then another noise came from beyond the wall: feminine, and less a groan this time than a long, sighing moan. It sounded as if the woman's head was right next to the wall, about a yard away.

The masseur finished with my upper back and shifted down my legs. He flipped the robe up so that my back and arms were covered, exposing my legs and butt. I again felt self-conscious, especially about my clean-but-not-brand-new underwear.

The sounds from next door intensified. As my masseur silently folded down the top of my panties, to massage my hips, the woman began to pant and moan more loudly. Also then there was a knocking, as a bed was shoved repeatedly against the flimsy wall.

Though I suppressed my giggles, several times I almost said something—"What massage is *she* getting?" But I remembered that the masseur didn't speak English, so I hid my embarrassed grin and my blush in the pillow.

The woman began to mingle words with her moans, and her accent was American. She finally and noisily climaxed while the masseur was working on my shin. She subsided, the bed stopped knocking, and my massage was completed in perfect, Oriental silence.

Shanghaied

As I was getting off the plane in Shanghai, it occurred to me for the first time that I had not prepared well for arrival in a tightly controlled foreign country where I didn't know the language. I had neither currency nor contacts. If no one showed up to meet me, I couldn't even call the ship, because I'd neglected to bring along a phone number. Since it was Sunday, I'd be reduced to waiting in the airport for twenty-four hours, until Olaf got in to work in Houston.

Fortunately, at the arrivals gate, I saw someone waving a sign with my name on it. Two young-looking Chinese men were waiting for me. I said hi—"*Ni hao*"—to the one holding the sign.

The taller of the two men—who came up to my chin—said something.

"I'm sorry," I said. "I don't speak Chinese."

He laughed in a way I was to get to know—with a quick, overly happy expression, his eyes disappearing behind cheerful crinkles. It meant I had done something wrong. "Miss Ken-da Teach-ah. Verra-happy meetchou."

His accent was so heavy I could barely make out the words. I realized he had probably spoken English the previous time, too, but I hadn't recognized it. "I ahm Chan," he said. "Translatoh."

I hoped I wouldn't have anything urgent to translate.

Since I was bigger than both men put together, I refused to let them carry all my bags. We took two each and headed out. Of course any international airport looks much like any other, but already I felt my senses going on alert, excited by the knowledge that I was in a new place. Taking in my first glimpse of China, I noticed smoggy yellow air and a complete lack of greenery. There was a car, the translator told me proudly. He pointed across a jumble of automobiles to a small square vehicle parked in some saffron-colored mud.

It wasn't a parking lot so much as it was a barren patch where cars randomly stopped. There were no markings on the ground to show you where to park or drive. Furthermore, I couldn't tell how the car was going to get out. On both sides and behind it, other vehicles boxed it in, and in front of the wheels, a steep mud bank fell away into a running gutter. I doubted that the little tin box had four-wheel drive.

We shoved my luggage in—it filled the trunk and most of the rear seat—but the translator and I could not get in. There wasn't room to open the doors on the passenger side.

The two men began shouting at each other in an alarming way, but I remembered my teacher saying that to Westerners hearing Chinese, it always sounded as if the speakers were arguing. The strong emphases, the loudness with which Chinese people often speak, and the rising and falling tones sound to us like a fight. I consoled myself that probably my escorts were just analyzing the situation.

I had plenty of time to ruminate, since the discussion continued for many minutes. Finally the translator turned to me. With the air of a person explaining something to a child, he announced, "Cannot move car."

Unfortunately, I had no suggestion to offer. After days of traveling, I had gotten myself to Shanghai; it seemed that they should be able figure out how to get me out of the parking lot. Weary, I looked around for something diverting, but all I could see were more badly parked vehicles and more mud. The two men kept yelling at each other until the driver left: I assumed he was going inside for help. The translator welcomed me to Shanghai again.

"Thank you," I said. "I'm sure I will like it very much."

"Pardon me?" he said.

"I said, 'I think I will like this city.'"

"Pardon me?"

After a while the driver came back with four other men, and they all stood around arguing, looking at our car, and frowning at the tiny brown truck parked behind it. Everyone talked at once. There was a lot of gesturing and pointing to the truck and at the mud bank.

After about five minutes, the men fanned around the truck and hunkered down. With manly shouts, they lifted the rear end up a few inches. The translator yelped, and they dropped it. The fender bounced as the men stood up.

More excited conversation went on, and then they bent and lifted again. This time they swiveled the rear of truck about a yard, and let it down again with much grunting and yelling. Everyone then looked very pleased.

Scrutinizing the new space, the driver nodded. We managed to open the doors a few inches, and after the translator and I squeezed in, the driver began maneuvering the car back and forward, into the mud bank and back out of it, angling each time a little more to the left. We slithered back and forth, with every movement gaining a few centimeters of clearance. Mud from our front wheels spattered the surrounding vehicles and splashed the legs of the men who had helped move the truck. They stood around in a careful circle, close enough to call encouragements—or perhaps criticism—through the windows.

When our car was finally free, the men sent up a polite cheer. We jerked into the narrow, winding aisle, then bumped at high speed toward the jammed street. The luggage jostled in the trunk.

The Shanghai Portman was the fanciest hotel I'd ever seen, let alone stayed in. The massive arches of the entryway rose above everything else in sight, and we drove under them, along a smooth, sweeping driveway. As soon as we stopped, white-gloved, black-uniformed porters jumped to let us out and collect the luggage; others sprang to hold back the lobby doors while we were still eight feet away. The glass panes gleamed in the afternoon sun; a royal red carpet led through an enormous, marble-floored lobby furnished with antiques. Someone was playing a piano in one of the overlooking balconies; old ladies in beautiful silk suits sat in love seats, chatting in muted voices over tea and sherry.

My room on the eighteenth floor had a bed wider than the Chinese buses I'd seen on the road. An antique writing desk awaited me by the window, and nearby stood a rosewood dining table and four chairs, for my solitary meals. The bathroom was marble, with dark green fixtures. I hoped that the ship's departure would be delayed for weeks.

I couldn't wait to unpack and to stretch out on the enormous bed and revel in the quietness. But for some reason I couldn't figure out, both the driver and translator stayed in the room. I'd read that it was an insult to tip anyone in China, so I couldn't get rid of them that way.

"Very good," the translator said, staring out my window. He'd been standing there for several minutes.

"Yes," I said for the fifth or sixth time. "It's a beautiful view."

There was another long pause. I went to the minibar and opened it, hoping for some bottled water. "Would you like something?"

The driver looked up hopefully, but the translator shut him down with a glance. "No sank you," he said.

I didn't know if it was okay to drink in front of them, so I shut the fridge, still thirsty. "Well!" I said, brightly. "I really appreciated your help. I'm sure I'll be very comfortable here."

The translator nodded.

"Did you want anything else from me?" I said. "Do I need to meet someone else or go somewhere with you?"

"Beg pardon?"

Slowly, I repeated myself.

"Oh, no," the translator said. "You rest." He paced back and forth on the balcony. The driver sat on the edge of the chair I'd offered, glancing around the room.

"Well," I said, "maybe I will have a rest now." I gestured modestly toward the bed, indicating that I would lie down.

The translator averted his eyes. There was a long pause. Finally he said, "Very good view."

I sat in my other chair, debating. I was thirsty, tired, and ready to be alone. "Um, maybe . . ." I began. They watched me, looking as weary as I felt. "Maybe it would be best if I were alone now."

"Beg pardon?" The translator's politeness was wearing off. I didn't know if I'd offended him or not.

"Maybe you could leave now," I said.

The translator shot in from the balcony, beaming. He offered his hand happily, speaking to the driver in alert Chinese. They were out the door in a second, smiling and waving good-bye over their shoulders.

Once I'd washed up and drunk some Swiss mineral water from my minibar, I wasn't tired at all. Excited by the prospect of the huge, new city below me, I changed in to my new Rockports and found my way to the elevators.

Leaving the confines of the hotel—ushered out by dozens of polite, pleasant-faced doormen—was like leaving the Western world. The borderline seemed to be the edge of the hotel's property. Outside the giant archway, the sky loomed, grayish yellow and low, over the long, cacophonous street. Automobiles moved in both directions, but for every car there were dozens of bikes weaving before and behind it. Bicycles swished and clanked and creaked by, the riders ignoring the noise and threat of other vehicles. Hindered by bicyclists, unencumbered by mufflers, the drivers making free use of horns, the cars made more noise than progress. I resisted the desire to plug my ears.

The streets couldn't have been more crowded. It was early evening, and apparently everyone was going shopping as they walked home from work. With the hotel behind me, I was the only Westerner in sight. Chinese faces filled the streets and sidewalks; feeling like a giant, I walked through them, trying not to stare and trying to handle their stares with good humor.

Weaving though the wide sidewalks, I constantly had to swerve around parked (but not always locked) bicycles and dodge people who wanted to speak to me. I thought it best, from my time in other countries and from what my teacher had said, to keep moving on the street. If I stopped, there would be demands for English conversations, English information, and impromptu English lessons. After that would come the requests for visas, jobs in America, travel money—no matter how I tried, I couldn't convince people that I had neither authority nor ability to help them emigrate.

I walked fast and aimlessly, staring at the buildings as the people stared at me. My Chinese teacher had told me that, although it was officially discouraged, the Chinese people invariably stared at foreigners. It was not rudeness, my teacher explained, just interest: they are curious people in general and don't see many Westerners in some parts of the country. I would have thought that those living near the Portman Hotel in Shanghai would have seen plenty, but they looked at me as if I were not only Western but also ten feet tall and purple. However, living in Egypt had prepared me not only to be gawked at but also leered at, called to, poked, and touched in a variety of ways (in Alexandria, I'd even had stones thrown at me when I went outside in jeans).

At least the Shanghaiians didn't purposely encroach on my space. As I walked, as rapidly as possible, down the street, some of them did stop to watch me, but if I caught their eyes most of them would smile or at least alter their expressions to acknowledge my discomfort.

Older people stared the hardest. One elderly lady, about four feet high, peered up at me like a curious dog, her face flat and unexpressive except for large, amazed eyes. I smiled back, but she stood there, blank-faced, as if I were a miracle or a horror show. I kept looking back, trying to make contact. Finally, in a friendly voice, I tried saying hello—*Ni hao!*

Her eyebrows shot up and her mouth dropped open in a smile. She laughed loudly, shook herself out of her trance, and continued walking down the street, looking back at me every few steps and laughing over her shoulder.

I liked seeing the little children. While I knew some Westerners thought China's one-child rule was extreme, if not cruel, I could not agree with that assessment, and I found the small families charming: everywhere I went in Shanghai, I saw babies and toddlers, well-dressed and healthy, being cared for by obviously devoted parents. As I walked by, tiny children would call "Herro! Herro!" to me in sweet, high voices.

As I approached one family, I noticed a father coaching his little girl. He was carrying her in his arms, so she was nearly at eye level with me, and as he approached he whispered, "Hello!" in her ear. Then he jogged her lightly as I passed. On cue, she called out to me.

When I answered, she giggled and then hid her face in her father's neck. All I could see was her black, shining hair and the little collar of her dress. He continued whispering to her, and she peeped over his shoulder with a pure smile.

Only once in Shanghai did I see a child who looked unhappy. I was walking by the interminable concrete wall of an enormous department store. In the entrance alcove, a woman squatted in front of a tiny boy. The baby was also squatting, his plump little legs bent double as he tried to hide his face from his mother. She was screaming at him like a harridan, and slapping at his knees. Her voice was cruel and scary. I couldn't see if she was hitting him hard or not, but the boy was wailing. I stopped and glared at the woman, hoping to attract negative attention to her, but after a minute I kept walking, thinking that I didn't understand enough about the situation to condemn it. And even if I had, what could I have done? In America, maybe, I would have at least spoken to the parent to try to calm her, but here I couldn't even attempt that.

About a mile from the hotel, the buildings on my right gave way to a long iron fence. Turning in the gate, I found myself in a green park, quieter than the street and—because of its two-cent entrance fee—somewhat less crowded. The people in the park weren't carrying bags or bundles; they ambled down the wide paths between the trees or sat on benches talking to their children. On the grass a few couples sat courting, bright color in their cheeks. They faced each other intently, leaning inward with every gesture, while keeping a foot or so of space between them.

Here I felt less like a giant than a zoo oddity: the park-goers studied me as they would an interesting nature exhibit. I felt comfortable enough to sit down on a bench, where I had about thirty seconds alone before a young man joined me. Well, I thought, I was tired of moving away. Why not give a free lesson, get to know him, enjoy his company for a while? I wasn't going to be in town long enough to make friends, so I might as well talk to strangers.

He sat staring at the ground, too embarrassed to speak. To help him out, I smiled. He sat up straighter, fidgeting. After preparation, he asked, "Do you speak English?" The question was fairly clear despite his singsong expression.

"Of course," I said. "You can tell that!" I talked a little, to get him to relax. In a few awkward minutes we established that I was American, that he was Chinese—from Beijing but working in Shanghai—and that he would like to show me the park.

So we strolled around the park I'd already seen. It wasn't very big—only about a block across, with one path looping through it. We created a spectacle; every time we stopped to examine a flowering bush or a piece of machinery, other pedestrians would stop, too, peering over our shoulders to see what we found interesting. My new companion, obviously proud of his alliance with a foreigner, treated the other people with an offhand superiority that I found annoying. Still, it was nice to have some of the attention taken away from myself.

I tried to seem impressed with the dull little park. "What's that?" I pointed to a delicate-looking orange crane, covered with soot and parked on top of a pile of rubbish. It appeared not to have been used in a long time. It looked like an abandoned Tonka Toy.

My guide said proudly that the machine was part of the new China. "We make it here," he said. "Not from United States."

"Great."

He looked at me thoughtfully and repeated the word. "Ga-rate?" he said.

"Great. It means good. Very good."

"Good?"

"Yes, good."

After we'd done the park circuit twice, my guide gestured to one of the empty benches. I sat down, wondering how I could politely extricate myself and continue my walk down Nanjing Road. Then he muttered something I couldn't catch. "I'm sorry," I said. "What did you say?"

He stared at his feet, looking a little angry.

"Try again," I said. "I'm sorry I didn't understand you. Your English is good."

"I want make kiss you."

A shock: I wasn't expecting to be hit on in China. Not knowing what to say, I scowled at him and shook my head.

"In America," he said petulantly, "is okay to kiss."

"No," I said, folding my arms.

"Why not?" Trying to seem brash, he managed only to look sheepish and confused. I felt sorry for him, but I had a reputation to live down. And as I had in Southern Europe and Northern Africa, I tried to explain that, like most American women, I was not given to kissing—or doing anything more than talking with—strangers. After that, he left.

Walking back to the hotel, upset, I wondered why I'd reacted so strongly. I was as shaken as if a stranger in the United States had suggested that we go behind some bushes and have sex. Having men hit on me hadn't been part of my experience for many years. I was glad that, in my early thirties, I got less attention from men than I used to. Male attention and sexuality had always seemed intrusive and aggressive, rarely welcome in my life.

Of course I'd made exceptions for boyfriends; having a lover seemed the natural course of things, even a good idea much of the time. I'd cheerfully entangled myself with man after man, with each affair lasting several years. Never wanting any further commitment, I'd ended each relationship, always moving on to a new man who seemed, at first, enticing. The relationships of the last decade had been more work than fun, but they'd provided security. I didn't want to be alone.

In between the stretches of relationships with men, there had been a few flashes of romantic brightness: twice in college, and once since then, I'd been with women. Those few times came back to me often in dreams, or in daydreams. With those women, I'd felt an intensity, a fervor like the kind that men seemed to feel. If a woman had asked me for a kiss in the park, I might have said yes.

Back in my hotel room, still pondering my romantic relationships, I had a message to call Barry Bradley. He was the other American who would be riding the ship, representing Olaf's company and helping with modifications to the seismic equipment en route. He sounded pleasant on the phone—Southern and gregarious—and we agreed to meet for dinner.

I changed and went downstairs hoping to like him. Having spent a fair amount of time on ships with people I couldn't stand, or who seemed unable to stand me, I was anxious to befriend or at least not alienate Barry. He opened the door to his room looking as nervous as I felt, and attractive in a boyish, unthreatening way: about six feet tall, with a big build. He had thick, wavy hair, cut clean and short, and as golden as Olaf's. Was everyone in this company blond?

We shook hands in a hearty, American way. I liked my first impression of him and sensed that he approved of me, too. Judging by appearances, I think we both felt that we weren't going to have to spend six weeks with anyone too weird.

Having seen a Japanese-style restaurant in the hotel, I suggested that we eat there. "We could get some sushi," I said.

"Get some what?"

"Sushi. You know, raw fish. Sashimi."

"Raw fish!" His Texas accent made each word two syllables. *Rah-aw fe-ish!* "I was hoping maybe we could get a big juicy steak some-wheres, but I guess this ain't the place for that."

"I'm sure it's not," I said. "Sushi's good. I got used to it in Califor-nia and I haven't had it in a while."

"California." He dropped his jaw, looking mock-alarmed. One of his front teeth was crooked, making his smile look like a little kid's grin. "Uh-oh. I'm from Oklahoma. Think we can get along?"

In the Japanese bar, Barry was more interested in the *sake* than in eating. His conversational entrée, as we sat down, was to say how sick he'd gotten the night before on Chinese wine. "I just barely made it up to the room," he said. "Peter had to practically carry me in there."

"Peter?"

"Oh, you'll meet Peter. He's on the phone to Houston right now. He's the operations manager, helping us get organized to go. He's not riding on board, though. Last night we just hooted in that bar across from the lobby; these guys know how to party."

My California roll arrived, and I started mixing the wasabi and soy sauce. I figured I had Barry pigeonholed pretty quickly: a good ol' boy from Oklahoma who liked his beer and beef. Well, I'd been shipmates with worse.

As I ate, Barry drank and talked. "Ain't seen one damn thing in this port outside the hotel. Peter's a damn slave driver. Gets me up at seven every morning and drags me down to the ship. We're pissing around there all day, and by the time we get back here and get washed up, I can't even think about going out."

"What are you doing down there? Isn't the ship ready?"

"Ready? She's about as ready as a spayed dog, I'll tell you that. We were supposed to pull out of here tomorrow, but we can't." *Cain't.*

"Why not?"

"That ship ain't safe, that's why. Olaf's in a big hurry for us to get there—we got a contract in the Gulf starting August 11, but no way we're going to make it. I been here a week already, and nothing has happened. Nada. You can't get these people to do anything."

I nodded warningly toward the sushi chef, who was eavesdropping as he patted fish eggs into bundles, but Barry shrugged. "These guys don't speak English. Not a damn word as far as I can tell. But I guess that's your problem, huh?"

"None?" I said, alarmed. "*None* of them speak *any?*"

"Hell if I know. I use the translator every time I want to get something across. Wang's the translator—he's pretty good. Mostly I sit on my butt and watch Peter get riled up. He hates the Chinese."

"So, what's the problem with the ship?"

"Oh, man." Barry groaned and poured himself another *sake*. He drank it like a shot of tequila, tossing the contents of the little glass back into his throat, then chasing it with green tea. "You don't want to know."

"Yes, I do." Secretly I was delighted to hear that we might have to spend a long time in Shanghai. Nothing could have delighted me more than a paid-for Chinese vacation.

"Well, the auxiliary shaft sheared. You got a clue what that means?"

"No . . ."

"I didn't think so. Well, it runs the generator and the compressor both, okay? But it broke, so now they're both shot. Without the compressor, your air conditioning don't work. Without the generator, you got no electricity. You still want to go?"

Before I could answer, he went on. "Also, all the equipment they've got on board is a pile of shit—I'm supposed to be making modifications on the way over, right? We got to build a deck back there to hold the cables that drag the platform. But there's no way I can do it with the tools we got.

"I'm trying to order stuff, but everything takes years to get here, these people are so damn slow about everything. It's like, in the States, you need something, you tell the boss and he gets it, right? Here, I tell them what I need, and they call a damn conference. I've got to justify why I need it, explain what it's for, say why we can't get along without it, and do a five-page written request, with the translator, for practically every bolt." He shook his head, dramatically. The *sake* was taking effect.

"I'm glad I brought my whiteboard," I ventured.

"That reminds me." Barry reached across the counter to pick up a paper napkin. "You got a pen? There's nothing to eat on the ship. We've got to come up with a list of food items we want."

"There's no food?"

"There's food for *them,* but nothing I want to eat. You like that shit?" He gestured to my rolls of white rice and seaweed. "There's about twenty tons of rice on board. But nothing else. I swear—I don't know what these guys are planning on living on."

"Well, I don't mind," I said. It didn't seem right to me to order special provisions. "I can just eat whatever they're having. I like Chinese food."

"Listen, babe, no, you don't. I went down into the storage locker to check it out, right? Because I been on a lot of ships and food is important."

"I know that." I wanted to explain that I, too, had experience on ships, but Barry wasn't listening.

He continued, "So in the storage locker, you know what they got? One case of soy sauce and a big thing of white pepper. That was it. So I went in the freezer room, and I saw this box marked 'chicken.' And I'm thinking, great, here's something I can eat. So I opened it up, and you know what was in there? Chicken *feet.*" He held the last word, looking for my reaction.

"Feet? You mean, like, thighs?"

"Nope. Not thighs, not wings. Feet. Claws." He held his hand in a tense, rounded shape, as if he were holding a baseball. "Thousands of the suckers. You want to eat that?"

"Let's make the list."

Barry took a chewed pencil stub from his pocket. "Better start with meat. How about some steaks? Let's see, we'll be out six weeks, that's forty-two days. Better get about forty pounds of steak."

"Forty pounds?" I said. "I won't eat any of it."

"Oh yeah, other people might want some. Forty pounds was just for me. Some of these guys never even had steak, I bet. If they're nibbling on chicken feet and I'm fixing steak, they're going to want mine. Better make it eighty pounds."

"Isn't that an awful lot? Steak's pretty expensive over here. "

"Listen, this ship . . . they're spending two, three grand a day to get everything ready. A couple steaks are a drop in the bucket."

I thought about what I ate at home. "How about some vegetables?"

"Yeah, they'll get fresh stuff before we go. Trouble is, that stuff goes bad after a couple weeks. You can keep it refrigerated awhile, but then it rots. They're getting some oranges, though. They last a long time."

"Well, how about canned stuff, then?"

Greg wrote down "canned vegetables," and then, as an afterthought, "canned meat."

Pretty soon we had compiled a list of long-lived foods we thought we could live on, including crackers, cheeses, orange juice, and peanut butter. "I wish we could take milk," Greg mused. "But a week or two after you're out, it's bad. I hate sour milk."

"How about canned milk?" I said. "Or powdered? It's better than nothing. Good in coffee, at least."

"Coffee." Greg snapped his fingers and wrote it down. "Instant coffee. And some kind of milk and creamer. You want any snacks? Candy bars or anything?"

"No." I had an ongoing battle with sugar, one that I'd been winning for the last year. I hadn't eaten any sweets since the previous summer, and didn't want to. I knew from past experience that, like an alcoholic, I couldn't control my intake. Strange as it sounded to other people, once I started eating sweets, I couldn't stop. "Don't get any candy. If we've got nuts and fruit, that's enough snacks. I've got some chocolate if you want it—I brought it to give out as gifts."

"Okay." The list covered both sides of Barry's napkin, which he folded into his shirt pocket. "We'll see how much of this they can find. But we better eat well while we can, man. Going to be a long six weeks." He sighed and stretched his long arms overhead. The motion pulled his shirt cuff away from his wrist, exposing a new tattoo. The freshly colored skin still looked sore, the blue letters vivid against the red flesh: PAULETTE.

"Who's Paulette?"

"My mother."

I fell for it. "Really?"

He snorted, rubbing at the tattoo with his other hand. "My wife. I got drunk the night before I left and this was here the next morning. Stupid-ass thing to do." He sighed through his nose, and shifted his weight. The little Chinese chair creaked, on the verge of breaking, and the waitress stared at him. Catching her eye, he ordered another bottle of *sake,* and a Coke.

Because of jetlag, I fell asleep early and then woke up at 4 a.m., alert and energized. It was still dark outside. Although I'd eaten dinner only six hours before, I was starving. I tried to convince my stomach to stop rumbling and my brain to go back to sleep, but it didn't work.

I recalled advice I'd received from a world-traveling flight attendant about dealing with jetlag: "Eat when you're hungry, and sleep when you're sleepy." So I got up and helped myself to orange juice, soda water, and peanuts from the minibar. This repast I ate sitting on my balcony, looking over the dim, uneven lights of Shanghai. My window faced west, away from the sunrise, but as I sat, the darkness turned transparent, and gray light rose behind the foggy outlines of the city. I went inside and showered, and when I came out, the sky was white and I could see slight human movement down below.

It was about five o'clock when I left the lobby: the desk clerks and the ubiquitous doormen looked sleepy and quiet. Outside on the cool street, morning was starting with the hoarse sound of a truck engine turning over and a few boys on bicycles cranking down the street.

Just beyond the hotel entryway stood a group of figures. At first I thought they were statues, but as I got closer I saw that it was a group of Chinese people doing tai chi. The "statues" were breathing—taking in air deeply and evenly, without hurry. They were all facing the same direction, watching a middle-aged woman who seemed to be their leader. All of them followed the teacher's movements, the group making one slow motion, like a swish of air through heavy leaves. Then they stood still again, just breathing.

It was the only time in my visit that I got to see Chinese people without their seeing me and changing their behavior. Because I was walking softly, and because I came upon the group from behind, none of them noticed my presence. A few passersby stopped to see what I was looking at, but not enough gathered to cause a commotion.

I couldn't see the faces of the people doing tai chi and couldn't judge age anyway in the Chinese, but these people seemed middle-aged: they were not so slender in the middle, and they wore dark, conservative clothing of the older style. Their pants and shirts were plain, and baggy enough to allow any movement. In a corner lay a pile of bags: the people had evidently stopped to exercise on the way to work.

They moved again, shifting their weight from one foot to the other, and twisting their upper bodies slightly. This allowed some of them to face me, but for once my presence didn't elicit stares or smiles. Focused on their breathing, they seemed not to see me.

A commotion came from across the street, where another group of exercisers had gathered. They were jumping up and down, doing windmills and jumping jacks. An instructor, a young man wearing an orange leotard and nylon wind pants, was exhorting them in a loud, drill-instructor voice. Their faces were flushed, and their clothes were coming untucked or unbuttoned, the edges flying around as the people hopped and flapped their arms.

The leader shouted out the count, and his class's pace increased as his voice grew louder and quicker. A few of the members struggled to keep up, red-faced and panting. Since I stood facing them, they could see me easily, and though I was a long way across the street, several of them pointed me out to their neighbors. They then jumped higher and pumped harder, showing off their Western-style aerobics.

Everywhere I walked that morning, pale yellow light was seeping into the corners of alleys and concrete buildings; everywhere the light fell, and everywhere it hadn't touched yet, people were doing tai chi. Old people—gender often unidentifiable—stood in doorways, at bus stops, or even between parked cars on the street, moving slowly and deliberately. In People's Park, where I'd been the night before, people were exercising on every patch of grass. At six o'clock, there were more people doing tai chi than there were cars on the road or businesses open.

As the sun grew higher and warmer, people picked up their belongings and went on with their days. Bicyclists filled the streets, weaving between cars, while people walking to work filled the pedestrian bridges over busy intersections. The little shops clanked open windows and doors; old ladies sat down on the sidewalk, stringing flowers to sell.

As they had the previous night, people stopped to stare at me. If I quit moving for even a few seconds, small crowds gathered. People peered into my face in a friendly way, talking at me in words I didn't understand. I walked as I had learned to do in Egypt, my head down or tilted way up, avoiding eye contact. Even though it was still early and not very bright, I wore sunglasses.

Although the people in Shanghai seemed gentle and friendly, I wanted to observe them, not to be observed. Every now and then I'd feel that I should talk to someone, and it was easy to smile at anyone I liked and have company. I tried to choose women for this interaction, to avoid getting into more misunderstandings like the one the previous evening. But mostly I walked, quickly, and alone, trying to see as much as I could.

Rushed along in the crowd, I felt my legs brushed by something, and I sensed a presence below me. I looked down and got a swift view of a bent head and a basket of creamy flowers. I couldn't stop, but as I continued, on each block I noticed an old lady sitting on the pavement, stringing flowers. Some had baskets in front of them, containing a few coins, but no one seemed to stop and buy from the women. They were the closest thing I saw to beggars.

Curiosity pushed me. After passing another flower lady, I angled out of the crowd, turned around and went back to her. My camera was at the ready, but I preferred to get permission to take a portrait, since some elderly Chinese people had an aversion to being photographed. Mostly I wanted just to see her, but the camera gave me an excuse.

As soon as I turned back, other passersby stopped to see what I was looking at. The woman was not as old as many flower ladies; her hair was still black, and her plump flesh filled her Western-style shirt above the baggy Chinese pants. She sat on the bare sidewalk, holding in her lap a straw dish of tiny, cream-yellow blossoms. They were unlike any I'd ever seen, like tuberose blossoms in their long trumpet shape, but thicker. I squatted down by the woman, showing her my camera with a questioning gesture. She glanced at me, squinted, and then put her head back down, possibly thinking it better business strategy to ignore me. By then a dozen people were peering at her over my shoulders.

I had already set the exposure and f-stop as best I could—I was using an old German camera that had no light meter—so I began taking pictures. I leaned toward her for a close-up, catching in her glasses the reflection of her checked shirt. Then I focused on her speckled brown hands, tying tiny knots as she strung together lines of flowers.

Bodies pressed in on me as the crowd grew bigger—people were closing around, chattering about what I was doing. Quickly there were thirty or more people pressing in. She twitched her head as if shaking off flies, and flicked her wrist in a gesture of annoyance. I would have liked to put some coins in her basket, but my purse was tucked away and to stay a moment longer, groping for change, would attract even more people and would be even more annoying for her. As I stood up, I had the sensation of sending people reeling, because the crowd backed away to make room. As I moved on, so did everyone else.

That afternoon I trekked to one of the "friendship stores," huge galleries of beautiful objets d'art, open only to foreigners. Though Nanjing Road was one of China's most famous shopping districts, comparable to Fifth Avenue, little in its stores had attracted me. Most of the clothes were polyester, and most of the vases and knick-knacks were of low quality. But the friendship store showed off aisle after aisle of desirable booty—including an entire elephant's trunk, carved centuries ago into a complex scene that included one thousand Buddhas. The price tag was in millions of yen.

I had an assignment to buy a small silk rug for my mother's living room, and I wanted one for myself as well. But to choose two, from the thousands available in that warehouse-sized room, seemed impossible. The carpets were displayed in deep piles, perhaps thirty rugs in a stack, and there were at least ten sizes to choose from. Further, I had to choose not only between silk and wool but between lower or higher numbers of knots per inch. I could spend no more than two hundred dollars for my own rug, but for that I could have anything from six feet of cotton runner to a yard-long rug to a tiny, gleaming wall-hanging of pure silk, as soft and dense as velvet.

Again and again the patient clerks—a man and a young woman—dragged out my selections from the heavy stacks. Although I was bigger and stronger than they, they refused to let me help. When I tried to pull out a carpet, or at least hold up the stack so that someone else could pull one out, I was politely, firmly reproved. Between my selections they waited, hands folded, as I paced around the showroom floor.

Late in the afternoon I was still trying to choose among four rugs: three traditional designs in earth colors, and one modern one in pale blue. About that time, the clerk showed me that the rugs looked completely different depending on which way you laid them down—with the light across the nap, they were light and colorful; with the light against the nap, they became shadowed and mysterious, with completely different moods.

I despaired. I could never choose. Every time I came close to knowing which two I wanted, I'd look again at another one from another angle and be thrown back into bewilderment. Every time I asked the advice of the woman who worked there, she'd just agree with my selections. "They are beautiful," she would say, diplomatic but unhelpful.

Finally I selected two that I knew my mother would like; she could choose which one she'd have and I'd take the other one. One had a soft beige background, circling a central image of a bird on a blossom. The other was brighter, with a floral design. After ringing up my purchase, the man closed his briefcase and prepared to leave. I walked out of the room with him and his assistant, all of us chattering about the sale. They informed me that—amazingly—I had selected the two very best rugs.

Then more and more employees came clattering down the stairs behind us, all laughing and talking to me. Several of them were pointing to their watches, and telling me that they were hungry. "Are you late?" I asked, not understanding.

"We want to have our dinner!" one man said, smiling.

Then I realized. "You were waiting for me?"

A dozen heads nodded; others had my question translated and then they too affirmed it: the whole "friendship store" staff had been held up, unable to go home until the last customer was done.

Embarrassed and flattered, I didn't understand why they hadn't told me they were trying to close. "Why didn't you tell me?" I asked, despairingly. But the Chinese people only smiled.

I got back to my room late that night, hauling my two rugs and a few armloads of dishes. Exhausted from walking, excited by the people I'd seen, I was half-asleep as I came in but looking forward to more explorations the next day.

Turning down the blankets, I noticed with some satisfaction that two Belgian chocolates had been placed on my pillow. Less appealingly, my phone was blinking to indicate a message for me. I dialed the switchboard and learned that Peter had called, telling me to be ready at 7 a.m. to go to the ship.

The *Tan Suo Zhe*

At 7 a.m. I was waiting with Barry in the hotel foyer. Still thrilled with my purchases, I was trying to tell him about the friendship store, but he seemed hungover and uninterested. "So anyway," I trailed off, "I hope you get to see it before we go."

"No way," he said. "We're leaving tomorrow, sure as shit. Get your stuff packed tonight."

My enthusiasm waning, I sat down on the edge of a big planter, which was like a backless bench—cold and uncomfortable. I'd wanted to see a museum; I'd wanted to buy some silk; I'd wanted to walk down Nanjing Road again, people-watching. We waited for half an hour, me shivering and resentful, Barry pacing back and forth between the planter and the door, hands in his pockets. "Damn Peter, anyway,'" he complained. "I could've used more sleep."

Peter, it transpired, was on the phone. He had been on the phone much of the morning, talking long-distance to Olaf's office: a couple-hundred-dollar conference. He finally barged out of the elevator at 7:45, the veins around his nose flaring, prominent against his pale skin. Like everyone in Olaf's company, he was barely middle-aged, but his thin limbs and hunched back made him look old and frail. He looked over my head and snapped at Barry, "Is the van here?"

"Do you see a van?" Barry said, holding himself in.

Daunted, but trying to be professional, I stood up. "I'm Gillian Kendall. Glad to meet you."

Peter allowed his eyes to meet mine for one second. He had the pale, stiff face of a businessman, with gray eyes as cold as clouds. He did not take my offered handshake, but wiped his wrist behind his ear, pushing back an oily strip of hair. "I hope you are prepared to be uncomfortable. This is not a luxury cruise."

I glared at his averted face. "I've been around two oceans on working vessels. I'm not expecting to be coddled."

When the van arrived, I sat in the front. I had to fold my legs into a tiny space, but it was as far from Peter as I could get. He barked at Barry a little as we rode, but mostly we sat in tense, unhappy silence. Embarrassed by the atmosphere Peter created, I felt sorry for the driver, the same man who had picked me up at the airport. He glanced at me with curiosity, no doubt wondering why Americans were so gloomy. I couldn't have told him what was bothering Peter.

It was a long way to the dock. We went beyond the downtown area I'd seen on my sightseeing tour, then through flat, dull outskirts where the buildings and streets seemed to repeat themselves like a film loop. Thousands and thousands of gray-white apartment buildings loomed like huge dominoes, rows of them stretching as far as I could see.

The traffic thinned out in the suburbs, and the driver accelerated. We bounced over the rough road—the van's shocks must have been jostled to death long ago—and the air coming in the tiny windows smelled putrid. Feeling ill, I leaned out as far as I could, and watched.

No one paid attention to the van, so I was able to look at the bicyclists and pedestrians without feeling self-conscious. People carried heavy loads on old rusted bicycles; one boy rode towing a cart stacked higher than his head with wicker hampers of chickens.

After about an hour, Barry tapped me on the shoulder. "Should get some fresh air soon. We're near the harbor." We turned a few more corners and came to a rusty gate, where the van stopped, rattling and coughing. A man in an official-looking uniform came out of a guard shack, acknowledged Peter, and peered hard at me.

"Give him your *passport*," Peter ordered, as if he'd told me to do this several times already.

"Oh!" I fumbled in my bag. It was lucky that I happened to be carrying it: no one had told me to bring I.D., and I might well have left it in the hotel room.

The guard stared at my passport, squinting at the dozens of stamps, stickers, pasted-in visas, and handwritten addenda. The stuff for Egypt alone took up four pages. When he finally happened across something in Chinese, relief spread over his face. He returned my passport and waved us on.

We jolted down a dirt road toward what looked like a cliff, with some ramshackle buildings on one side, until Peter shouted "Stop!" The driver braked.

Peter and Barry got out, and I started to follow, but Barry said, "Stay put. This guy'll take you to the ship." Peter slammed the back door, and they disappeared. The driver continued up a little hill, and then parked where the road petered out on a flat area overlooking the quay.

I got out gratefully, shaken from the ride and the proximity to horrible Peter. It felt good to move my legs, and I followed the driver down the hill. All the ships docked along the quay seemed pretty rugged; none was even a fourth as big as the Navy ships I was used to. Since the names were in Chinese, I couldn't read them. I asked the driver, in my dreadful Pidgin Mandarin, which ship was the *Explorer,* called in Chinese the *Tan Suo Zhe.* He understood the nature of my question, if not the words, and pointed to the vessel that would be my home for the next month and a half.

With a bright orange hull and a white upper deck, she was squat and sturdy looking, though very small. I was going to cross the Pacific—world's largest and nastiest ocean—on a vessel the size of a rich man's yacht. Although I had been told the specs—206 feet long, 46 across—I hadn't been prepared for those measurements to look so tiny.

The *Tan Suo Zhe* seemed front-heavy, like a tugboat, because of the three stories of living quarters piled on her forward deck. Above the living quarters I could see the complicated equipment and antennae of the upper bridge: it looked as if a radio or TV station had been set up in the open air. The back half of the ship was flat except for a large double smokestack.

Proudly, the driver pointed to an upper deck, where the two lifeboats were hoisted—they looked like little orange toys—and to the helicopter deck in the stern. It, too, seemed improbably small. On Navy tenders, the landing decks had enough space to support two basketball games at once (when no helos were landing), and they were covered with a gritty, nonskid surface that took the rubber right off your athletic shoes. This helo deck looked, like the rest of the ship, greasy, unused, and unusable.

It also looked unkempt, not at all shipshape. Even from the quay, thirty feet off, I could see dozens of lines lying around uncoiled, and what seemed to be paper and cardboard trash stuffed into the corners.

The driver chattered at me in Chinese, pointing to an area below the helo deck. The aft section of the ship, just above the waterline, was open, looking like a garage door. I guessed that eventually, the seismic cables would come out through that opening.

"Hey!" A rough shout came from above: Peter, on an upper deck, was jerking his thumb at us. "Get up here!"

"How?" I shot back. I hadn't even seen a way in yet. "Where's the—" I didn't know what to call it. On Navy ships the entryway was called the quarterdeck, but there had to be another name for it on this smaller vessel. "Where's the door?" I finished, lamely.

Peter pointed down, indicating a heavy, waterproof metal door, open against the white side of the ship. Too late, I remembered that the word for this kind of portal was "hatch." A long plank of thin wood, held approximately in place by knotted twine, swayed over the water, leading to the ship from the quay.

I let the driver go first, and after the gangplank didn't collapse I followed him in. He vanished ahead of me, and I had to grope along the dank passageway, blinking while my eyes adjusted to the dimness. I tried to find some markings on the walls to tell me where I was (Navy ship training, again), but all I saw were plastic-framed signs in what looked like Norwegian. I later learned that the vessel had originally been built in Canada and was used by a Norwegian company before being bought by the Chinese. Unable to read the signs, I tried to memorize the ship's layout as I scrambled up ladders and along dark corridors.

It wasn't as hard to reach Peter as I'd expected. He was still on an upper deck, but he'd come indoors and was looming at the top of the ladder. "About time," he grunted, and then indicated a group of Chinese men in a corner. "Get to know the crew."

He turned back to the driver, and snapped at him in fast English. "Where's Barry, huh? Barry? Don't you even know where *Barry* is?"

As he and the driver clattered down the ladder, I was left facing my new students, alone and without introduction. About ten Chinese men were staring at me. I smiled—not very convincingly, I'm sure—and walked toward them. Several of them jumped up, and at least four chairs were pushed in my direction, with a lot of Chinese I couldn't understand.

I sank into a seat and, to hide my shaking hands, pulled up to the table. All the men backed off to the other side. Although all of them kept staring or smiling at me, and talking in my direction, they huddled together like puppies. My half of the table was bare except for my bag; they squashed their cards, ashtrays, and hands together on the other side. Several cigarette packets were thrust toward me.

"Hello, and no, thank you," I said, but there was so much noise I doubted that they heard. Two of the men started talking over the others' heads, apparently arguing. One of the younger-looking ones, with buckteeth and an earnest expression, stared at me soulfully, ignoring the clamor.

"Hello!" I whispered to him. *"Ni hao!"*

"Ni hao! Ni hao!" several of them yelled as if they'd never heard the expression before. They waved their cigarettes delightedly.

Some of the men turned to one person in the middle, slapping his back, patting his arms, and urging him to speak to me. He stood out from the others, because he was wearing a navy blue smock over his trousers, while the others wore dirty T-shirts. Also, his smile distinguished him—he had very high, rounded cheekbones, as prominent as a Native American's. And his eyelashes were striking—long and rich, curly and dark, like an ad for mascara. When he removed his cigarette and smiled, showing square, even teeth, he was very attractive.

As the other men jabbered, he laughed, shushed them, and looked down. He seemed to be concentrating. He stared at his cigarette, watching it burn without focusing on it. The others quieted, and I waited to see what would happen. Finally the man in the blue smock spoke up, very slowly and softly: "You—" he stopped, laughed, and then composed himself, taking a breath. "You will be our teacher?"

"You speak English!" I said. I could have hugged him.

"No, no. I cannot. I am bad student."

I was so delighted that I said about a hundred times how well he spoke. I had to say everything very slowly, in very simple sentences. "You are good student. Very good English." The other men laughed at the strange sound of our words, and peered at my mouth as I talked. Some of the men, recognizing the word "English," took it up, chanting, "Eeenglish! Eeenglish!" at top volume.

Above the clamor, I learned that the "bad student" was named Zhao, and that he had traveled to the United States before. He got this out haltingly and with many apologies, but I understood. I kept encouraging him, relieved that I had one person, at least, who wasn't an absolute beginner. Every word he or I said was followed by discussion in Chinese; poor Zhao had to translate everything to the crowd.

We were sitting in the dayroom, or what would have been called the mess in Navy terms—an eating area off the galley, lined with padded benches and tables bolted to the floor. It was about the size of a living room. There were twenty or so loose chairs, a large freezer, a few cabinets, and not much else.

Zhao and the other men were using a metal jar lid for an ashtray. Since they all chain-smoked, the lid quickly filled up with ashes and butts, and it smelled atrocious. Hardly able to breathe, I gently moved it further away from myself. The kid with the buckteeth picked it up, leaned toward one of the open portholes, and dumped the ashtray's contents outside.

I was so surprised I forgot to simplify my vocabulary. "Won't that litter the quay?" I asked Zhao.

He looked at where I pointed, to the porthole, but didn't understand my question. He shook his head. "I bad student," he said. He translated something for his friends, who whooped either agreement or dissent, clapped him on the back some more, and kept smoking. It was obviously the high point of their day.

After an hour or so of being shouted at in Chinese, refusing cigarettes every ten seconds, and exchanging monosyllabic sentences with Zhao, I was ready to leave, despite his beautiful cheekbones. Since I had no books with me and no lesson prepared, and since people constantly wandered in and out of the dayroom, all talking, there was no way I could teach anything. I was exhausted from having to answer barrages of questions in Pidgin English, from having to write down and spell every word, or draw pictures—in general from being attentive to ten people at once. I couldn't even look away for a second without seeming rude. Being "on" like that with no break had always been the hardest part of teaching for me. That first day with the Chinese students, it was like being with young, demanding children, except that I couldn't say it was break time now, or that they had to be quiet. I had to remain polite although my voice was giving out, my eyes stung from the cigarette smoke, and my ears hurt from all the yelling. I felt I'd done my bit as far as "getting to know the crew" went, and I was anxious to get back to the hotel and continue exploring Shanghai. Besides, there would be plenty of time during the journey to get to know everyone in minute detail.

Occasionally Peter and Barry appeared among the various people wandering through the dayroom. Every time Peter came in, I'd try to catch his eye, so I could ask for a ride back to the hotel. But he evaded me: he had either forgotten my existence or he didn't want me to escape.

Everyone else at the table ignored the people traipsing through, except when another crew member would see me, start, and come over, grinning and full of questions. Then the others would explain to him who I was, he'd join the pile of men on the padded benches, and we'd have to start over with hello, what is your name, and so on in cartoons and Pidgin English and Chinese. I kept patting the chairs next to me, indicating that others could sit there, but instead they lined up against the wall, leaning against each other, jostling for space.

Suddenly everyone stopped talking and turned to look at someone who had just come in. It was Peter, with two Chinese men looking curiously at me. To one of them, Peter said, "Tell the captain that's the teacher."

Pointing to me, the new translator said something to the captain. I had not seen this man before but was relieved to think he might be our translator en route. He was older than most of the crew, not very tall, with a square face and quick, small eyes. Everyone in the room hushed, watching the captain's reaction.

I stood up, my mind whirling with the Chinese phrase I'd rehearsed for this moment. In my head, I heard my Mandarin teacher's voice saying the Chinese phrase that meant, *Hello, my name is Gillian Kendall. I am the English teacher.* I had practiced it many times for meeting the captain.

The captain's handshake was as soft as a kitten's paw, and he barely glanced in my eyes. I got out my sentence slowly and carefully: *"Ni hao. Wo shi Kendall Ji Lian. Wo shi Yingwen lao shi."*

The captain muttered something. Looking sideways, he said "Herro!" and ducked into the hall.

That night was the farewell banquet. I didn't want to go, since it meant I'd see less of Shanghai, but I knew I'd incur more of Peter's wrath by not showing up. Also, I was hungry, and I'd been told that the food would be superb. Plentiful, too: there would be one course for each person at the table. So I dutifully donned the only skirt I'd brought, as well as all the jewelry—button earrings and a chain necklace.

Neither Barry nor I knew the way to Shanghai's other Western-style hotel, so I told a taxi to take us there: it turned out to be only three blocks away. As impressive as the Portman in size and design, it sported turquoise and mauve carpets, padding the foyer and halls from wall to gleaming wall. Waist-high, gold-etched vases held fans of peacock feathers, and Casablanca fans turned overhead. This hotel seemed *nouveau riche*, whereas the one where we were staying seemed to have been built by and for old money.

Peter was lurking with a group in the dark lobby bar. Joining them, Barry and I were introduced to Peter's friends, a French couple who were touring China. So far as I could tell, they were unrelated to Olaf's company. Once again I sensed an odd coldness from Peter: he was friendly enough to the French people and civil to Barry, but after the introductions he ignored me utterly.

My gin-and-tonic came instantly, and I held it as a prop, watching the others go through a bottle of scotch. Most of the conversation was in French or Chinese, but occasionally Barry or the interpreter would speak to me in English. Barry couldn't follow the conversation either but kept busy by ordering beers, experimenting with different brands. I was bored, and glad when it came time to eat.

About thirty of us filed into a private dining room. We sat at three tables, ten people at each, and I looked forward to a ten-course meal. I was seated by Barry and the Frenchwoman, across from the interpreter, and far from Peter.

Obsequious, perfect waiters brought our first course: a small piece of fish for each person, arranged in little bowls on dark green leaves. We each had the food set in front of us, and I knew from reading guidebooks that Chinese protocol required the most important guest—in this case Peter, since we were the Chinese company's guests—to initiate eating.

Peter either didn't know this fact or didn't care to observe the custom, and no one told him. So we sat there with the food cooling on our plates, drinking tea and beer, while Peter conversed in French with his friends. His rudeness or ignorance irked me. The Chinese looked uncomfortable, and, I thought, hungry. I tried to get the interpreter's eye, to tell him that Peter didn't know the protocol, but he was busy translating for a Norwegian engineer talking to the captain. The rest of the table sat silent, staring at Peter, willing him to begin.

I thought about picking up my own chopsticks to start the meal, but my doing so—me being a woman, and low on the totem pole—might be misconstrued. Like everyone else, I sat there cursing Peter's lack of courtesy.

Peter drank beer and kept talking, oblivious to the food and the people glumly regarding him. Evidently a number of details had to be worked out before the ship could depart. I picked up a few things about final exit papers for one of the crew, and the necessity for repairs to one of the radio systems. Getting parts seemed to be an issue: things mailed from the States had never arrived.

As Peter ordered another round of drinks, the captain looked at all of us, then he and the interpreter exchanged a few rapid words in Chinese. With an embarrassed expression, the interpreter raised his chopsticks. "Let's begin," he said with feigned enthusiasm, and we ate.

The food was terribly disappointing. Eight of the nine courses were bland, room-temperature pieces of fish, beautifully decorated but watery and tasteless. I couldn't tell if it was equally disappointing to the Chinese or whether they enjoyed the plain, soft food. Somewhere around course number six, we had some terrific prawns, wonderfully broiled, pungent with garlic. Unfortunately, we got only one prawn each.

During course number nine—a dreadful, hot pink, Jell-O–like mixture, oversweet and laden with pale, mushy fruit—Barry spoke up. He wrestled Peter's attention away from his French friends and asked, "Did they repair that hull?"

After the question was translated, an excited discussion ensued between the captain and first engineer, all in Chinese. Wang, the interpreter, turned from side to side to follow it. The men talked loudly at each other, gesticulating, then called to someone at another table.

As they questioned the other man, Barry explained to me sotto voce that the previous week, a safety check had revealed a three-inch crack in the metal fabric of the front hull. Ignorant as I was of engineering, even I could grasp the undesirability of a gap in the shell of a ship. At length the Chinese talk quieted down. The captain issued a final statement to the translator, who turned to Barry to answer the question. "Well, the problem is resolved," he said. "They have painted over the crack."

Wednesday morning the phone woke me up at six. I leapt to get it, thinking I was late for the departure. "News," said Barry. "We ain't leaving today. We got to get that hull fixed right."

"Darn!" I said, cheerfully. "I'm crushed."

"Huh. Looks like one of us gets to play tourist some more. I gotta go to work."

I got up and dressed quickly, delighted that I could see more of Shanghai before turning around and heading back for Texas. If the hull got fixed, we were due to leave the next day.

As I was breakfasting from the minibar again—nuts, an apple, and more spring water—I contemplated Peter's apparent dislike of me. I couldn't figure out what I'd done wrong or why he had been so nasty ever since our first interaction. I tried to surmise what he might have heard about me before we met: only good things from Olaf, I was sure, unless Peter objected to the fact that I was female. Maybe he was like the Navy men who thought that women were bad luck on ships.

From Barry, Peter might have heard an account of our initial dinner conversation, but there was nothing wrong in that unless Peter objected to our listed food requests. That seemed the only possible problem: maybe the list Barry and I had prepared was too long (or its items too expensive), and Peter was blaming me for wanting special treatment.

Since it was only 6:30 a.m., I thought I could catch Peter before he left for the ship. I dialed his room number and got a sleepy answer.

"Peter? It's Gillian. Kendall. The English teacher."

I waited for some acknowledgement, but got only silence.

He must really dislike me, I thought. "I'm just calling to mention something that's been bothering me. You know that food list that Barry and I made up? Well, don't worry about it. I imagine it's not very convenient to do special shopping for us and I really don't care what—"

"Is that all?"

"Yeah, that's about it, so, I guess you're on your way out the door, aren't you? I'm sorry, Peter—" I found myself apologizing to a buzzing, hung-up phone.

He'd hit a new low. If he was too stubborn to tell me what was wrong, and too rude even to accept an apology, I wasn't going to bother with him. Besides, he wasn't coming on the journey. My only fear was that he might make a negative report to Olaf, but I put it out of my mind, determined to enjoy my last day ashore.

As the first sunrays stretched across Nanjing Road, I slipped along the little side streets—still quiet—to a residential area. It had been raining, and as bicyclists went by, their tires whispered on the wet pavement. In a little alley, a boy in pajamas was pumping water from a communal well, and through apartment windows I caught glimpses of people spooning up food. I stood far enough back from the houses and yards that I wasn't intruding, but I looked as hard as I could.

On one corner stood a man with a bicycle, apparently waiting for something. At his feet lay a number of bottles and cans. I lurked behind a wall so he wouldn't notice me, and watched. A woman walked up and offered the man a small plastic bag. From it he withdrew four small, empty cans. He weighed them, then gave the woman a few coins, and added the cans to the pile near his feet. He was running a recycling center.

I spent the morning taking pictures in an open-air market. In the warmest part of the afternoon, knowing it was probably my last day in the city, I wandered for miles and toured some attractions. That evening, as I changed for bed, I noticed that I had worn out my new walking shoes, the Rockports. I'd taken Rockports on previous ships because the rubber soles stood up well to the metal decks, and the flat heels made it easy to climb ladders. My two other pairs had both lasted over a year. This one I'd trashed in three days of tramping around Shanghai.

Peter seemed to be in a reasonable mood as we checked out of the hotel and headed to the ship on Thursday. I was grateful for the relaxation of his usual nastiness, since I'd been dreading his complaining about my luggage. If he didn't like me for being female, he'd hate me for carrying too many suitcases. To my relief, he just shrugged when he saw the bellman appearing with the trolley-load of my stuff. Perhaps the prospect of leaving China—for him, by air, to go back home—brightened him up. His silence that day seemed almost civil.

On the quay, we made our way through a crowd of Chinese people who were talking and shouting to the men on board. I gathered that they were family members, come to see the crew off. When we reached the edge of the quay, beside the gangplank, Peter said to me, "You can manage this all right then."

"Well . . ." I dithered. I didn't want to have to carry all my stuff across the narrow footbridge and up the ladders by myself.

Barry winked at Peter and picked up one of the bigger suitcases. "Come on, let's give her a hand." The suitcase looked like a pillow tucked under his arm. Gratefully, I took the whiteboard and the two smaller bags myself.

Barry led me to my stateroom. Along with his and a few of the officers' rooms, mine was on the second-to-top level, one level above the dayroom where I'd met the crew, two down from the bridge. It was an honor to have berthing so high up, since upper parts of a ship tend to be more comfortable. The only quarters above mine were the captain's and the first mate's, both of whom slept directly beneath the bridge, the command center for the ship. Not only was my stateroom up high, but it had two portholes: one overlooking the port side, the other the bow. I felt like an executive who had landed a corner office.

The room itself looked great: about seven by ten feet, with one corner taken up by a separate, shut-off bathroom. "Wow," I said, "it's got a private head!" I'd been wondering if I was going to have to share with the men. My bathroom comprised a shower stall, which contained a tiny sink and toilet. I turned the shower on for a few seconds, and water filled the sink and poured onto the toilet lid.

"It works," Barry said. "You can brush your teeth, wash your hair, and sit on the toilet all at the same time. By the way—" he picked up the toilet paper, and set it on the floor outside the bathroom. "I learned this the hard way. If you keep it inside, it gets soaked."

The rest of the stateroom was a white box. My rack, or bed, lay across one end of the room. Again, I was grateful—on my first ship,

I'd been sleeping in a high rack, out of which I had fallen and broken my wrist. Across from the rack was a little table bolted to the bulk-head, or metal wall, as well as a good chair, which was tied to the table so it couldn't fly up during a storm. A cushioned window seat ran under the side porthole, and under it was a storage space. I also had a minute closet.

Barry watched me check the place out. "You still want to come?"

"Are you kidding?" I said. "This is palatial!"

Barry shrugged; he wasn't going to complain about roughing it if I didn't. He went down the passageway to his room, and I started unpacking. Hanging my clothes and stowing toiletries took about ninety seconds, since I'd brought so little. I was organizing my school stuff into folders and boxes, a more laborious task, when someone knocked.

The door was open, and I was in plain view of the man standing in the doorway, but he was averting his eyes. I said, "Yes?"

He glanced at me, murmured in Chinese, and with an embar-rassed little half-bow thrust forward an armful of towels, soap, and toilet paper. Equally awkward, I thanked him in both languages. He tried to dart off, but I stopped him, stammering my name in Man-darin. *"Wo shi Ji Lian."* I pointed to my door, where I'd taped a name sign my Chinese teacher had made for me. She had chosen the name *Ji Lian* because it sounded vaguely like "Gillian." It meant "beautiful healthy lotus flower" or some such thing.

Seeing the name, the man nodded vigorously. He pronounced my name and then pointed to himself: "Lin" he said, and added something in Chinese that I understood to mean that he was a steward, there to see that my room was all right, and so on.

Lacking the right Chinese vocabulary, I pointed to the trash can under my desk, which was full. He reached for it, but I picked it up before he could get it. "I'll empty it," I said, even though he couldn't understand. "Just tell me where. Where? *Nar?*"

He pointed out the porthole, and then out my door toward the weather deck. He made a gesture, as if throwing the trash overboard, and a splashing sound.

"What?" Again, Navy experience had not prepared me for this. On my last ship, all trash had been disposed of in an orderly, if environmentally undesirable, fashion. It was sorted into heaps, and burnable waste was hung over the side of the ship in a metal cage and burned. Non-combustibles were recycled or, more often, sunk.

On this trip, I had received firm directives from Olaf not to dump any garbage overboard, but to store it on board until we reached Galveston. He didn't want the crew polluting the water, and I had the impression that doing so could incur fines for the company. However, I couldn't explain all that in Pidgin Mandarin and hand gestures. I nodded at Lin and thanked him again, letting him think I would throw my trash into the ocean. I might not approve of his waste disposal technique, but I had met someone kind and helpful.

A few hours later, the engines, which had been humming for hours, turned up several decibels. Shortly afterward, I heard a loud scraping noise, and the whole ship shuddered as if we were washing up against something big. Wondering if I'd missed our departure, I looked out my porthole. On the forward deck, three men bent over the anchor chain as it rose from the depths, slowly wound up by a small motor. Wet, melon-sized metal links emerged from the opening, the deck vibrating as each section of chain shuddered up and onto the spool. After a few minutes, the chain stopped, with a heavy, metallic groan, and the anchor reached its storage well on the hull.

Barry came to my door and shook his head at my unpacking. "You going topside? There's a big party." As we jogged up the ladder, he called back over his shoulder, "This ship is a real big deal here—part of the new China, I guess. Opening up trade with the West. This is one of the first ships ever to go out for a Western company. There's TV cameras, the whole works."

At least a thousand people had crowded onto the quay, all waving like mad to the crew, who were leaning over the rail, laughing and calling down to their families. A band thumped out brassy Chinese music, and on top of it someone was making a speech into a megaphone.

When I came on deck, the crew greeted me with applause and started pointing at me and shouting explanations to their friends below. Seeing me, a lot of the people on the quay yelled and laughed in surprise. Babies were held up to look at me. I waved down, smiling genteelly and generally into the crowd like Queen Elizabeth.

Two primitive TV cameras rolled, taking in the scene from their fixed positions. One was focused on the deck of the ship, and I waved at it, wondering if I'd be featured on Chinese TV that night. If I were, would anyone recognize me? Maybe Peter's French friends, if they watched. Maybe that guy from the park.

Below me, on the lower deck, a few last crew members scrambled on board. Before going up the gangway, Zhao, the man who could speak English, hugged his daughter and said something close to her face. It was all so different from an American, Navy departure: no one was crying.

The captain was gesticulating, talking with two reporters by the side of the ship; he had one foot on the bridge. He waved them off, jumped across the plank, and pulled it in behind him. Then he shut the hatch.

With the bridge gone, nothing except the ropes—which I remembered were always called "lines" on a ship—connected us to the shore. The engines grew louder, and a few of the men scurried down the outside ladders, getting to their positions on the weather decks. From my place on the stern, I watched dockworkers untying the heavy lines, and tossing them, uncoiled, aboard. Within seconds all the lines were on our side of the water, and the distance between us and the quay widened.

In half a minute the gap expanded to several yards. It was too late to jump off. As the ship began moving forward, a few children ran along the quay, calling up to us. The crew members on deck kept waving good-byes. I waved, too, although no one was looking for me. The band played louder and the faces became indistinguishable. Soon they were just a mass of people, farther and farther away. The man speaking into the megaphone shouted good-bye, the crowd cheered, and the band gave us a huge crashing of cymbals.

The ship channel widened, and the *Tan Suo Zhe* moved toward the middle of it. The shore, now visible only as a long, low row of factories, was several hundred yards off. If I'd wanted to, I might have been able to swim. But soon the horizon grew smaller and flatter. I was hypnotized, and sad, watching the end of China slipping away. I'd had so little time there.

After half an hour or so, there was land on only one side of us. Everyone except me had gone forward or below; I stayed on the bow, watching the countryside disappear. Below me, a man in orange overalls moved slowly around the lower deck. I thought that he would coil up the messy lines that lay there like huge wet snakes, but instead he was knocking at some piece of machinery with a wrench.

I watched the last pieces of China receding. A few blobs of islands glided by, and then we passed the bouncing orange sea buoy that marked the end of the channel and the beginning of the East China Sea. As the land disappeared behind us, the engine roar grew steady and loud, and the smokestacks blew back gray lines of burnt oil. The breeze picked up, bringing the first fresh air I'd smelled in days, and the ship's roll became more noticeable as we reached the real waves. We were at sea.

One Arm's Distance

As the journey began, I took preventive measures against depression. Something about a long sea journey—probably the confinement and lack of stimulation as well as separation from loved ones—tends to bring people down. True sailors (Tristan Jones, for example, whose books I'd been reading, or Thor Heyerdahl) possibly didn't feel this way, but practically everyone on Navy ships, including me, had shown signs of distress, even emotional illness. On those other trips I'd slept too much, eaten too much, worried too much, and suffered too much homesickness.

On the *Tan Suo Zhe,* I expected to miss Martin, and I was concerned that conflicts would arise between me and other people on board. Also, as the only woman, I'd have special pressures—not least the possibility of sexual tension or harassment. I dreaded the idea that one of the men might become interested in me so I tried to assume it wouldn't happen, but, with the men being at sea for six weeks, I thought I might become the object of random lust or, worse, some kind of predatory pass.

However, as much as I dreaded personal confrontations, I was even more afraid of boredom. To fend off inertia and apathy, I came up with a daily schedule. The captain had told me that he wanted me to teach two classes, two hours each, every day. That was considerably less than the schedule Olaf had suggested, which meant less work for me, but I didn't like the idea of seven-day weeks. I held out for six days a week, knowing that students (and certainly teacher) would do better with regular breaks. Having a day off would give the lessons a rhythm, a sense of starting fresh every week, so that anyone who'd been bored or discouraged (again, including the teacher) could get a new wind.

Through the interpreter, I asked Captain Tan if I could separate the classes by levels, one for beginners and one for more advanced students. He agreed but said that the beginning students must meet in the morning, the others in the evening.

My teaching schedule set, I set about filling in the empty hours. Exercise was the best antidote to my depression. On other ships I'd used the officers' gym regularly and sweated through aerobics classes on deck, even in the Gulf of Oman, where temperatures soared well over one hundred degrees. On the *Tan Suo Zhe,* where my stateroom was chilly and I would have liked more exertion, exercise would be limited to walking around and around the decks, circling like a goldfish. It would be boring, and if the seas were rough, there was a slight danger of toppling overboard, since the deck had such a low guardrail. Still, I planned to walk every evening. In the mornings I decided I would stretch, write in my journal, and get some sunshine; in the afternoons, I'd prepare for my classes and study Chinese.

Also, I planned to see as many sunsets as possible, sunsets being the one reliable source of beauty on a working ship. Tempers might flare, personalities might grate, the routine might grow too familiar and the water turn muddy gray, but—as long as it wasn't raining— every night I'd have an unobstructed view of one of the best shows on earth.

My first day on board, as we moved out of the Chinese waters and into the East China Sea, I was delighted not to be seasick. Since the water wasn't rough, the ship's movement was just a slow, flat rolling. Things left lying didn't even shift, and my stomach felt normal. This stability was convenient since I had a lot of unpacking to do.

After the first half hour or so I forgot about being on a ship. Just as if I were moving into any new home, my first priority was to arrange my desk, which in this case consisted of the small table bolted to the deck. On the single bookshelf above it, I put my best textbooks, some paper, and a few pens. The shelf had sides, like a box, so the things would be safe if the ship started rock 'n' rolling.

Also, I put up a calendar and a map of the world. Actually, it was only a map of part of the world, consisting of two pages that I had enterprisingly torn from an in-flight magazine. The map showed everything from eastern China to the Atlantic Ocean; all of the United States was included, as was the whole Pacific. For interior decorating, I taped the two 8 1/2 x 11 inch pages above my desk, making a pale blue picture against the dull bulkhead. Martha Stewart, I thought, watch out.

That first day, I felt nervous about leaving my stateroom. So much depended on first impressions, and for a woman in my position, that meant appearance. In consultation with my Chinese teacher, I'd picked my "wardrobe"—the few things that fit into the tiniest suitcase I owned—primarily for comfort and function on board a ship. I'd brought one skirt, but that I folded away, since it didn't work to scramble up and down ladders in a skirt. I had some relatively new jeans, two other pairs of loose cotton pants, and various plain shirts and sweaters. All of it was calculated to look as androgynous as possible. I didn't want to call attention to my femininity, but still, preparing for my first underway appearance, I brushed my hair back from my face with a band and put on a little makeup: just enough blush to look healthy, and some mascara for confidence.

My cabin opened onto a small passageway that crossed the ship from port to starboard: at either end, the passage opened to the outside weather deck. Across from my room was a companion ladder, or interior stairway; down the ladder was the dayroom, on the first deck above the waterline.

The ship was shaped like an oversized tugboat. Most of her body was flat, but four decks, or stories, were stacked in front, like a miniature apartment house. In this "house" were the offices and living quarters: the staterooms; the galley, dayroom, and lounge; the sick bay; and the radio room. Most of the crew slept and showered in the bunk rooms below water level.

Since I was most familiar with the dayroom, I went down to that area. The ladders between decks were less steep than those on Navy ships, which had resembled house-painting ladders, almost straight up and down. The ladders on the *Tan Suo Zhe* went at perhaps a thirty-degree angle. Still, it wasn't the kind of stairway where you would let go of the handrail.

In the passageway, I noticed the ship's movement much more, probably because the hatch to the weather deck was open, so I could see, hear, and smell the ocean. As I climbed down the steps, holding on against the rocking, several people at the bottom watched me descend, waiting for their turns to go up. The ladders were too narrow for two people to pass, so who went first depended on rank, timing, or politeness. I said hello in Chinese and then English, and then "*Xie xie.* Thank you."

In the dayroom, at least a dozen men were sitting around, watching TV and smoking what smelled like the cheapest and harshest of cigarettes. I felt nausea as well as a rush of disappointment: I hated television and hadn't expected to have it on board. As soon as they saw me, the men straightened up and shifted to alertness, looking at me instead of the screen.

Someone called, "Hi! How are you?" Although I recognized Wang, the interpreter, by his English, I couldn't have picked out his face. I wondered how I'd ever learn my students' names, because the men all looked the same to me. Approaching the group, I tried to see how I could distinguish one man from the next. Their faces seemed very similar, and all of them were wearing baggy, worn gray trousers. However, Wang had a narrow, foxy face, with pleasant, heavy-lidded eyes, and he was smaller and thinner than most of the men. Also he was wearing a pale green nylon jacket, buttoned over his T-shirt.

I asked Wang what everyone was watching. "Chinese soap opera," he confided, waving toward the set and giggling. The gesture reminded me of my gay friend Bill's campy moves.

As I sat down, several of the men got up and moved away, taking the jar lids they used as ashtrays. I didn't understand what was going on, and I even wondered if I smelled bad to them, but I wasn't offended, since most of the men smiled as they reseated themselves and they continued to face me, watching my face as I talked with the translator. About ten people offered me a cigarette, urging their packs toward me even after I'd refused several others.

Some of the men had moved to one of the padded benches near the table I'd chosen. Since several people were already occupying those benches, the newcomers had to squeeze in. The men cuddled up close, putting their arms around each other, perfectly at ease. They looked like children crowded into a car. I was pleased to see that Chinese men were so relaxed about touching each other. In fact, I wanted to stare at them as they stared at me, but instead I asked Wang why all the men had moved away from where I sat.

He glanced from me to the men, and his clever face looked amused. "Well, maybe it is Chinese custom. I think you do not have. But in China, if a man sit next to a woman, he must keep some distance if she is a person he does not know. With sister, or wife, is different. But for you, since we do not know you well, we think is polite to keep some area, some space." He held his arm straight out from the shoulder, and I saw that his fingertips didn't quite reach me.

"About this far," he said. "Maybe one meter—one yard. Maybe is strange for you. Foolish custom."

"Strange, but good," I said. "I think it's very considerate. I can think of plenty of times when I would have liked American men to keep a yard away."

My remark didn't seem to go over very well. Without replying, Wang shifted his eyes sternly back to the television. Had I offended him by even hinting at impropriety?

To change the subject, I asked about the soap opera.

"We-ell . . ." he drawled, obviously relieved. "I think it is silly. I do not watch it usually. We are just watching it while we wait for our dinner." He nodded toward the kitchen, where oily smoke billowed toward the ceiling.

"Is it like an American show?" I asked.

"Well—" Wang crinkled up his face in a frown. "I do not think so." He laughed again, too embarrassed, I guessed, to talk about the romance in the program. We seemed easily to get onto difficult topics.

Then I asked what was for supper, and Wang looked pleased and translated my question for the others. Immediately everyone started chattering. They pointed to the kitchen, nodding. "They say the cook is very good," Wang told me happily. "I think you will have some food that is all right for you."

Someone ran into the kitchen and summoned the cook, Mr. Ding, who trotted over to my table. He was a lovely, rounded man, with a broad face and thick, coarse hair that was different from everyone else's smooth black locks. He looked like a little lion, I thought, with a big dark mane. Mr. Ding spoke in Chinese to the interpreter, sounding eager.

Wang turned to me. "He wants to know if you are hungry."

Mr. Ding's face lit up. "Hon-gree!" he sang, obviously remembering the word from some English lesson. Everyone laughed and repeated it. Mr. Ding stood about three feet away from me, peering into my face. "Hongree?"

"Yes! *Shi.*" I said. "Hungry. I'm hungry!"

The noise level grew exponentially. Communication had occurred. Everyone knew what it was to feel hungry, so they understood something about the stranger on board.

The assistant cook called from the kitchen, and the crew stood up, put out cigarettes, and started bustling around the room, opening various cabinets and drawers. One man reached into the cupboard below where he was sitting and got out a white plastic bowl. Another went to a drawer under the TV and fished out two chopsticks.

I started toward the galley to find things to eat with. But as I reached the doorway, Mr. Ding trotted toward me, jabbering in Chinese, and flapped at me to sit down. I looked at Wang, still sitting where I'd left him. "He says they will serve you here." Wang stood up gracefully, making a place for me at the table. "Please have a seat." Feeling honored, but also overprivileged, I sat.

The dayroom was partly divided by a wall, but I could see the other half of the room, where the men were sitting down at tables, talking, clanking their plates, and opening cans of Coke and big brown bottles. In between the dayroom and the galley was a cafeteria-like serving line of food, from which the men helped themselves.

Barry appeared in the doorway, having been summoned by Mr. Ding. The young assistant cook, Zen, came in with an armful of tableware. He set plates, bowls, chopsticks, and cans of Coke in front of me and Barry. I looked at the soda with dismay: sugar was not in my plans—in fact, avoiding sugar was a big part of my mental health strategy—but I didn't want to be rude and refuse anything that was so kindly offered. Also, I knew that Zen spoke no English, and he looked so young that I feared offending him even more than I did the other men. He looked almost like a teenager to me.

Fortunately, Mr. Ding saw me looking at the Coke, and pointed to it. "Hongree?" he asked. "Good-ah? No good-ah?"

Relieved, I said, "Maybe some water? Could I have some water to drink?" I pointed to the fountain by the television. "I'll get it, I just need a glass." I pantomimed drinking from a cup.

"Yes, yes." Mr. Ding went into the kitchen, hurrying in his bent-over little trot. He returned a minute later with two empty jars, which he filled with water and set before Barry and me.

The assistant cook brought out bowls of fragrant soup for us: a clear broth, bobbing with wontons, with soft green vegetables floating in it. Mr. Ding anxiously watched us take the first mouthfuls.

I was disappointed—the soup was salty and slightly greasy, but otherwise tasteless. But Mr. Ding was watching with evident concern, so I said, "Thank you! Very good."

Barry set down his spoon in disgust. "You like this?" He snapped open his can of Coke. "*This* good," he announced.

I didn't have to eat much of the soup, fortunately, because the assistant cook came back with a huge plate of noodles, which he set between us and which Barry dived into with his fork.

I served myself with chopsticks, which made Mr. Ding laugh. He waved at me and yelled something into the other side of the room. A few of the men came in, carrying their bowls of rice under their chins and laughing at me. The translator came, too, blowing on his soup and grinning hugely. "Well, he says you are using your left hand for the chopsticks! They have never seen it before."

I could have told them a few stories about what the Egyptian students thought of my left-handedness—a sign of evil, an unclean habit—but food was coming fast. The noodles were hot and covered with a sauce that was oily but tangy. It might have been seasoned with miso, or it might have contained a thousand other things I couldn't identify. A platter appeared at my elbow—a few dozen small fishes, fried with onions and spices. They were delicious and I had two or three of the filets with some rice from a steaming bowl.

"I can't believe this here's just for the two of us," Barry said, chewing. "We got enough here for the whole crew."

I tried offering the plate of fish back to Mr. Ding, thinking he might take it over to the other side of the mess, where the crew had retired to finish their meal. "A lot to eat," I said, waving at the huge plates of food, trying to show that it was too much.

The cook shook his woolly head and returned the fish to the table. "Little bit."

I'd stuffed myself with fish, noodles, and rice and was ready to quit eating for at least a day when Wang came back, bearing a platter of beef ribs stacked as high as his chin.

"Now we're talking!" Barry slid half a dozen ribs onto his plate.

I couldn't believe we were supposed to eat more. "Too much!" I said again, as politely as I could. But the ribs were fantastic and I managed to eat one, and then part of another. They were cooked in a thick sauce that tasted of fennel and chili. I wasn't crazy about the flavoring, but the meat was so tender that I overcame my anti-red-meat scruples and enjoyed it.

Barry was making his preferences known to Ding, who was still watching us eat. "This stuff," Barry said, waving a rib, "is very good. The rest, so-so."

"So-so?" Mr. Ding looked confused.

"I like the fish," I said, pointing to the platter, which still held enough food for several meals. "But please, don't make so much. Not so much."

"Na so mush?" Mr. Ding was good at imitation, and he seemed to be catching on to what I meant.

The assistant, Zen, came out of the kitchen. Thinking he wanted to clear up, I offered him my plate, but he couldn't take it: he was carrying a vat of chicken, potatoes, and green beans, cooked in a brown stew.

"Oh my God," Barry said. "We are going to get fat."

We both tasted a little of the vegetables, which were good, if slightly overcooked. But even if they'd had the finest preparation in the world, we were much too stuffed to appreciate them. My stomach hurt and I leaned back in my chair, overcome.

Meanwhile, the men were drifting back in. I wondered if they wanted to turn the TV on. They went into the galley and rinsed their bowls, then put them away in their various cubbyholes all over the day room. Several men leaned over a long freezer that stood against one wall, peering in and choosing ice cream desserts. Wang joined us, perching on the seat at the end of the table, hands around his jar of tea. "Well, I think it is not very good." He nodded toward my heaped plate of stew, from which I'd taken only a few bites.

"Oh, it's not that!" I said. "I'm just totally stuffed."

"Eat up," Barry grinned. "Don't you know there are children starving in China?"

I held my breath, looking to see how Wang would take this. His eyes crinkled, and he smiled behind his hand.

"Don't listen to him," I said.

Wang waved away my apology. "I have heard it before, what Barry said. Is it true, the fathers and mothers in America say to the children that we in China are hungry?"

I let out a gust of air. "I heard it about India," I said. "But I guess parents do say that about China, too. Just to get the children to eat, you know."

"Well, I will tell you something," the translator said. He sounded shy but eager. "In China, the English book are very popular with many people. Do you know the story, 'The Little Match Girl'?"

I remembered something about an orphan peddling boxes of matches for pennies in the snow. "Sort of," I said. "She's very poor, right?"

"Yes, and no one will buy her matches from her. And it is Christmas Eve! She is hungry and cold, and she has no parents. My mother and my aunts always told us, 'That is how children live in England and the United States. Be grateful you have rice.'"

I laughed hard at this story, and saved it up to tell my friends later. It seemed the translator was getting more relaxed, and I was glad that we were moving to more casual, candid exchanges.

Mr. Ding came toward Barry and me, proffering handfuls of ice-cream bars and popsicles. The labels, in English as well as Chinese, identified the flavors: chocolate, vanilla, and something labeled not green tea but "green pea." Barry and I shook our heads, apologizing through the interpreter for not eating more. I said, "Please tell Mr. Ding that it was delicious—"

Wang interrupted me to translate, and the cook looked ready to hug me. Beaming with his whole round, snub-nosed face, he chattered back, and Wang explained: "He is glad you enjoyed your dinner. He wants you to tell him anything else you would like him to make."

"Anything *else?*! Please tell him that I won't want to eat again for a week."

"Tell him," Barry added, "that we don't want to get fat on this ship. He could make just one dish and that would be fine. Maybe some veggies and those ribs, and I'd be happy."

The translator talked with Mr. Ding for a minute and then turned back to us. "Well, the cook says he is sorry that he got a late start with cooking today, because they were bringing supplies aboard. He knows it is not enough food. He will make more tomorrow."

The tobacco haze in the dayroom had cleared a little while Barry and I ate, but when the crew wandered back after their meal, they were all lighting up again. Boxes of cigarettes were offered continually; matches were struck; and gray, noxious columns wafted upward, increasing the cloud. Clearly, I was going to have to accept secondhand smoke as an EFL occupational hazard. Someone switched the TV back on, and we watched gray, fuzzy figures move around in a mist. Wang explained to me that as we got farther from land, the TV would become less and less functional. I hid my delight.

While several of the men pulled chairs close to the TV, others seated themselves at a respectful distance, watching Barry, Wang, and me talk. Every time I moved, I sensed a great deal of interest. If I lifted my glass to drink some water, someone would comment on it, saying "Thirsty?" or offering, in pantomime, to get me another glass. I refused more Cokes and cigarettes than I could count. Although I appreciated their kindness, I didn't like so much attention, and so felt relieved when several of the men gathered around the next table to start a card game.

Someone had opened a couple of portholes, and fresh sea air blew in, carrying away some of the smoke. Mild crashes came from the galley, where the cooks were cleaning up. Although I didn't see the captain or the first mate, nearly everyone else was hanging around the dayroom. Some stayed intent on the foggy TV, several were following a game of chess in one corner, but most of them—at least a dozen men—gathered around the card table. The four men playing were seated, but the onlookers were standing, leaning on the backs of chairs. Every single person was smoking, and most of them were talking. The cards moved fast, each hand of whatever they were playing resulting in a cheer and some argument.

Trying not to directly inhale any of the lines of smoke, I pulled my own chair closer to the game. Immediately the little crowd opened up, and I was invited to play.

Fortunately, Wang was playing, and he explained the rules while the cards were shuffled. "Well, this game is called 'Pig,'" he said. "You know how to play bridge?"

I said I'd played bridge a few times.

"Oh, then I think it is no problem for you. Just remember that club is trumps and heart is strong and if you have a lady spade try to pass it away, she doubles the bad points."

"What?" The cards had been dealt and put in my hands. Everyone else threw down a card, too fast for me even to see, let alone think about. Wang played one of my cards, someone snatched up the trick, everyone cheered, and the first hand was over. The next six or seven went the same way: while I was still trying to see what the first people had played, someone behind or next to me would grab a card from my hand and slap it onto the table. I had no idea what was happening. Sometimes I "won" a round and the men would point to the pile of cards, exclaiming loudly, until I took it. Ferocious discussion continued the whole time.

As the smoke thickened and the ashtrays filled up, the air smelled worse and worse. My clothes and hair were going to reek, and I didn't know yet what kind of laundry facilities we had. I tried breathing through my mouth so I wouldn't have to smell the fumes, but that made my throat hurt. I was distracted from the game, which was difficult for me anyway.

"Wait!" I said finally. "I can't follow this! Can we slow down a little?"

Wang translated and there was a stunned moment of silence. All the men stared at me, looking worried. "Well, I am sorry," Wang said. "We were playing slowly for you."

"Oh, no," I said. And then, after a moment, "Oh, dear."

"I think I did not explain it very well," Wang assured me. After that, he made the men freeze the game after each card. "This is high card," he said, "because trump. But this trump is bad now, so is good for Lin to put down. You can put down king now."

"But I thought the king was a trump!" I said.

"Doesn't matter. Ace is down already, and king is no good this time. You have Jack so no difference."

"What about the queen?" I said, but the other players' patience was worn out. They had played another three cards before Wang could answer. He touched my Jack and told me to play it. I did, and it took the trick. A lot of cheering followed.

"See?" Wang said. "You are good player."

After half an hour I grew disgusted with my inability to catch on, even though it wasn't really my fault, since the game went so rapidly. The crowd tightened around the card table as I excused myself: now they could do some *real* card playing.

In a corner of the dayroom, a few men were watching a chess game. I sidled closer for a look, feeling relieved. At chess, I wasn't championship material, but my boyfriend at Stanford had been a serious, competitive player, and he'd taught me a few things. As I approached, the men acknowledged my presence with quick hellos, but then turned back to the game board, on which nothing was happening.

One player looked especially intent; someone pointed him out to me and made me understand that he was called "Mr. Chess." He seemed older than the rest of the crew. In general I couldn't ascribe ages to the crewmen—to me they all looked about eighteen, and I had been astonished to learn that they had wives and children. But

Mr. Chess was partially bald, and his remaining hair was light black, almost gray. His long forehead made him look even taller than he was, and he was one of the thinnest people I had ever seen. He was not sitting in his chair, but squatting on its seat. Doing so put his head forward, in front of his feet, and he gazed down on the board with the stare of a vulture. When he sensed my arrival, he acknowledged me with a tiny smile, but then turned back to his game.

This Chinese chess used round disks that looked like checkers with figures etched on them. I thought I recognized a broken line of pawns in front, but otherwise the gold imprints on the little disks bore no resemblance to the rooks, knights, and queens I'd been expecting. The skinny, bald man sat on his haunches and smoked, and his opponent smoked and sipped a Coke. The people watching smoked and made comments about what the players should do, but no one was grabbing the pieces the way they'd grabbed my cards.

Suddenly Mr. Chess moved a piece twice, jumping over another piece to do so, and took one of his opponent's pawns. His move was followed by a ripple of discussion that I couldn't understand. I had no idea what had transpired, and there was no one to explain it to me. Also, I had to get some air. Murmuring good nights, I moved out toward the weather deck.

In the passageway, I heard strange sounds coming from the room labeled "officers' lounge," but which Wang and Barry called "the bar." There were odd, metallic noises, a quick series of explosions like television gunshots, then laughter. In the bar the porthole was covered, and no lights were on. It was so dark I had to blink my eyes to adjust. Squinting, I saw Barry's silhouette in the blue light of a video screen. He was leaning back in a chair, feet propped on either side of the monitor, punching at a remote control. "Zap! Got that sucker!" He jabbed the control again, eyes still on the game. "You seen this yet?"

Four small blocks, representing tanks or alien aircraft or something, appeared on the bottom of the screen. Barry controlled a spaceship flying above them, dodging the missiles they sent up. He could shoot down at them and chip pieces off the blocks. Suddenly the screen seemed to explode, then went dark.

"Aw, shit!" Barry slammed down the control. "I was almost to level two." He turned to me, jubilant. "I guess we're gonna have plenty of time to get this down. I'm glad it's here; it's so damn smoky in that room I couldn't take it."

"I know what you mean," I said. "You don't smoke either?"

"Just quit two months ago. I still chew sometimes, but I hope these guys don't talk me back into it. That's why I'm doing this." He held up his Coke can, signaling. "I've gained ten pounds since I quit smoking. My wife told me to get in shape on this cruise."

As far as I could tell, he was in pretty excellent shape. He was a broad-shouldered, muscular man, twice the size of most of the crewmen. He could probably gain quite a bit without its showing. I felt self-conscious about my own excess weight (about twenty pounds, which shows a lot more on a woman) and wondered if he were being judgmental of me. "Well," I said. "I was just on my way to get some air. You want to come?"

"Maybe later." Barry turned back to the machine and clicked it into life. "Let me kill these dudes and get to level two first."

Outside, the moon was peering over the edge of the flat, black ocean. I wondered how far we were from land, and as I walked back to the stern, I felt some of the loneliness I'd known was coming. None of the games inside appealed to me, and no one else seemed to want to share the night air.

Inevitably, I wondered what Martin was doing, if he were thinking of me at that moment, if he were missing me. I'd been gone about a week. Had he joined one of the groups I'd suggested; had he found someone to hang out with over the weekend? I considered how I'd feel if he found someone else he wanted be involved with, but the prospect seemed unlikely. Besides being shy, he claimed to be in love with me. I didn't think I needed to worry, and, vaguely, I felt that I would not be inordinately troubled even if he were interested in someone else.

Being alone on the weather deck was odd. On Navy ships, you couldn't move without stumbling across another person. When we were in the Persian Gulf, sailors had stood round-the-clock watches all along the deck, every few yards. And at the stern there had always been two people posted, whose job it was to look and listen for anyone falling overboard. But if I'd fallen off the *Tan Suo Zhe,* no one would have known. I was as alone as if I had already jumped.

I peered over the aft railing at the black, salt water. Water splashed and slapped against the hull, and a diagonal white wake rippled away from the side. Judging by the size of the wave, I could tell we weren't moving very rapidly. I thought about how fast the card game had been, how foreign the chess, how unappealing the death-and-destruction video game. For a long time, it was going to be just me and the ocean.

Ma, Not Ma

My first duty as teacher was to establish a baseline record of the students' skills. Olaf had explained that I could earn a bonus, depending on how much improvement the students showed in their speech. I figured that in order for him to see improvement, he had to know where they were starting from. So, my second day on the ship, I took my cassette recorder down to the main deck.

As usual when I came into the dayroom, several men looked up expectantly. I nodded hello, beckoning. Three or four men stood uncertainly, then followed me into the bar. Wang, the interpreter, was there, and he explained that I wanted to tape each of the men for a minute or two. The men nodded, looking surprised and nervous.

To demonstrate how the machine worked, I pressed "record" and started talking. But the little recording light stayed black; I had to hold the machine to my face and speak into the microphone before it would pick up. Too late, I realized that I should have brought a remote mike. This arrangement was awkward even for me; it might make the men even more uncomfortable.

I hit "rewind" and "play," and we then heard the tape I'd just made: "It's Friday, June 28, 1991, and we're in the East China Sea. It's a cloudy day outside, but the ocean is pretty calm. I'm sitting in the bar with Wang and a few other people. We're about to start recording their English." The men laughed at hearing my voice coming out of the box.

To give the others confidence, the interpreter demonstrated how to make a recording. He held the little box squarely in both hands, and addressed the small opening in a serious voice. "Ah, well, this is Wang. Wang. We are very happy to have Ji Lian for teacher. Thank you." Then he spoke in Chinese for a minute, telling the onlookers what he had just done. We played back his speech, and the others applauded. Hearing the noise, a few more people came into the bar. That was all very well, but none of the future students wanted to go next. They nudged each other toward me, but every person shook his head and backed away, afraid to talk to the box. I set it in the middle of the table so that whoever talked wouldn't have to sit so near to me. A few of the men sat down and hunched toward the machine, staring at it as they might a bomb.

"They say they cannot speak English," Wang explained. "So do not want to make voice recording." I told Wang that that was the whole point, that I needed proof that they couldn't yet speak. He told the group, and everyone nodded understandingly but no one volunteered.

I picked up the recorder and passed it to one young man who was sitting closest to me, the one I'd noticed before with soulful eyes and buckteeth. He waved it away, but he smiled slightly.

"Please tell them," I said to Wang, "that this would really help me, if they will just speak a little, even Chinese." Wang interpreted what I'd said. Everyone looked dubious.

Then the man I remembered from the first day, Zhao, came to the door and was quickly called in by the others. Hearing what I wanted, he sat down in the chair closest to me, his knee jogging up and down. I showed him the recorder and how it worked. Very slowly, I asked him, "Can you speak English?"

He looked at me, fingers drumming on the table. When he spoke, his voice was so soft that the red light didn't come on. "I can—I cannot speak English," he whispered.

"Good!" I said, loudly. "Try again!" I gestured to the opening he should talk into. He closed his eyes. "I can—I can speak a little English."

"Thank you!" I took the machine from him and spoke into it, sounding like a game show host. "Thank you very much! Now, what is your name?"

"My name is Zhao Hong Qiu," he said. He opened his eyes, saw everyone peering at him, and giggled. "I am—I am Chinese." This time when he passed the machine back to me, his eyes were shining.

"You speak very well," I said, slowly, into the tape. "What is your job?" Zhao blinked, and tilted his head.

"Your work? What do you do?" I said. Wang translated it.

"My work! My work is—my work is computer!"

A few of the men recognized the word "computer" and tried it out. "Cow-poo-tah!" "Ka-pu-tah!" Some of them grew bolder and pronounced it loudly, leaning toward the tape recorder.

I thanked Zhao and held up the microphone so that it would pick up everybody saying "computer." Speaking in a group seemed to encourage them: soon they had their heads together like a doo-wop group, chanting "Ca-pu-ta!" and "Herro!"

I played the tape back for them, and everyone seemed delighted, pointing to each other as they recognized their voices. After that the toothy guy shrugged, indicating that he would try the machine on his own.

"*Xie xie,*" I thanked him. "Do you speak English?"

Wang translated behind him. Slowly, he spoke into the machine. *"Bu shi."* No.

"No English at all," I repeated, so Olaf would get the point. "What's your name?" I pointed to the list of names I had in front of me. They were spelled out in Pinyin, Anglicized Chinese, but I didn't know whether he could read them.

He looked at where I pointed, then back at me, confused. He had a well-shaped head and clear, intelligent eyes. I liked him. His teeth, sticking forward, gave his mouth a pleased, hopeful expression, like a little boy's.

"Your name?" Wang translated.

"Chen Li Jie," he said.

Someone laughed. It was Barry, leaning on one arm in the doorway. "That guy's name ain't what he said. His name is Fang."

A few days later we were off the coast of Japan. When I woke up and went outside, three white mountains were rising in the distance like a Hiroshige painting. It was strange to realize that I had been in that country a week ago, sleeping in the Narita Holiday Inn and getting that memorable massage.

I sat outside for a while on the weather deck forward of my stateroom, which I liked to call my "balcony." It was a small deck, so I could sit on it and look down at the main level, or sideways across the water. Because no one ever had reason to walk around forward of my cabin, that area felt private. I watched for flying fish, which I could make out when they leapt away from the spray of the hull. They flew out of the water like arrows, gliding five, ten, sometimes twenty feet, their tiny wet "wings" outstretched, before diving back into the water. Often they'd reappear instantly, like a skipping stone. Once I saw one go skimming and dipping into the water and reappearing for over a minute.

Leaning forward to watch the fish, I held onto the rail, and it left oily soot on my hand. Still, the rain at sea had taken away some of the port dust. Things were improving.

Barry and Ma tromped out on the main deck below me, their heavy steps audible even over the engines. Ma was the largest Chinese man I'd ever seen—almost Barry's size. From my perch, I could see them clearly, but they didn't sense my presence. They were bending over some piece of machinery, Ma in his huge, stained orange overalls, Barry in clean blue ones.

"I need a pipe wrench!" Barry said. "Do you have a wrench?"

Ma looked back at him, large and eager, but oblivious. "Oh, God . . ." Glancing up as if for divine assistance, Barry saw me sitting on the upper deck. "Hey! Do you know the Chinese word for 'wrench'?"

"That vocabulary word has not come up in the first week of lessons," I said primly. So far we'd been working on simple pronouns and verbs and greetings. But to be helpful, I pantomimed a wrenching motion to Ma.

"Aaahhh!?" Ma made a high, startled noise and he lumbered aft. I assumed he was going to the toolshed.

"He'll probably come back with a screwdriver." Barry came to lean against the bulkhead near where I sat. He reached in the pocket of his overalls and took out a paper packet of Chinese cigarettes.

"I thought you—" I stopped myself from reminding him that he'd quit. Smokers had enough to worry about, I thought, without being hassled about their habit.

"I know it." Barry tapped a cigarette out of the package, and lit it with quick, practiced movements. "But these guys smoke like fiends, every one of 'em, and they keep offering 'em to me. I'm so bored I picked up one of these things and now I'm a pack a day again. They are nasty, too." As he smoked, the sharp smell of cheap tobacco wafted upwind. I moved my head to avoid the stream. "You'll be smoking too before we hit Panama," he said. "I predict it."

"Your prediction is wrong," I said. "I may be eating sugar, but I'll never smoke."

"Sugar, huh?" Barry squinted against the smoke. It made him look slightly rakish. "You eat a lot of that stuff?"

Self-conscious about my weight and afraid he was about to recommend a diet, I changed the subject. "When are we getting to Panama, anyway? What's our ETA?"

"Oh, Jesus, don't you start. I called Olaf this morning and he's got his shorts all in a wad; he's harassing me to turn up the engines to make better time. This tub's only doing eight knots now, so we're not going to get in till August 8, if we have good weather. They want me to modify the engine so we can get up to twelve knots, be there by the sixth.

"But how am I supposed to do that when I can't even get a wrench to open a damn valve? It's practically impossible to modify these engines even if you're on land, if you've got a whole machine shop, if the people you're working with speak English—"

Ma came struggling through the hatch, his thick arms wrapped around a long metal box, rusty but filled with an assortment of hand tools. He proudly presented it to Barry, who slapped him on the back in thanks. "All *right*, man, you did all right!"

Ma set the box down and put his arm around Barry, hugging his shoulders. "Okay," Barry warned. "I don't like you that much."

"Good job, Ma!" I called down. "Thank you! *Xie xie!*"

"Shay shay?" Barry said.

"Means 'thank you' in Mandarin," I said. "Try it sometime."

"No way. These guys are going to have to learn to speak our language; I ain't learning theirs."

"Xie xie," I said again to Ma. I thought Barry should learn to use

it, even if he didn't want to. Ignoring the hint, Barry threw his cigarette over the side and bent to pick up a wrench.

A bit daunted, I returned to my stateroom to review an article I'd somehow acquired, called "Foreign Teacher Expectations in Chinese Universities." It had come from the April–May 1991 *TESOL Matters Newsletter,* a publication I could not recall ever hearing of. However, this article had appeared in my papers as I had unpacked, so I read it with interest.

The two Chinese authors suggested that the ESL students in Chinese universities would be going on to be teachers, interpreters, or translators. But on the other hand, my sailors would be going on to be sailors. They wouldn't have much opportunity for upward mobility, regardless of their language skills. My job was to teach them how to receive orders from Norwegian and American bosses and how to give information, when necessary, to the same.

When the ship got to Galveston, a crew of American mechanics would swarm aboard to make the final preparations for the seismic operations in the Gulf. Once the "shakedown," or trial run, was completed, American seismic specialists and Norwegian managers would join the ship for its one-year contract in the Gulf. The Chinese crew would be demoted to the ranks of swabbies. They'd still run the ship's engines and support systems, but apart from the top officers, the radio tech, and the computer operator, their jobs would be menial.

Therefore, unfortunately, my students' English skills needed to be purely functional. Grammar, writing, and reading didn't matter—understanding spoken commands did. They needed to know how to do things like fetch a wrench. I was nervous about the idea of my students getting used to my accent, and then being faced with Norwegian accents, or Texan ones, but there was little I could do about it.

These Chinese authors—who, in absence of any other supervision, I began to think of as my mentors—said that native English speakers often spoke more rapidly than did Chinese English teachers and that students were hesitant to ask questions. Silence in the classroom, it said, usually signified confusion. *Great,* I thought. *They won't understand me and won't ask questions.* But the article suggested that it would help if I slowed my speech and used the blackboard frequently. Well, I could certainly do that, and I was cheered to read that "patience and good humor achieve the best results for teachers in China."

Captain Tan had scheduled two classes a day: in the morning, beginners, and in the evening the more advanced students, that is, anyone who could speak a whole English sentence. That was fine with me: I could handle four hours of work for $170 a day.

My beginner-level class included three mechanics, all classified as air gun operators, and designated by Olaf as "lower priority" students. During seismic operations—if the ship ever got that far—they'd be responsible for controlling the "guns," the camera-like machines that took seismographic pictures of the ocean bed. These guns had to be lowered in exactly the right spot in the water, or the image of the seabed would come out wrong, so the mechanics had to act fast once the ship had reached the correct position. These three men, Wu, Gu, and Xiu (whom Barry called "Huey, Dewey, and Louie") were not as educated as the captain and officers, and two of them had never had English lessons. Still, they all came to class cheerfully and paid rapt attention.

The three air gun operators worked under Chen, the small man with an overbite, whom Barry called "Fang." I was afraid to use the nickname out loud in case it might hurt Chen's feelings, but to me it became endearing—I liked his perpetual, expectant smile. Fang was one of the best bosses I've ever seen. Because he knew a little more

English than his workers, he sat between the three of them at lessons, helping them. Not only did he take notes for himself, diligently following every word I said, but he would check the others' notes, occasionally correcting them or quickly translating. When he did so, Xiu, the tall, skinny mechanic, or Wu, the younger one, thanked him with a quick nod.

Gu had had zero exposure to English, and I doubted that he'd get very far. More from a sense of duty than any real hope that Gu would learn it, I sat him down one day after class, and gave him a copy of the English alphabet. I had printed the capital and small letters as clearly as I could, leaving space after each one for him to copy them if he wanted. Fang stayed after class too, leaning over the alphabet sheet with a rapt expression.

I pointed to the first letter. "*A,*" I said, and made the two sounds, short and long, that the letter signifies.

Gu tried to say the sounds after me. "Aiiee?"

"Good. Yes." We did it a few times, till both his *a*'s were acceptable. I then pointed to the next letter and made the *b* sound. I didn't bother teaching him the name of the letter, since it wouldn't be helpful to him in reading, but just tried to associate the shapes with their sound.

We worked through the alphabet, and as I taught him each letter, he wrote cryptic Chinese figures next to it. Sometimes he and Chen put their heads close together and discussed what Gu wrote, trying a few variations before settling on a translation.

When we had reached *z,* I thought I'd go over the alphabet again, and I pointed back to the beginning. Before I could speak, he pronounced the letter for me, long and short. Then he went on to recite the alphabet, inflected like Chinese but unmistakably in the sounds of English. He had used Chinese sound-symbols to reproduce the correct sounds and was translating each one out loud.

About a week after the first class, Barry and I were still being served gargantuan meals. One night, stunned by all the food, I was still sitting at the table long after supper was over. Wang came over, and stood a respectful distance away. "Well, I hope you have enjoyed your dinner."

"I enjoyed way too much of it," I said. "I can't move."

Wang smiled. "Well, it is good to eat. The captain has asked for—a favor." His face furrowed. "That is correct? I can say 'favor' for small job without payment?"

"That's perfect," I said. "And yes. I'll be happy to do the captain a favor."

Wang looked relieved. "Well, you were asked to teach only two lesson a day, I know that. But chief mate cannot come to afternoon class. He is on bridge at that time, guiding the vessel."

"That sounds more essential than English lessons," I said. "And besides, he can speak a little, can't he?" I wasn't sure if I could detect a blush on Wang's face, or if he was simply looking down in a way that made him seem embarrassed. It was a look I'd get to know—a lowering of the eyelids that meant an apology that could not be spoken.

"Chief mate says that he can speak English. Captain ask you to help him."

"Sure," I said, wondering what the problem could be.

Half an hour later, the chief mate came barreling into the classroom. His yell preceded him—I heard his hoarse, cigarette-ruined voice while he was still on the stairs. He came in sweaty, with his clothes disheveled, trailing Lin and a few other subordinates. When he saw me waiting he became louder. "Inglish tich! Inglishtich!" Then more Chinese, very rapid and at such high volume that my ears hurt.

"Hello!" I said. "How are you?"

"How do do?!" He extended a hand for me to shake, then

snatched it back as I touched it. He laughed loudly, showing yellowed teeth. "Hello!" he yelled into my face. "I fine!" Each phrase was followed by a shout of loud, self-conscious laughter.

I covered my ears with my hands, though I kept smiling. "You don't have to yell!"

"I chief mate! I good English! Good! Good! Chief mate good English!" Taking over the bench near my chair, he shoved a book in my face. I'd brought the tape recorder, planning to start with that since I hadn't gotten a baseline recording of him, but I put the machine and my plans aside. Clearly, he was desperate to make a good impression, and I was not in charge of this lesson.

His hardback grammar book had onion-skin pages and pale gray ink—probably a Chinese rip-off edition of an old English textbook. He held onto one cover, and flipped through the pages faster than I could see them.

"Hold on!" I flattened a hand on the book and read through my fingers.

> Would you care for sugar, Mr. Brown?
> Yes, thank you, Mrs. Jones. I would like two lumps, if you please.

These phrases were going to come in very handy while he was trying to fix the engine with the Texan oil riggers.

"I good English!" The chief mate leered at me, grinning with his stained teeth. Grabbing the book back, he tore through it, looking for something. He didn't leaf through the pages—he shoved wads of pages around roughly, bending them and nearly tearing some out. It amazed me that the text had survived so long. Then he planted it in front of me, opened to an early dialog.

> How do you do, Mrs. Jones?
> Fine, thank you. And how do you do?

The book fell open to that point, the spine broken. "How do do!" he bellowed, jabbing at the dialog. "I good English! How do do!"

Well, if he wanted to learn from a British book of manners, I wasn't going to argue. "How do *you* do?" I corrected him. "Four words." I held up four fingers, then showed him the line.

But the chief mate held up his own hands with several fingers extended. "One two thee foh siss eight sehveh ten!" He grabbed the pencil out of my hand and started writing double-digit numbers all over my paper. "Two-ten! Thee-ten! Four-ten!" The whole time, he was shouting as if I were halfway across the Pacific.

Again I covered my ears with my hands, and shook my head. "Loud!" I pointed to my ear and made a wincing face.

His eyebrows arched in shock. "No, no good-ah. No good-ah. Bad student! Bad English!" He slammed the book closed.

"No, not bad," I whispered. "Just loud." I kept talking in a quiet voice, hoping he'd get the hint. I picked up my tape recorder and turned it on. "This is the chief mate," I said into the machine. "And he speaks a little English already. I think he—"

The chief mate grabbed the machine from me and yelled into the microphone. "I chief mate! Chief mate good! I English good!"

Although I admired the chief mate's willingness to interact in English, his attempts were hard on my ears and psyche. Tutoring him meant being shouted at, and constantly having to give approval. He was like a young child with me, though in his interactions with the other men he seemed perfectly mature.

One of my favorite students in the beginner class was Ma, the beefy, cheery man who seemed to live in orange overalls. Since his job was to serve as an "able-bodied seaman," or general ship's handyman, he often worked outside on the decks. He always seemed to be carrying something heavy, or leaning over an awkward piece of machinery, or climbing ladders to paint in difficult spaces. His hair fell over his eyes uncombed, and grease and paint stained his overalls and sometimes his hands and face.

Whenever he saw me he would smile hugely, wipe the sweat from his temples, and wave as if we were old friends. When he spoke English, nervousness made his voice high: he'd squeak "Hello!" at me and then laugh at his own strange sound. I was always glad to run across him, and I wished very much that I could talk to him properly, but the best I could do was say hello.

In the class of beginners he was the rawest and shyest. He reminded me of the Navy sailors who, knowing they were destined for lives of grunt work, never even attempted to get into the college classes. But here was Ma, eager to learn, fitting himself into a small chair in a classroom at age thirty-something, and probably finding sitting there easier than whatever he did for the rest of the day.

The other students quickly let me know that Ma's name meant, amongst other things, "horse." Considering that none of them could speak English, this explanation was quite a feat. There was a lot of pointing at Ma, saying his name over and over, horse sounds, and drawings on the whiteboard of horses along with what seemed to be a mother and child.

Dimly, I remembered my Chinese teacher saying that the word "ma," used with a rising tone at the end of any sentence, made the sentence into a question. It was like saying "right?" in American English. But she told me that if I used the wrong tone with "ma," I'd be ending my statements with the word "curse," "mother," or "horse."

Unfortunately, I couldn't distinguish between most of the tones, and while teaching I didn't have time to think about which tone I was supposed to aim for every time I used Ma's name. My unintentional puns delighted the students and they repeated them endlessly. They would patiently correct me, "Ma, not ma, not ma," but I just couldn't hear or copy the different inflections without a great deal of careful thought.

"Ma is horse!" someone would inform me every day as I greeted the students. "Mr. Ma—horse!" the others would repeat, making galloping motions and whinnying laughter. Ma seemed alternately pleased with the attention and embarrassed by the animal nickname. He retaliated by pointing out that the others' names also had second meanings. Mr. Tsu, the radio operator, had a name that sounded like "pig." And another's was "Fox," which everyone seemed to think was slightly indecent. But for some reason—perhaps because the horsey name suited Ma's big build and sanguine temperament—his name was the favorite pun. Every time I called on Ma, the whole class would shout his name after me.

A frequent warm-up was to go around the room saying hello, starting with whoever was closest to me. The students sat on comfortable, padded benches that lined three sides of the room. Since Ma often came into the room last, he usually sat at the end near the door and me, so he'd be first for the greetings. I'd say, "Hello, Mr. Ma!"

"Ma!" "Ma!" His name was parroted from every corner of the room. For the first week or so I thought it was just a continuation of the Ma/horse joke and didn't pay much attention. But when it happened in front of Wang, the interpreter, one night, he explained it to me. "They are trying to correct you!" he said, amused. "It is Ma, not Ma."

"I know," I said cheerlessly. "But I can't hear any difference. Ma, Ma."

"You are saying 'Ma,' with level tone." He explained that, using typical American flat intonation, I'd been beginning every class by addressing Mr. Ma as "mother."

One day I took the beginner class down to the "gun shack," the tool room that opened aft onto the work deck that eventually would house the seismic cables. The mechanics proudly showed me around the three rooms where they worked. Scraps of wood, linoleum, and metal lay in every corner and under every table. The closet doors bulged open, showing piles of paperwork and manuals in English, Chinese, and Norwegian. Drills hung from the wall, their noses pointed down like horses, and hundreds of glass jars, holding screws and nails, crowded the tops of the tables. Wood shavings littered the floor, giving the room the pleasant air of a carpentry shop, and various handsaws, drill bits, levels, planes, and other dark metal tools were heaped in rotting straw baskets.

We had been working on counting and on learning the English names of tools, so this was the perfect place to put the lessons into practice. Barry had told me that once the Americans came on board, the mechanics would mainly act as gofers, getting tools and carrying messages to and from the bridge. The only exception would be when the seismic surveys were going on and the mechanics would be operating the air guns.

I held up a flat-head screwdriver and asked, "What is this?"

Fang looked at the other three, his teeth making his glance look hopeful and optimistic. He knew but he was letting the other students try to answer.

"Sca—" said someone.

"Sca-da-da," they all chorused.

"Yes, okay, try again," I said. "Screwdriver. Screw-dri-ver." We'd done this term at least a hundred times.

"Scao-da-da."

"Okay," I said, resigned. I wished I knew anything at all about how to teach accent reduction. But their understanding of received English was more important than pronunciation. I said, "Bring me a ball-peen hammer."

Chen blinked a few times, processing what I had said, then ran into the other room. He returned with the correct tool.

"Great!" I said. "Xiu, what is this?"

"Ba-pee hamma."

"Yes! Good! How many?"

Xiu knew a trick question when he heard one. "One!" he grinned.

"Bring me three screws," I said to Xiu, casually. Trying to imitate the future commands he'd be hearing, I didn't inflect it particularly clearly. Xiu wrinkled his eyes at me, and I repeated, "Three screws." He turned to a jar near him, undid the lid, and brought out three nails.

"No, these are nails," I said, patiently. "I want screws."

But Xiu shook his head, pointing to the ball-peen hammer. "Hammah, scew, no good-ah. Hammah nail."

After a few weeks on board, it became clear that while I might help the Chinese men's English along, my own Chinese wasn't going to get very far. In the evenings after class, I generally went into the day room, intending to study. My big, shiny, cartoon-like Chinese book attracted a lot of attention—no one could believe it was a text.

"We do not have such things in China," said Wang, touching the cover reverently. The workbook included several pages of stick-on tags, in Chinese and English, most of which I hadn't yet attached to their intended objects. They said things like "clock" and "mirror" in both Pinyin and English, the idea being that you'd see the label on the object and learn the Pinyin word. Quite a few of the stickers weren't appropriate for our ship—stickers like "dishwasher" and "bathtub" and "car" remained in the book. Wang read every one of them, running his finger over the smooth surface.

"Would you like to take those?" I asked.

"Well, thank you, but I think it would be wrong. It is your book," he said.

"No, no, take them! You will use them more than I will."

Wang kept his eyes down, obviously averting his gaze from the pages of glossy labels. "Well, thank you. But I would not use them."

"Oh, sure you would. Or maybe you could give them to some-one who is studying English."

"Well—I think—they are yours."

"Yours," I said. "Please. I'll never look at them."

Wang looked up at me, his foxy grin appearing. "Well, thank you. I think my daughter would like very much."

From there we went on to discuss his daughter, who was eleven. Wang worried that she did not always get top marks in her school's grading system. "In English is okay," he said, "and history and Chi-nese. Always first in class. But mathematics, she is sometimes sec-ond, even third! She says one boy in her class always is first. We do not understand. My wife ask her, 'What is wrong with you? Why don't you study more?'"

Astounded, I said, "It sounds as if she's doing great! How many people is she competing with?"

"Not many. Maybe forty or fifty in her class. Do you have such lazy students in America?"

I couldn't answer him simply. I said that I had no children, but that the schools in some parts of the United States were so dangerous that they had to have police in them. Not much learning could take place. Others, I said, had small classes, gifted students, and dedi-cated teachers. From there we talked about school in general, and city schools versus rural schools, and then a few more people joined our table, and soon another evening had gone by without my learn-ing another syllable of Chinese.

One odd effect of being around so many non-English speakers was that I, too, began to speak in "Chinglish." One night Barry and I were eating dinner when Mr. Ding shuffled up to ask us if we needed anything. Because the cook was always preparing lunch and dinner while I was teaching, he never came to classes. But he was a smart, outgoing man, and he knew some English words that he liked to use. We could usually exchange simple ideas, though his accent was pretty strong. "Eat-ah rice-eh?" he said. "Rice-eh good-ah."

"Yes," I said. "Rice good."

"You Coke-eh?"

"No Coke-eh," I said without thinking. "Coke-eh no good."

"Coke-eh good," Barry said.

"Good-ah? No good-ah?" Ding tossed his head back and forth in mock confusion.

"Rice good, Coke no good-ah," I pronounced.

Barry contradicted me, pushing his fork into a piece of chicken. "Coke good-ah. Chicken good-ah. Rice no good-ah."

Understanding perfectly, Ding went off to the kitchen, singing.

Another effect on my speech was that, after learning that I was repeatedly calling Mr. Ma "mother," I tried to develop more awareness for the tones I used. In the first weeks, I was trying to teach the beginner-level class some vocabulary. We'd gotten through the pronouns and names, and we were working on simple verbs and nouns so that they could begin to make sentences.

I had put a big world map on the classroom wall and was pointing at the country where they'd be spending the next six months. "U-ni-ted States," I said. They repeated after me, each one garbling the words in a different way. I slowed down, and focused on the first word, "U-ni-ted."

This time their repetition was more uniform. "U-niya-teh." It was still wrong, but at least they were all wrong in the same way.

I stressed the second syllable so they'd hear it plainly. "U-*ni*-ted."

"U-*ni*-teh."

"Good!" We practiced that version for a while, and then I decided to work on the final consonant. "United!" I said, emphasizing the "d."

Ignoring the final letter, they copied my inflection perfectly, stressing the final syllable: "Uni*teh!*"

The members of my second class, the "advanced" students, ranged widely in their knowledge of English. At the top of the class came Zhao, who stood out not only because of his lovely face but also because he could, given enough time, translate things between me and the rest of the class. I called him my teaching assistant.

Classes met in the bar: about the size of a suburban dining room, it was neither so big that I felt distanced from the students nor so small that we were crowded. On the left as you entered was the bar itself, with room behind it for someone to stand and serve drinks, but that space was now full to waist height with hundred-pound bags of rice. The other three walls were lined with padded benches, in front of which stood several tables, bolted to the floor. After a couple of the men had tied my whiteboard across the bar, it formed a good backdrop for me as well as a focal point for the class.

The bar itself was a wonder of educational resources; the brass rail was about chest high, and surrounded by padded barriers to keep things from rolling off during a storm. You could find all manner of things behind and under the bar—pencils, scraps of Chinese and Norwegian writing, worn chopsticks, ashtrays, remote controls for the video game, and, after I got there, magic markers for the whiteboard as well as pens and notebooks. Daily I gave thanks for my foresight in lugging the whiteboard along—we used it not only to write sentences and words but also to draw pictures.

One day in the first week of class, I was learning about the men's jobs. "You are all sailors. You work on the ship." As I spoke I pointed to them, and to the general environment, the ship as a whole. We had been over this vocabulary before, so I knew they were getting it. "Mr. Tsu, what do you do? What is your job?"

Tsu's face screwed up tightly in effort. "I am radio officer," he said.

"Good! You are a radio officer." I pointed to the man next to him. "What is *his* job? What does *he* do? Is Lin a radio officer too?"

Many giggles from the class.

"Lin is steward," Tsu said.

"Yes! Good! Lin, are you a steward?" Lin almost always answered questions correctly. He carried his English notebook around with him and practiced for an hour before every class. Also, he had the advantage, in language-learning, of being the youngest crewmember—he was only thirty.

"I am steward," he said, more or less by rote. "I clean the ship and take care of passenger."

"Yes!" I beamed at him. "Very good! Today, what did you do?"

"Today I work. I help Mr. Ding . . . in kitchen."

"You helped Mr. Ding?"

He began to answer in Chinese, then corrected himself and changed to English. "Today Mr. Ding is cook. Today he cook fish."

"Very good! I like fish!" Appreciative smiles from students. I asked everyone: "Do you like fish?"

"Yes! We like fish!" said Zhao, and then everyone copied him. "We like fish!"

"Today we fish!" said the captain.

He hardly ever spoke, so I wanted to reinforce his effort right away. Misunderstanding, I said, "You fished today?"

The captain looked nervous. "Today, ah—today." He spoke rapidly in Chinese to the chief engineer, sitting next to him.

There was consultation with Zhao, who then looked up at me politely and translated. "Today captain worked hard. Captain Tan talk telephone to Mr. Olaf. Also captain work bridge."

"Good!" I made my response directly to the captain. "Today you worked hard!" He stared at me blankly, so I began again. "What do you do? What is your job?" We'd been over the lesson every day that week.

"I—I captain!" he stuttered out.

"Yes! Very good!" I nodded and even clapped a little. "You are the captain."

"I captain!"

That seemed fairly well established, so I ventured further, pointing to myself. "What do *I* do? What is *my* job?"

"Ah—" The captain was older than the rest of the crew, perhaps fifty, perhaps sixty. From his facial expressions and body language, and based on how the others treated him, I could tell that he was intelligent and sincere, but it was difficult for him to recall his English—if he'd ever known it. Really he belonged in the beginners' group, where he would have shined for knowing a few words. But he'd placed himself in the advanced class, where he was doomed to embarrassment. I knew this, but my asking him to move down would have been as insulting as telling him how to navigate.

"Me," I repeated, slowly. "What is my job?"

"Teacher," the chief engineer whispered. The captain echoed it, looking relieved.

"Yes," I said. "I—am—teacher."

"I—am—teach-ah," the captain parroted.

"No, *you* are *captain!*" I pointed to him, then back to myself. "*I* am teacher." I tried to say it in Chinese.

Voice low, he pointed to himself, saying, "You—captain. I—teach-ah."

Not wishing to embarrass him, I gave up. Turning to the next student, I said, "Who is teacher?" The chief engineer beamed at me, pointing. "You are teacher! I am chief engineer." He was a big panda of a man, with graying hair and a wide, boyish smile. He was wearing a pink shirt that brought out the slight sunburn on his cheeks and made his skin glow.

"Yes, Chief Engineer! You have a nice shirt today! Pink!" He tilted his head to one side, confused, but got it when I repeated "shirt" and pointed to his garment.

"Thank you!" he said, turning a shade pinker.

"Who is captain?" I asked him. The chief looked respectfully to his right, where the captain, hearing one of the few words he knew, had straightened up. "Tan is captain! He is good captain!"

The others chimed in at this. "Good captain!" Tan slumped a little less, and acknowledged the praise with a nod.

Then he said something quickly to Zhao, who translated to me. "Captain must go to bridge." The captain nodded at me and then ducked out of the room, fifteen minutes into his fourth lesson.

After class, the students had thanked me and exited for dinner, and I was gathering my books and papers. By seven everyone was usually pretty intent on eating, so I was surprised when Wang came into the room, followed by the captain. Barry, on his way to dinner, stopped off to eavesdrop. He hung in the doorjamb like a curious ape.

Wang spoke softly and seriously. "Captain says he is sorry, but English classes take too much time. The men are tired and cannot work."

"What?" I didn't even try to hide my amazement. "What do you mean? I think everyone likes the classes a lot." Except the captain.

"Tomorrow and rest of journey, classes must be one hour long."

That's ridiculous, Wang! Wait, don't translate that. But, say—please say politely that I can't teach anything in just six hours a week. Say—ask him if we can try an hour and a half."

"His word is law," Barry warned me. "He is the captain."

Snake, I thought. I knew Barry had been having his own power struggles with the captain, over modifying the engines—why did he have to side with Tan now? What did he care how long I taught? I ignored Barry.

"Okay," I said to Wang. "Please tell the captain that I respect his opinion very much. But the men have a lot of English to learn. In six weeks, they will have an American crew to work with! Doesn't the captain want them to succeed?"

The two Chinese men conferred for a while, and then Wang turned back to me. "Captain says you are very good teacher. One hour a day, each class, is all you need." I was furious, but it would do no good to argue. The men left to have dinner and I went outside to rant at the ocean.

I strode aft where no one could hear me over the engine noise, ducked behind the storage locker where no one could see, and screamed into the wind. My throat was already sore from sleeping in cold air and from talking so much, so the screaming was particularly unpleasant, but it felt necessary. "This is *not fair!*" I yelled. I went on, cursing Tan's shortsightedness and his authoritarian stance. By the time I was done, I'd denounced not only him but also the entire Chinese system of manners based on rank.

By the time I went in to find some supper, I was winded and hoarse as well as hungry. Obviously, word had gotten out about the reduction in hours and the argument: the men in the dayroom seemed subdued and didn't look at me. It was little consolation that my hourly wage had just doubled.

Two Miles to the Bottom

Underneath me, waves thumped the keel. Every now and then, we hit a massive wave at a bad angle and the impact sounded like a cannon going off. Vibrations shuddered down the hull, and the whole ship shook as if coming apart.

It worried me that I'd never felt such pounding on Navy tenders, but I realized it was because they displaced about twenty thousand tons. I'd never felt anything like it on little yachts or sailboats either, but of course, those small boats hadn't been in the middle of the Pacific, with a gale whipping in from the Aleutians. I said prayers for my family and friends in the event of my death, and then, even more earnestly, I said some for myself.

I wasn't sleeping but had reached a point of vague relaxation in my prayers and meditation, in which the sounds of the storm weren't so frightening and my mind calmed down a little. Just when I might have fallen asleep, someone knocked on my door.

I heaved myself from the bed and pulled on my jeans. Mr. Ding stood outside. "You sick?" he said. He looked a little sick himself—pale and cheerless.

"Yes," I said, trying to sound brave.

He held out a piece of freshly cut ginger. "No sick."

"Really?" I took the ginger—its sharp, fresh smell was certainly bracing. I nibbled a corner of it. "This will make me feel better?"

"No!" He took the ginger back from me and rubbed it inside his wrist, telling me something in Chinese. I copied his movements, rubbing the rough edge of the root on my skin. It didn't have any effect on me, but at least Mr. Ding looked pleased. "Rest-ah," he said. "Have a rest."

I didn't know if he meant me or himself. It was midafternoon, the hour of the *xiu xi,* or universal nap. I thanked him and staggered back to bed, my arms fragrant with ginger.

No one but the cook and me seemed much bothered by the worsening weather. After lying down for a while, I went downstairs ready to cancel class, but everyone was up and about their business, inquiring about my health. Feeling inferior, I crept back to my room and took my first anti-seasickness pill.

I'd had a stateside doctor prescribe the medicine, but I'd been hoping to make the journey without using it. An hour or so after taking it, I felt well enough to teach, although I had to brace myself against the bar to stand up.

At the end of class, my second-level students seemed unusually eager to leave the classroom. Their "thank-yous" were a little rushed, and on his way out, Zhao explained why. "Today dinner is chicken feet."

"Chicken feet. I'd been wondering when they were going to break those out." Zhao didn't follow what I said, so I just nodded him on his way, grateful that the cook had so far ignored my requests to be served the same food that the crew ate.

No matter what Barry and I said, Mr. Ding continued preparing special food for the Westerners. For us two he fried pork chops, stewed beef, sautéed chicken, and grilled steaks, while the Chinese crew got rice, steamed veggies, and occasional fish. Besides feeling laden down by all the meat, Barry and I were getting sick of eating together. Not terribly compatible in our interests or values to begin with, we were no longer enjoying our nightly tête-à-tête, sitting across from each other in American exile while, in the next room, the rest of the ship feasted on rice and beer.

Not that Barry was a bad guy: apart from his politics (slightly right of Ronald Reagan), he was agreeable enough, and we had some nice supper conversations. One night, after a few Chinese beers, he'd unbent to tell me about his personal life.

"I think about it all the time," he said. "All day. I can't stop thinking about my son, Randall. It's stupid, I know. He's eighteen, too old for me to tell him what to do, but—listen, I'll tell you the situation and you tell me if you think I'm crazy."

"You don't look old enough to have an eighteen-year-old son." In fact I knew that he wasn't old enough; the sheet Olaf had given me had put Barry's age at thirty, the same as mine.

"Stepson," he explained. "From my wife's first marriage. But I've raised him since he was eleven: he calls me Dad. Anyway, he's in a pile of trouble." Barry went on to detail a soap-opera chronicle of the boy's adolescence, starting with his being the strongest and biggest kid in the junior high school, and getting into too many fights. "I think a guy has to fight *some*," Barry said. "But not every day. Not even every week."

Figuring prominently in the recent scenarios was an older girl called Lavina, who had a tendency toward dropping by Barry's house in Tulsa around dinnertime and then not being able to start her car to leave. "I told her last time," Barry went on, flicking his thumb on the neck of his beer bottle. "She's welcome to come by the house once in a while; we want to know his girlfriend, but every day is too much. It's like she wants to move in."

"Do you like her?" I asked.

"Can't stand her. It's Randall's business who he dates, but I just don't want him to be so involved with her."

As he talked I felt a new sympathy for Barry—this big, muscular man with the easy, swaggering stance and the neoconservative values. He was not especially savvy to the nuances of any lifestyle except his own, I could see that, but he was tolerant enough of me and my leftist leanings, and his son seemed to give him a lot of heartache.

Obsessively, he went on. "I told him I don't want her coming around all the time while I'm at sea, but I don't know what's going on. I can't stop thinking about it."

Of *course* she'd be coming around while Barry was at sea, I thought. What better time? And it didn't sound as if Randall was spurning her advances. I felt bad for whatever Barry would have to face when he got back home.

Other nights, when Barry didn't drink the Chinese beer and we had little to talk about, and when the sounds of laughter, companionable arguing, and conversation floated over from the other side of the room, I felt desperate to escape our nightly dinner date. I tried coming to dinner right on time, since Barry was usually a little late; sometimes I skipped the meal altogether, since I was never hungry after lunch, but that resulted in hurt looks from Mr. Ding and apologies for the inadequacy of his cooking.

Really, I wanted to go eat on the other side of the mess, with the crew. Barry had already done so a few times, simply taking his plate and walking over there with no explanation or apology. When he'd done that, it had made me feel like a pariah—I'd hated eating alone and had hid my embarrassment by reading. It was especially bad since the cook still prepared special dishes for us and waited on us—or waited on me alone, if Barry left—as if it were a restaurant. Everyone else served themselves from the serving line, but the cook insisted on bringing us our food.

The obvious thing was for me to move over and eat with the crew as well, but I hesitated to do that. After all, I'd be the only woman, and who knew what that implied? For all I knew they'd expect me to pour the tea—or, worse, they might feel inhibited about joking around in front of me or speaking Chinese. I didn't want to usurp attention during their precious free time or turn dinner into another English lesson.

But on Chicken Feet Night I made my move. After everyone had served themselves and was sitting down, I told Barry what they were eating.

"I know it," he said, and made a retching noise. "I'd rather starve." He dug into a grilled drumstick. "This here's downright edible, though."

"I'm going in," I said. Trying to be inconspicuous, I moved along the serving line to the Chinese half of the room. En route I held onto poles and tables, bracing myself against sudden lurches.

My fears about intruding were instantly banished by the welcome I received. "Teacher! Yes! Eat Chinese food! Chicken! Teacher sit!"

Too shy to sit next to anyone, I sidled to the end of the nearest table, where Zhao, the chief engineer, and a few others were chewing heartily. A bowl of chicken feet graced the middle of the table, braced by several large bottles of beer and some jars of evil-looking pickles. I pointed to the central dish, saying "I would like to taste this."

Several plates and chopsticks were thrust in my face, the owners cheerfully offering me their uneaten food.

"That's okay." I bent over the communal bowl. The greasy steam made me gag. A dozen or so gray-yellow claws poked up at me. Each foot had four long, skinny toes, and each toe had a tiny, oval nail on the end. The joints, where the skin wrinkled, looked like human knuckles. I picked up the smallest foot, but it looked like the hand of a sick old lady. Shuddering, I dropped it.

I thought about Barry chomping into the chicken leg in the other room. Why didn't that make me sick? Although I was 90 percent vegetarian at home, I'd certainly eaten plenty of chicken in my life—the *other* parts, though, not the feet. But everyone in the room was watching me, Mr. Ding already mewing, "No good-ah?"

Trying not to inhale, I picked up the claw; with my eyes shut, I nipped at it with my front teeth. I felt shifting layers of tough skin, fat, tendon, and bone. I ate a tiny morsel, which tasted and felt like the gristle on the end of a drumstick, but softer.

Ding's face was right in mine as I chewed. "Good? No good-ah?"

I put down the foot, trying to look pleased. "It's strange for me. It's good, but strange. Different."

"Good-ah?" He peeped at me from under his black fringe of hair. "Teacher say good-ah!" He laughed proudly, and handed me a plate of Kung Pao chicken. As I was eating it, happy to be in the company of the crew, one of the men said something that nearly made me choke.

"Teach-ah like penis," the chief engineer observed.

I was so horrified I couldn't even look up. "Pardon?" I said, hoping I'd misheard him.

But he repeated it, enunciating clearly. "You like-ah penis! Penis very good!"

This time I looked up, seeing not only the chief engineer but also the others at the table watching for my reaction. They had set down their bowls and were all looking at me. This was worse than my deepest forebodings about joining their table.

"Teach-ah like—" Zhao said. He spoke slowly, trying to help me. "We like. Chinese like very much penis." Seeing the confusion on my face, he pointed helpfully to my plate, which held chicken, scallions, and—his chopstick directed my gaze to what they were talking about—peanuts.

I got very little sleep that night; the vessel tossed too much. I was afraid of being thrown from my rack, so I tended to stay awake to hold on to the guardrails. Adding to my discomfort, the stateroom was over air-conditioned. I had already requested two extra blankets, which Lin had provided, bringing my total to four heavy, scratchy, not-very-warm covers. Since I'd forgotten to pack a nightgown, I slept in a T-shirt, underwear, and socks, all cotton and lightweight. What with shivering under the blankets and trying to keep a hand on the rail, it wasn't very restful.

Also, it was noisy—I stuffed earplugs into my ears to dim the constant clatter of anonymous doors, but the small wads of foam didn't block much sound. Although I had searched the passageway, I hadn't found any unlatched lockers or hatches. But with each slow roll to port, two or three doors opened and shut: I heard each individual unoiled groan, as each door creaked open, then the clatter of metal doors hitting metal bulkhead—bang! bang! pause, bang! Then, as the ship righted itself, they crashed closed. Then *those* doors would stay shut when the ship rolled to starboard, but others would swing open. It was more than maddening.

At about 3 a.m. I got up and went downstairs, hoping to warm up. Barry was playing video games, his face haggard in the green light shining out of the screen. "Seems like I can't sleep any more at night," he said. "I swear, every night I'm down here till daylight. Then I get sleepy."

"Me too," I said. "I thought I was over jetlag, but I can't get up in the mornings."

None of it made any sense. When I'd been in China, I'd been waking up before daylight and feeling sleepy at dinnertime. Now, as we were going back East and getting gradually closer to our accustomed time zone, I felt as if I had just flown to Europe. I stayed up later every night.

The ship took a deep roll, and Barry's chair shifted under him. "That felt like twenty-five degrees."

"Really?" I knew that ships' rolls were measured by the degrees off center that the keel moved. I pictured it as a straight stick coming up the middle of the ship; if that stick moved five degrees off center as the ship tilted, the motion was barely perceptible at the lowest decks. But if you thought about the top of the stick, the top decks—officers' country, in Navy terms—that five degrees became a lot more noticeable, particularly if you were on the side to which the boat was leaning. At forty-five degrees, one whole side of the ship was getting dunked. Somewhere between forty-five and ninety, measurement became academic, because a ship would be lying on its side in the water, starting to sink.

While working on a Navy tender, I'd heard that that massive ship had once taken a thirty-five-degree roll. No one had been hurt, but filing cabinets bolted into the deck had ripped free. In ammunitions lockers, weapons went flying into one another, and in the clinic, a doctor performing minor surgery had almost cut off someone's foot. A sailor who'd been standing watch on the weather deck saw the water rising almost to his face. When the ship righted itself, the sailor was hyperventilating, and he couldn't release the rail he'd been holding onto; his friends had to pry his fingers loose. I thought about telling the story to Barry, but he was already looking ill.

"Going to get worse before it gets better," he said, shooting something with his joystick. "There's a hell of a storm off Alaska."

"I heard. Chief mate told me it's an Aleutian gale."

"Aleutian gale," Barry mused, staring at his screen. "Sounds like a stripper from Fairbanks."

"Well, I was wondering—if it's such a bad storm, why doesn't the captain alter course?"

Barry shook his head, eyes fastened on the flashing green figures. As he talked, he pressed the buttons automatically. "'Cause he's an idiot, that's why. I tell you I found a porthole open? It was taking on water."

I considered the implications of this remark. I didn't know how dangerous it was to take on water, but it didn't sound good.

"You know what else happened today?" Barry said. "I spent three hours talking to the seismic company about how to modify the engine. You know how much that satellite phone costs?"

"Olaf told me ten bucks a minute."

"Right. So three *hours*—you can do that math—getting these guys to tell me how to do this thing, right? And I don't have the right tools. It's very complicated—I don't know if I can do it, to tell you the truth. But then Captain tells me I can't do it, he won't allow it—the weather's too rough. He cut the engine speed to six knots."

"Great," I said. "We'll wallow in the middle of the storm."

"Hell, yeah." Barry squinted at his screen and then maneuvered his spacecraft sharply sideways. "But at least if they're drunk up there, they're going slow. Not too much can happen."

"What?" I said. "Are they taking their beers up to the bridge? To relieve stress or something?"

"Jesus, didn't you know? Every night! Everyone except the captain gets loaded after dinner."

Not only hadn't I known, but I was shocked. On Navy ships there was one rule about drinking on board, and that rule was: no drinking. No beer, no wine, no alcohol of any kind in the staterooms, in the mess, or anywhere else, except in storage locked up by the disbursing officer from start to finish of a cruise. People could buy booze overseas but not keep it in their cabin. The only variant

I'd ever heard of was, once, in a Mediterranean port, there had been a two-hour reception for foreign dignitaries at which white wine was dispensed in doll-sized cups. But even then we weren't underway, and officers on duty were forbidden to partake. But here in the middle of the Pacific, on an old ship, the people responsible for my safety were partying on the job.

There are times when you have to look reality square in the face and deny it. "I'm sure they're not drunk today," I said. "No one would be that stupid."

I went back up to bed and took another pill, and I finally fell asleep. When I woke up it was 10:30 a.m., technically daylight, but outside my porthole all I could see were whitecaps. All over the ship, things clicked and rolled and clattered back and forth. The boat seemed to be listing to starboard a long time on each roll before she righted herself. I was afraid we had hit something and were taking on water.

I dressed and hurried up to the bridge for a weather bulletin. The ship was rocking so violently that I didn't so much climb up the ladder as crawl across it, clinging to the railing. The bridge ladder faced port, so when we rolled that way, it tilted horizontal under me. When we rolled to starboard, I had to hang on so as not to fall off backward. I alternately staggered and floated up to the bridge.

Barry and the translator were muttering to each other on a bench in the aft section; forward, by the panoramic front window, the captain hovered over the controls. Outside, spattering, crooked streams of rain were washing down the glass. You could have cut the tension with a chicken foot.

The captain nodded to me sympathetically. "Weather no good-ah."

"Right." I went over to the chart table to study our position. Although I was ignorant of navigation, I liked to see the ship's progress, recorded on the giant sea maps every eight hours with fine, straight lines of pencil. Each day when I checked, the mark would have advanced a few millimeters along the paper, ending in a neat cross, our position marked in sharp, tiny numbers.

The present chart showed no land at all; it was just a yard of blue paper interspersed with latitude and longitude lines, and curvy, free-form circles showing depth measurements—measurements, lately, over ten thousand feet. A corresponding map showed our planned route; its smaller scale included the Hawaiian Islands, faint green dots some fifteen hundred miles to the southeast. I was holding on to the chart table with both hands, trying to keep myself vertical, when the chief mate came over to me. "Captain alter course," he said.

"He *has* altered course already, or he's going to?" I asked. There were too many tenses in English. "He finish alter?"

The chief mate jabbed a finger at the chart, using his other hand to hold onto the table and keep his footing. Outside, a wave smashed against the window. I turned; water covered the glass, foaming down in torrents. We were four decks up, on the highest level of the ship; if waves broke here, couldn't they wash right over us? And if they washed over us, couldn't we capsize? No one else seemed perturbed, so I said nothing.

"Captain alter course," the first mate repeated.

I sighed. "When?"

"This morning. About five degrees north," Barry called across the room, sounding disgusted. "We're practically heading for Alaska now. And he's going so slow that the winds are going to catch up."

I stepped over to Barry's bench and sat down—or rather, the seat came up and I bumped onto it. "Is this as dangerous as I think it is?" I said.

Barry shrugged. "You got life insurance?"

Another wave struck the underside of the vessel, sending a shock of nausea through me. I pressed my stomach in and groaned, realizing I hadn't taken a pill that morning. "Isn't it about time for a port of call?"

Barry snorted. "In your dreams. You know how far the nearest land is?"

"Yeah. Hawaii." Remembering the beach at Maui, I sighed. "We could be there in a couple days."

"Nope. The nearest land is two miles—straight down."

I felt bile rising in the back of my throat, and I looked for something to throw up in—Barry's lap, perhaps?

"Well, you look pale," the translator observed. "Have you eaten your breakfast?"

"No, yuck," I said. "I don't think I ever want to eat again."

"No, you got to eat." Barry gave me a light, sympathetic punch on the shoulder. "Even if you think you're gonna barf. At least eat some crackers, to dry up your stomach. Maybe sip a little Sprite, too. Just don't drink the whole can. The idea is to get your stomach juices to dry out."

"Really?"

"Listen, I know this shit. One time, a guy I couldn't stand came out shark fishing with us, down in the Gulf. And it was his first time, and he was sick as a dog. And I kept telling him, 'Just drink a lot of water, man, no matter what.' And he'd go gulp down some water and then he'd get worse. He was barfing all over. I kept telling him, 'You're not drinking enough, man,' and he'd go drink some more, and throw it up. Man, I was *torturing* him. It was hilarious."

"You have a great sense of humor," I told him. "Anybody ever try to choke you?"

"Go eat a cracker," he said. "You'll live to thank me."

In the mess, it took me five minutes to eat one cracker, because I could only bear to take tiny nibbles. Feeling even worse after the food, I took a Sprite and dragged myself back to my cabin, which also took a long time as the ship was rocking more and more violently.

I'd left my closet door unlatched, so shoes, dirty clothes, and all the bags of trash I'd refused to toss overboard lay strewn across the floor. I kicked them back in, slammed the door and latched it, then immediately had to open it again to find my seasickness pills.

I had the sense, though, that just a pill wasn't going to be enough, so I brought out the heavy artillery of the war on seasickness: the patch. It was a small gauze pad that you taped behind an ear—I'd worn a similar one on Navy vessels. My doctor had warned me that these patches were very strong, only to be worn in heavy weather. Well, this was about as heavy weather as I ever hoped to see, so I stuck one on.

Lying in bed was intolerable. Once a minute or so, the mattress slid three inches up the bed as we rolled to starboard, then back down as we rolled to port. In between, the inevitable, unfindable cupboard doors slammed open and shut. Every few moments, a huge wave would crash into the hull, making the whole ship shudder.

I thrashed about my rack, trying to brace myself with rolled blankets, until my legs were sore with chafing against the sheets. I couldn't curl into a ball, which would have felt the safest, because the guardrail didn't allow me enough room. No matter how I turned, it seemed to be digging into my arm or my hip.

Finally I got out of bed, moved the desk chair into the bathroom, and dragged my mattress off the bed. I tumbled onto the floor and then lay down in the tangled sheets and blankets, ready to die. The patch was starting to have an effect—making me drowsy and thirsty. Just before I fell asleep, my throat felt dry and rough, and I wondered if the lifeboats were stocked with drinking water. If we had to abandon ship, would I remember to take my Sprite?

I dreamed not of storms but of deserts; I was dry and dying of heat; parched, I sought an oasis but found only sand. Sand lined my mouth, and sand ground into my eyes, and then I was awake, wrapped in a tangle of sweat-damp sheets, my throat feeling ready to crack.

Holding onto the bulkhead, I staggered up for my water bottle and downed it in a few swallows. The damned patch! It had dried out not only my stomach but the rest of my body, too. I drank the Sprite, then went in the head to splash my face and hands in cold water. The good news was that the nausea was gone.

The bad news was that we were in forty-foot seas. I could estimate the heights because average waves broke just below the main deck. In normal conditions, my cabin was two decks above sea level, but "sea level" became meaningless in the storm—the wind and rain whipped the waves into froth and the whole ocean rose and fell, roaring, tossing the ship like a toy. Remembering a boat I'd sailed on once, cleverly named *Toy Yot*, I thought how, really, all ships were like bathtub toys in the ocean.

I heaved the mattress back into place and braced myself in my rack, facing the porthole. The ocean was churning with black waves and whitecaps. The water flew up past the opening, gray slushy foam covering the porthole. For ten or fifteen seconds as the boat rolled to port, all I could see was swirling water. Then as we slapped back down, the horizon of water fell, sending water foaming across the deck. From an invisible sky the rain hit straight down like bullets. The boat tilted to starboard for a long moment, as if balanced, ready to tumble over. I couldn't breathe until she again crashed flat.

Most frightening was the noise of waves crashing overhead. Before, the heavy pounding had come from the keel, but now the waves were breaking on the deck over me, three levels above the waterline. Between giant waves, seawater sluiced off the deck in torrents. The steel hatch on my forward porthole was closed, since the glass was in danger of breaking, but on the other side of it, the waves sounded like a waterfall.

I prayed. Remembering the words of the Episcopalian liturgy I'd grown up with, I asked for protection "for all the ships at sea"—especially this ship, particularly on this sea.

I wondered if, should the *Tan Suo Zhe* sink, I might have a chance of getting into a lifeboat. I wondered if either of the two lifeboats could withstand the heavy seas, or if either would even float—we'd had no drills, no safety checks of any kind. My room was on the boat deck, so called because it was where the lifeboats were stationed, and such proximity might have comforted me, but I did not know whether my Chinese students would remember their beloved teacher in the event of an emergency.

I thought that probably the ship would sink that night, and that I should stay awake and listen for people going to the boats. But even if we did make it into a boat, and even if the boat proved seaworthy, we would still have to drift for weeks to reach land. Since we were a thousand miles south of the shipping lanes, we wouldn't see another vessel in time.

It seemed as if my life were about to end, and if I were going to die, I didn't want to be alone. I staggered up to the bridge, the ladder swinging up and down. The captain and chief mate were holding onto the ship's wheel and the rail around the instrument panel; they didn't even hear me come up. They were shouting at each other over the crashing water and screaming wind.

I went aft to look out the big back window. Seabirds were shrieking, circling around, fighting the wind. Some tried to land on the water, but they'd be dashed by waves and would ascend again, wet and squawking. Behind us, whitecaps dashed down over the boat's small, ragged wake, obliterating all traces of our passage. On the lee side, whitecaps rushed away, and between them swung deep black troughs.

Clinging to bolted-down furniture, I went forward to look at the few instruments I could read. Our course was seventy degrees east— that meant we were indeed heading for northern Canada, or Alaska. Great. The captain saw me and pointed to the gyroscope that measured the rolls. As I watched, we tilted to port and the needle moved to thirty-nine degrees. The captain smiled a hollow, false grin, his eyes flat and frightened. "Ga-leh," he said.

"What?"

"Galeh!" He was announcing the gale, in case I hadn't noticed. Underneath the mask was a very tired man, looking older and less confident than usual. I shook my head at him, and was about to ask a question when we were hit by a monster wave. We ducked, grabbing whatever fixtures we could reach.

When I looked back up, the chief mate was leaning over the chart table, spread-eagled, gripping the rail with both hands. The captain hung onto a bolted-down chair, staggering back to his feet. They both looked at me, and they must have seen my fear: still holding on, they nodded at me encouragingly. "No ploblem!" sang the chief mate, and the captain copied him: "No ploblem!"

Right. I decided I had enough information for the time being and made my way to the dayroom, where I hoped the swells might feel less dangerous. No one was in the radio room when I passed it, and the bar was quiet. In the dayroom, a few men sat quietly, smoking, looking exhausted. I sensed they'd come there for the same reason as I—to have company in fear.

Metallic crashes came from the galley. Alarmed, I groped my way in there to see what was falling. Mr. Ding was near the sink, looking white. He had one arm wrapped around a pole, and he was trying to tie down the huge rice cooker. Still, he tried to be friendly, asking, "Sick-ah?"

"Not any more. You?"

He didn't answer, engrossed in pulling at a knot in the ragged twine he was using. I felt terribly sorry for him—struggling to feed us and feeling sick at the same time. Then I thought of how I could help him. "Mr. Ding!" I said. "You want some Western medicine?"

He looked at me curiously, not understanding. I took the pill bottle from my pocket and tapped one into my hand. "Eat," I said, and pantomimed swallowing the tablet. "No sick-ah."

He laughed and picked up the little white pill, looking mischievous. "Wesah-ton med-sin?" his voice rose to almost nothing. I might as well have been offering him LSD.

"Go ahead," I said. "No sick!"

He swallowed the little pill and then stood still, as if expecting immediate relief.

Tapping his watch, I told him to wait. "Twenty minutes. You'll be better."

Mr. Ding nodded, obviously not believing me, and shuffled off to the sink, where he began washing rice in a plastic bucket. The ship swung sideways, and the water came out of the taps almost horizontally—he had to hold on with one hand and direct the flow of water with the other.

I crossed the dayroom again, nodding at the other people. Lin, the steward, had his feet propped up on a chair, which would rock out from under his heels every few minutes. He had become very adept at catching it before it fell. I wedged myself into a corner where two benches came together behind a table. I could brace myself there when the big rolls came, and lean back during moments of calm.

Calm moments were rare, however. Mostly I sat with my head down, holding the table edge with both hands. Although I'd expected the rocking to feel less intense down there, the swells seemed worse. Hoping they'd stop, I counted. We got five, six, seven big waves in a row, each one banging the hull like a gong and sending shudders through the vessel. Besides the rocking, the ship began pitching forward, too, and then the two movements combined into a terrible, up-and-down circling motion, like a spinning, sinking top.

After five minutes of the ship spiraling and shaking, I couldn't take any more. We'd been in rough weather for two days and I felt ready to jump overboard, just to stop the lurching. The ship tilted steeply to port, and hung there. Then, when she should have rolled back, something happened—it felt as if we hit a trough—and instead of righting, she went further onto her side. *This is it,* I thought, bracing myself. I figured the quickest route to the lifeboats. A snapping sound made me look over toward the galley, where the huge freezer was sliding along the floor.

The bolts keeping it in place had broken; it slid like a huge coffin along the deck, pushing chairs aside like wisps of straw. The movement was slow, with a long swishing sound as the heavy appliance dragged along the linoleum. It reached the far bulkhead just as the ship began to straighten.

The sound brought Mr. Ding out of the galley; he, Lin, and I stared at the freezer. If the ship swung hard to starboard, the freezer might go flying . . . Without speaking we ran and surrounded it, guiding it back into place as the ship rolled back. There was a moment's lull; someone produced more twine, and we wrapped the thin cord around and around the freezer, tying it to the steel wall brackets as tightly as we could.

As we sat back down, Lin shook his head at me, his mouth slightly open. He wasn't as old as the other men, I remembered, and someone had said it was his first trip. I raised my eyebrows at him, not hiding my own fear, and we understood each other.

Someone came down the ladder screaming. I thought it might be a message to abandon ship, but the chief mate ignored us and stormed across the mess, yelling something. Several other people followed him and staggered into the galley, where I couldn't see what they were doing. Lin got up and joined them; a minute later I heard several of them calling for Ma, sounding angry.

Ma appeared, his earnest, heavy face full of trouble as he trotted to the galley, where the chief mate was cursing him. I heard Ma gasp, then he ran back out of the room and along the passageway to the hatch, which he wrestled open. I couldn't believe it, but he went out on the weather deck.

I went to the galley where the men were standing, muttering to each other. When I asked what was up, Mr. Ding said "Box! Box!" and made a motion as if something were falling over. He signaled me to look out the porthole, and the others made room for me to see.

Five-gallon paint cans were rolling and spilling all over the deck, which was already heavily stained with paint. One can trailed a wanton rope of orange color behind it: it went banging along the deck, hit the bulkhead, bounced over a locker, and landed on a pile of line. The ship pitched, and a huge drum flew overboard, smearing the guardrail and dropping gallons of poison into the ocean.

"Jesus." Barry was standing behind me. "This is obscene. The paint locker must've bust open."

In the darkness, a dim white light appeared against the rain. It was Ma, roped to the bulkhead and struggling along on all fours. He crawled toward us, carrying a flashlight and shining it around. The thin beam lit a streak of the spattered deck, smeared with red-orange paint. Wet and gleaming in the light, running in thick rivulets and mixing with the seawater, it looked like blood.

A few days later, the interpreter admitted to me that it was the worst storm that the captain, the chief mate, or anyone else on board had ever known.

Enough Beer to Float the *Titanic*

By morning the worst of the storm had passed. The rain thinned and finally eased off, leaving a thick fog; the waves chopped against the sides of the ship, rough but no longer threatening. Delighted to be still alive, I went out on deck for my morning walk.

Heading aft, I came across the paint locker. About six feet high, standing at the top of an exterior ladder, the once-white cabinet now bore gaudy streaks of orange, black, and brown. Apparently the cans had crashed around inside, burst the doors open, and tumbled out. Strands of latex paint looped from the cabinet and all over the stairs. The deck was an inch deep in encrusted puddles, partly congealed, partly still open, like wounds. More colors had dripped and splattered down the ladder like a giant Jackson Pollack painting, pooling and spreading at the bottom into hideous puddles.

Someone had stepped through the mess and tracked orange goo down the stairs; multicolored footprints now walked across the lower deck, disappeared into the general smear of paint, and then reappeared and led to an aft hatch. To preserve what was left of my Rockports, I went back the way I had come, forward around my stateroom and down the ladder on the other side.

The main aft deck, which we'd seen from the galley the night before, was a swamp of paint. The same orange that the hull was painted in now covered the metal deck in swipes and streaks, lashed and interlaced with flung blotches of black, brown, and red. The fending-off tire—a huge tractor tire that was tied outside the ship when she was docked—shone in its new decoration. The sun pierced the fog, sending Jesus rays down into the ocean, and through the black and orange tire I could see streaks of light turning the gray clouds silver. Sodden, newly painted ropes draped around the tire, glistening like tinsel. Stalactites of white paint dripped down, sticky, swaying in the breeze.

The whole effect was disturbing. On a Navy vessel, such devastation could never have happened—paint was stored in marked cartons on designated shelves in a special paint storage room, fireproof and locked with strong bolts. Like everything else, paint was ordered, tracked, maintained, and controlled. But even if something did spill, anywhere on the ship—spinach, for example, or radioactive waste—lower-echelon sailors were sent immediately to scrub it up.

I'd never seen a line uncoiled on a Navy ship, nor a surface that was not shining clean. My staterooms had been sterile when I moved in, and I tried to keep them so, because even in officers' country, we'd had to endure inspections.

The first time the inspectors came, I was lying in my rack, reading. I had my robe on, my books were everywhere, and stacks of student papers littered the floor. When the first officer opened the door, I thought it was a social call, and invited her to sit down. Then I saw that she was flanked by six male officers and chiefs, as grim as riot police. Each person had had a mission—to check the lighting, the fan, the electrical outlets, the plumbing, the general level of tidiness, and so on. I think one person was examining the dust. The officer ticked off on her list that my bed was not made, and confiscated my blow-dryer for not having been registered with the ship's safety officer.

Here on the *Tan Suo Zhe,* I thought, the spilled paint would probably stay forever. She would become known internationally as the amazing Technicolored seismic vessel, whose crew never cleaned the deck.

But since my job description didn't include paint scraping, I headed up to the bridge. I liked to check the latitude and longitude every day, so I could record our progress on my own map. As I climbed up the ladder, the bridge seemed unusually quiet. Only the chief mate was on watch, lying at full length on the captain's chair, his feet propped on the controls. When he saw me, his eyelids fluttered a bit, and I wondered if he'd been dozing.

In the aft part of the room, Mr. Ding lay on a white sheet, curled on one side like a plump, Oriental lion. His hair was rumpled, and his hands crossed in front of his chest like paws.

This also had never happened on U.S. Navy ships. As far as I knew, it was not SOP for the cooks to take afternoon rests on the bridge, nor for the crew to accommodate them by tiptoeing, as I was now doing, so as not to wake them.

The chief mate pointed to the cook and whispered, "Sleep-ah!"

"Yes," I whispered back. "Why is he up here?"

But either he didn't understand, or the question wasn't important, because the chief mate didn't answer me. He cast a fond look back at Ding, still snoozing, then put his own chin back on his chest. I crept over to the chart table, making as little noise as I could.

At that point the daily weather telexes were coming from Hawaii, the site of the nearest National Weather Service station. Underneath the descriptions of prevailing conditions for various parts of the ocean, a bulletin stood out, typed in capitals: a motor vessel from Hawaii was "OVERDUE," that is, missing, whereabouts unknown. Called the *Reefer Queen,* she had been seen last near Mindanao, in the Philippines. I thought that, with "Reefer" in the name, she must be a pot boat, but the chief mate roused himself to tell me that it was "veddy big ship. Maybe fifteen tousan ton." He stretched his arms wide.

It scared me that a ship substantially larger and probably more important than ours could just vanish. The bulletin said: "All mariners are requested to keep a sharp lookout." Dutifully, I peered ahead into the hundred yards I could see in the fog. A lifeboat could be half a mile away, and we'd never know . . .

Disheartened, I went to my stateroom to record the day's position. I inked a dot on the blue wall map and then, studying the calendar, counted the days until we'd probably get to Galveston. Barry had claimed it was about three more weeks to Panama, and then another week or so to port.

We'd been out only about fourteen days, but the initial energy of the trip was wearing off. I began to list and schedule things to look forward to. There wasn't much the way of amusements or pleasure, but any small change was better than unvaried routine.

One high point of every week was the phone call to Martin. My contract stipulated that I could make one five-minute call a week, paid for by the company. Barry claimed that there was no accounting for this phone bill, that all the minutes to the States were billed in a lump sum, so no one could know how long we talked, but I didn't abuse the privilege of using the satellite phone. My calls sometimes went over by a minute or two, but I didn't want to cheat Olaf out of hundreds of dollars. Also, there was a kind of old-fashioned romance in the pressure of time, the hurried exchange of news and affection over long, crackling distances. Also, having the time limit made it impossible for us to discuss any of the really difficult things, like whether or not I would go to Iowa and whether or not Martin would accompany me.

I had been thinking that I would go. Being away from Houston, I noticed how little I missed that city. I had liked the other graduate program in Iowa very much when I'd visited it; I was inclined toward leaving Texas and going to the Midwest to finish my PhD.

Martin was about the only thing I did miss from home—so I looked forward to talking with him. Even though it was only a few minutes once a week, it was better than nothing.

Besides phone calls, I looked forward to tapes. Garrison Keillor never failed to make me happy, so I'd brought along six of his tapes. However, I was rationing them, allowing myself only one new tape each week. New tape days were on Wednesdays, to break up the time between phone-call Sundays. I kept myself to this discipline because I knew I'd get depressed without something to look forward to.

After tapes, the excitement got pretty minimal: I planned the dubious luxury of washing my hair every three days, timing it so that it never happened on the same day that we would cross a time zone. I loved moving my clock's hands ahead, feeling closer to home and Martin. Saturdays were special because they were my day off—though usually I just did laundry and took naps. To enliven other days, I'd plan special activities in my classes, such as games in English or a vocabulary tour around the ship.

The day after the storm was a Sunday, and I was happily anticipating calling Martin that evening. Since I never knew for sure what time zone I'd be in each week, and since I never knew whether or not the ship's phone setup would be working, I had given Martin a window of time during which he should try to be at home. I liked to call him at seven, right after my evening class.

My morning meditations over, I went downstairs to see if I could find some breakfast. Mr. Ding had adjusted to the fact that I was on a weird sleeping schedule, and no longer took it personally if I didn't show up at breakfast or even lunch. He'd leave me three or four platters heaped with food, and the huge rice cooker was always on, and often he'd interrupt his nap time to come in and hover around, asking what else I needed. I hoped to find a relatively light brunch—a little rice and grilled fish, maybe—amongst the inevitable piles of pork and greasy beef.

From the entrance to the galley I saw it. Stretched about four feet long, a big slaughtered duck dangled by its neck from the ceiling, slowly dripping blood into the sink. It'd been cleaned but still had feet, eyes, and beak. Black stubble clung to the gray, sagging skin. As the ship moved, the duck twirled slightly on its noose, revealing a red gash along its breast. Suddenly, I didn't want even a cup of tea.

That afternoon, I went into the galley as usual before my afternoon class, to sit with my students. After lunch came the inevitable Chinese siesta, *xiu xi,* during which the entire ship shut down, except for one person on watch. But several of the men, including Zhao and the chief engineer, would abbreviate their naps and then bring their books and notebooks to the dayroom to study. They would read or talk about the lessons, and I'd answer questions or talk to them in English before class started.

Today, however, a terrific game of cards was taking place: even the diligent students had been sucked into the group clustered around the table. Someone dealt four cards, and there was a second of rapt silence before someone pounded the table and called something, immediately echoed by groans and shouts of agreement.

Barry sat in the middle of ten or so men, his large figure almost hidden by the Chinese group. "Look at this game," he said. "It's just an addition game, but it's very clever how they do it."

Tsu, the radio officer, slapped down a deal. Everyone stared at the cards: an eight, a three, and two fives. Then Zhao knocked the table and spoke rapidly, pointing to the cards.

"You have to make twenty-four with these numbers," Barry explained. I don't know how he—Zhao, what did you do?"

Grinning, Zhao picked up the eight. "Eight without five."

"Huh?" I said.

"Minus," Barry said.

"I am sorry. Eight minus five make three." Zhao put those two cards down and pointed at the others, a three and a five. "Three with five make eight. So I get three and eight. Three multiplied eight is twenty-four!"

I caught on slowly. You had to use all the cards in any set of four, and whoever could make twenty-four first would knock on the table. The loser usually took the cards, but in this case so many people were playing that it didn't matter.

After a while I looked up and saw that the crowd had doubled. Captain Tan and Lin were looking over my shoulder. Lin flapped his notebook at me. "Class!" he said.

I'd completely forgotten. "Yes! Class!" I echoed, calling the others from the game. Ding came to the door of the galley and joined in, imitating me. "Class!" he shrieked, in a high voice. "Inglish class!" This made the others giggle, and they scrambled obediently for their books.

Moments like that made me feel deeply fond of the students—it was hard to see them as grown men with real lives and responsibilities when, around me, they behaved like perfect, adorable schoolboys. I knew that the way they acted mostly reflected a cultural difference, because Chinese people had more respect for teachers than almost any other group, but still I reveled in the attention and deference.

On the way into class, Lin looked at me daringly. I could tell he was composing an utterance he was proud of, so I waited, showing that I was ready to listen.

"Today is Sunday," he said carefully.

I was a little thrown. "Yes. Today is Sunday. Was that a question, or—?" The room had become quiet as everyone followed our exchange. Someone laughed.

"Sunday—" Lin began, and then couldn't go on.

"—Make phone call," the chief engineer added. His pink cheeks spread into a wide grin.

I began to understand. "Yes . . ."

"Not to parent. To—friend!" Lin burst out. He was joking, but the atmosphere in the room was nervous, as if the students thought I might get angry with them.

"Yes." I took a breath. "My boyfriend. Martin. I call him every week."

"Aahh." Lin scraped a chair from a table and sat down. Somehow the tension was diffused, perhaps just by my clarifying the situation.

For that day's warm-up, I'd decided to teach students that Americans say hello in a variety of ways. I was tired of hearing them always parrot back whatever I said to them, so I put greetings and typical responses on the board, in order of formality:

Hi! Hello!	Hello! Hi!
How are you doing? How's it going?	Okay. Fine! Great!
How are you?	Not bad. Well, and you?
How have you been?	I've been well, thanks.

I then explained when people might use each expression, with which kinds of friends or colleagues. I tried to get across that the exchanges were not as routine as Chinese greetings, that in the United States almost any of the answers on the list could go with almost any question. I pointed to each expression and had the students repeat it after me, which they loved to do. Pointing to the phrase, "How are you?" I read it and commented that it was "very common." And they echoed it back to me in perfect choral obedience: "How are you? Very common."

After the warm-up that day I began work on the radio announcements. Olaf had said that the single most important thing I could do was make sure the men could be understood on the ship's radio. So far they hadn't been using it, since we hadn't passed any other ships, but in a few weeks we'd reach the major shipping lanes, and then the Panama Canal, and then the Gulf of Mexico, which according to Olaf was thick with traffic—everything from international oil freighters to private yachts. A major hazard would be the thousands of small fishing boats operated by Vietnamese immigrants, who didn't speak English any better than our crew.

Once our ship started working in the Gulf, it would be trailing a seismic platform some miles behind it. Olaf had stressed that the men had to be able to communicate the platform's whereabouts to other vessels to avoid the cables or the platform being run over and destroyed.

The lesson was simple: I had a sheet of commands and announcements that the men had to be able to pronounce clearly. This had nothing to do with comprehension: it was pure accent reduction. I let the other students go early, and sat down at one of the tables with the crucial crew members, the ones who would be talking on the radio: Captain Tan; Cui, who was called second captain and would take over as captain in Texas; the radio officer Tsu; and the chief engineer Lin.

"Please read this sheet," I said. "From Olaf. Very important."

Since we had no photocopy machine on board, I'd copied the command sheet several times by hand.

The first sentence was, "This is the seismic vessel *Explorer.*" As the students read it to themselves, I silently questioned the linguistic sensitivities of whoever had dubbed a Chinese vessel *"Explorer."* There was no way the crew could ever pronounce it properly. The name *Tan Suo Zhe* meant something like "one who explores or searches," and I desperately wished that whoever had translated the name had decided on *"Searcher"* instead. Of course we, the Americans, were no doubt mangling the ship's real name, *Tan Suo Zhe,* every time we spoke it. And Olaf wanted to give the ship a Western name for her work with American companies; I could see that. But when my students tried to say it, the ship's name deteriorated to baby talk: "Essa-pu-luh-luh" they said.

"Try again," I encouraged them. I wrote the word on the board and pronounced it slowly: "Ex-plor-er."

The chief engineer tried it first. "Exa-pu-lu-luh." He added sounds without realizing it; it was odd for them to have a syllable that began with a vowel, because Chinese syllables start with consonants.

One trick I knew for teaching hard phrases was to start at the end, with the last sound. "Try saying 'er,'" I said. "Er."

"Uh," they said.

"Good! Now again! 'Errrrrr.'" I rolled the *r,* to show how hard the Western consonant was.

All four men giggled. The more I rolled the *r,* the more they laughed, but their attempts to imitate the sound resulted only in a long, drawn-out "uhhhh." Finally I drew a lion face on my paper, and pointed to its mouth, to show growling. "Grrrr!"

They cracked up. The captain laughed so hard he had to lean on Tsu for support. When they had their breath back, I went around the table, asking each person to try making the hard *r* sound. Zhao and

Tsu could do it a little, with effort, but the captain never would. But I tried again the starting-from-the-end approach. "Okay, say 'er.'"

Variations of the syllable came out. They were getting better.

"Good!" I said. "Now, 'plor-er.'"

"Pu-lo-luh," they chanted, raggedly.

We worked on joining the syllables "ex" and "plo" for quite a while, since they had trouble blending consonants: "exuh-pu-luh." After we'd been doing this word for about five minutes, I took a deep breath and modeled the whole word, slowly and clearly: "Ex-plor-er."

They took deep breaths too. Then: "Exa-pu-lu-luh."

It was the same with the word "seismic." Each time, they turned it into four syllables: "seis-ah-mick-ah."

"Seis-*mick*," I said, showing the hard ending to the word. To demonstrate how sharply the word ended, I clapped my hand over my mouth after the last *c* sound.

When the captain's turn came, he imitated my motion, slapping himself on the mouth before the last vowel could emerge. Then he giggled around his hand.

"Good," I said. "Try again! 'Seismic vessel *Explorer*.'"

The good captain of the *Tan Suo Zhe* lowered his glasses and frowned at the piece of paper in front of him. "This ah—this ah— Seis-ah-mick-ah bess-ah Exuh-pu-luh-luh." Between words he slapped his mouth, and after each slap he giggled. I was not convinced that the Vietnamese fishermen in the Gulf of Mexico, hearing his giggles, slaps, and Chinglish over the crackling, popping, much-interrupted ship's radio, were going to get the message entirely clear.

After class, while everyone else was eating dinner, I climbed up several decks to the radio office. This was a dark, claustrophobic room wedged between my deck and the bridge. Much mysterious equipment lined the walls: machines covered with gauges, antennae, dials, and knobs, all the flat metal fronts stacked in uneven, boring array. The other space was filled with cabinets stuffed with all kinds of junk—I could see books and papers, wire, tools, tea canisters, and pencil stubs. Only one person at a time could get into the narrow aisle between the piles of stuff. To use the satellite phone, you had to wedge yourself on a stool in front of the standing microphone, and hold down a red button while you spoke.

Tsu, the radio officer, was waiting for me. He was a quiet, blunt-nosed man who spoke English better than most of the others; he seemed a little apart from the rest of the crew, perhaps because his job was more technical than theirs. That evening, as always, when I got to the radio room, he'd already made the complicated connections to my country and city, and all I had to do was dial the area code and number. He sidled out of the room, giving me room to go in, and I watched as he went down the ladder to his dinner.

Barry had been getting paranoid about our phone calls, claiming that everything was taped and that later the translator listened to the tapes and relayed everything to the captain. I told him he was crazy. For one thing, there was no evidence of a tape recorder, and I couldn't believe that the Chinese engineers who'd refurbished the ship for seismic work had thought to include bugs. Also, I asked, why should the captain care about our private conversations?

"I don't know," Barry glowered. "Maybe they're not taped. But it seems like whenever I'm talking to Olaf, there's people hanging around outside."

Even if they were monitoring Barry's calls, I was sure no one listened in on mine. Everyone was far more interested in dinner. Still, maybe there was something a little secretive about Tsu. While the connection to Houston went through, I opened a few drawers in the big metal chest. There, in the front of the top drawer, I found evidence of what Tsu did up there all day: he had his English note-book open, neat notes in Chinese and English, and the tape re-corder I'd given him, halfway through a demo tape I'd made of the radio announcements.

The line was ringing, and then I heard Martin's voice, sounding sleepy and excited. "It's you!" he said. "Wow!"

"It's me!" I said. "We have five minutes!"

He chattered through his news: his contract work was going well; my tomatoes were ripe; he'd had dinner with two of our friends; and a stray cat had adopted him. The bad news was that our friend Tay-lor, who had AIDS, now also had pneumonia. "He can't talk any-more," Martin said, his voice low. "His parents came from Califor-nia to stay with him, and they're really nice, but they're sad."

I knew that Taylor might not be there when I got back in four weeks' time. "Give him my love," I said, helplessly. "Give him my best."

"I miss you a lot," Martin said. "You know?"

I knew. I would have been surprised if he had not missed me, since he had little else in Houston to feel attached to. I said I missed him, too, although I suspected that my feelings weren't as strong as his. I told him a little about the storm, and gave him my expected ar-rival date. I glanced at the clock: we had used up five and a half min-utes. "I have to go," I said. "We're over the time. I love you."

After he said it back I hung up, and the warmth of his voice was replaced by the buzz of long-distance nothing. My few minutes, one of the highlights of my week, were up—spent, as Lin had marveled, not with parent, but with friend!

I sat with the crew that night, at the table with Cui, Zhao, and the chief engineer. They were having fish and green beans, but for me Ding had prepared my favorite dinner—Kung Pao chicken.

Everyone knew it was my favorite, and they looked happily at the plates Ding brought to the table. "Chick," Ding announced. "Teach-ah like chick."

"I love it!" I offered the platter around to my tablemates. To be polite they tasted some of it, but said they didn't care as much for the nuts and spices as I did. "How can say, the taste?" Zhao asked.

"We call it 'hot,'" I explained. "Szechuan food is very hot. It has a lot of peppers."

"Ji Lian like hot food," observed the chief engineer. He handed me one of the jars that crowded the end of the table. In it, huge cloves of garlic swam in a dark, vinegary broth. Using the chopsticks, he fished out a couple of pieces and put them on my plate. I ate one and liked it.

"Hen hao chi," I said. *Delicious.*

"Eat with beer," he said. He popped a garlic clove into his mouth, then chased it with a long draught from a brown bottle.

"Sure," I said. "I'll take a little beer." They wanted me to have a whole bottle, but since they were quart-sized I didn't take one. Instead I let Zhao pour some for me into a clean jar. There were very few glasses or cups on the ship, for some reason, but everyone used empty jars to drink from.

Someone yelled behind me. I turned. Barry, coughing and flushed, was being slapped on the back by Captain Tan and Lin. "Have you tried this wine?" he sputtered. "Goes down like velvet."

"What wine?" I asked. Immediately a huge glassful was poured for me.

"Go ahead, chug it down," Barry said. "Better that way."

"Yeah, right." I sniffed at the clear, viscous liquid. It smelled like pure alcohol.

"Very nice," said Cui. Politely, he lifted his glass to me. "It is good, like garlic."

Cautiously, I took a tiny drop between my lips. My mouth blazed as if I'd drunk acid. I swallowed hard, feeling the stuff sear down my throat. Tears came to my eyes and I choked and coughed, each breath feeling like fire. My tablemates watched in dismay.

"God," I said when I had my composure back. It was all I could do to keep from mentioning the similarity to jet fuel. "That's a little stronger than American wine. French. Whatever. Our wine would probably taste like soda to you."

Zhao looked at me curiously, not quite getting it.

"This is very strong," I said more clearly, "To you, American wine would taste like Coke."

He translated quickly; I heard the international word "Coke," as "Coke-ah." The other men at the table laughed and shook their heads. "We do not like," said the chief engineer. "Coke-ah too strong."

The cook and his assistant stood to begin cleaning up. The others drifted away, taking their plates and chopsticks into the galley to rinse. Tsu stood up, and opened the porthole. "Clean up," he said to me shyly. He pushed together all the empty beer bottles, at least six on our table, and then, one by one, jettisoned them into the sea.

Later that night I was sitting by Barry in the bar, listlessly watching him play a video game. His score was now in the hundreds of thousands, and he had reached a new level that none of the rest of us had ever seen. Besides the usual spaceships and aliens, he was having to dodge whirling balls of fire and small, quick-moving meteors. It bored me silly.

It bored him pretty well, too, but he said that it gave him something to do besides worry about his stepson. When he couldn't sleep at night, he'd go upstairs and talk to the chief mate, and when he couldn't stand that anymore he'd come downstairs and up his score a little. When he reached a quiet spot between screens I said, "Wasn't that wine terrible?"

"Blech. Never again." The machine flashed to life and Barry hunched forward, his trigger finger shooting steadily.

"I can't believe they drink that stuff every night, then go on watch."

"The beer, too," he said. "Makes me kinda nervous. But it's okay when we're out here—there's nothing to hit, you know? The ship's on, like, autopilot, and really nothing can go wrong. But when we get to Panama, man . . ."

"They'll be out of beer by then. Just as long as we don't let them order any more from the shipping agents—"

"Are you kidding?" Barry's eyes were locked on the screen, but he pointed toward me with one elbow. "Check out that seat you're sitting on."

I looked down at the blue vinyl cushions. "Looks okay to me."

"No, dingbat. Check under it. The seat comes up."

Sure enough, the cushions were tacked to a piece of wood, which lifted off the base, exposing a coffin-like storage area. The space was packed with cases of beer.

Barry tapped madly at his joystick and an exploding sound came from the screen. He swore, put down the control, and leaned back. "Every single bench on board is sitting on a ton of beer. They got it in their rooms, too. There's even a shitload in the hold. As much as they've been drinking, they've barely made a dent. There's enough booze on this ship to float the *Titanic.*"

I replaced the lid on the stash, thinking of all the miles to go before we were remotely within reach of land, of all the ships we'd be navigating around in the Canal and the Gulf, of all the storms yet to come, of how tired the men were getting. "Yep," I agreed. "Enough to float the *Titanic,* or sink it."

Dolphins Are Not Fish

Along the journey between continents, certain customs changed from Chinese or American to Chinglish. Having read that it was most polite to address Chinese people formally, I'd begun by calling the men Mr. Wang, Mr. Zen, Mr. Zhao, and so on. And I'd thought the crew would like to call Barry and me by our last names, as well.

Barry put up with that for about three days, and then he came barreling into the bar in the middle of a class. "What's with this 'Mr. Bradley' shit? Can't you teach these guys to use my first name?"

"I'd be glad to," I said. "Only I understood that the Chinese custom was to use surnames." The students were leaning forward, trying to make out what we were saying.

"You got ears? They call each other just Wang, Gu, Pan, whatever. Right?" he addressed everyone in the class, speaking much too rapidly. "Don't y'all just call each other your last names? Gu, they call you Gu, right?"

Gu looked helplessly at me. "It's okay," I said softly to him. "Okay, Barry. We'll work on it."

"Great. Sorry to bust in on you." He swung off down the passageway, and I turned back to my befuddled students. "Now," I announced, "we will take a break."

While they filed out, to drink tea or to smoke, I looked over the crew list that Olaf had given me, which included all the crew's names, birth dates, and jobs. If Barry wanted a change, fine. I agreed that the Chinese men should get used to referring to Americans by their first names. In China the family name came first, but Gu couldn't introduce himself as Gu Hai Bin because then the Norwegians would call him Mr. Bin.

When my students came back I explained to them that in the United States and Europe, we have the given name first, then the family name at the end. This struck my students as exceedingly odd. I had to repeat it many times and give many examples on the board. "My name is Ji Lian, Gillian," I said. "My family's name is Kendall— that's the end of my name. Now let's try saying names in the American way. Mr. Gu, when you are introduced in the United States, you have to say your name is Hai Bin Gu."

Gu looked ready to explode with amazement. He stood up, straining over the table to see his name as I wrote it on the board: "HAI BIN GU." When he saw it, he shook his head wildly and sat back down. The others in the class laughed and sang out the name, pointing to Gu, and slapping each other on the back. I might have just told the best joke in the world.

"What's so funny?" I said. "Zhao, why is everyone laughing?"

Zhao could hardly sputter an answer through his glee. "He name—name not Hai—Hai Bin Gu—" Hearing it out loud made everyone laugh even more. I let them get it out of their systems and, when they were done gasping and wiping their eyes, I carefully asked Gu if he could say his name in the new way. He did so, but he barely got it out through spurts of giggling.

It was the same with every student. We went around the room, putting their family names last, and they could hardly breathe for laughing. The captain laughed so hard he turned purple in the face, coughed, and got hiccups. He had to leave the room, and we heard him guffawing down the hall.

No one could explain the joke to me—Zhao and the chief engineer just kept saying that the names sounded very odd to them. When they'd laughed themselves into a shiny-eyed stupor, I repeated that from now on we would be less formal. "You can call Mr. Bradley 'Barry,'" I said. "That is his first name. Barry."

"Bally," repeated Zhao, using the Chinese variant of the hard "r." The rest of the class copied him, reciting Barry's new name, the one he'd asked for. "No Mist-ah Bladley! Bally!"

From then on we dropped the "Mr." and "Miss" from our interactions, at least for the students who came to class. I still called the silent old man "Mr. Chess," and the cook kept the name "Mr." because he liked it, but the rest of the crew enjoyed using the informal names for me and Barry.

That lesson was my most popular class; all through dinner, the men kept pointing to one another and shouting out the reversed names.

By the time we reached the halfway point in the trip, trash was taking over my closet. Along with his other instructions, Olaf had charged me with reminding the men not to dump any trash into the water. I had reminded them, pointing out that Olaf himself had written it on the bottom of my crew list and on the radio commands sheet. But they all ignored the order.

Refusing to dump anything that wasn't biodegradable, I packed away every scrap of plastic and metal I used, and kept all the waste paper: notes for classes, notes from my Chinese study, game score pads, and the inevitable illustrations and cartoons that we sketched to communicate. I hated the idea of polluting the ocean with stuff that could easily be burned (or better, recycled) when we reached Texas, so I stuffed my rubbish into plastic bags and kept it. After a few weeks, the bottom of my tiny closet was covered with white, crackling bags. I had to balance my shoes on top.

Despite my efforts, every day I saw the men hurling trash into the ocean, and it always bothered me. I'd seen more Coke cans dropped in than I could count, and endless cigarettes. The cans, worth a nickel each, would have been hoarded in China, but because we were at sea and space was limited, the men didn't bother to hold onto them. Worse than the cans and butts, though, were the plastic bags I saw flying over the side—bags that wouldn't decompose, that would litter the ocean for years.

Virtually every hour I was outside, I saw trash floating on the water—trash that came from somewhere else, not our vessel. We were midway between Hawaii and California, over a thousand miles from either land mass, and almost as far from the nearest ship. (Although we were traveling on one of the Great Circles, apparently no other ships were taking our route. Other cross-Pacific traffic was far north of us, using the shipping lanes that ran along Alaska and then down the Canadian coast.)

Often, sitting on the deck forward of my cabin, I would catch sight of something perhaps a quarter mile ahead of us, bobbing between waves. As we approached, it would grow clearer and bigger until I could make out that it wasn't a seabird or a clump of weed, but floating garbage. Most of what I saw was packaging—there were at least two plastic bags for every other item. I decided I'd be more committed, when I got home, to "pre-cycling," especially to avoiding one-time packaging.

The trash dumped by my shipmates disappeared behind us, so

where was all the other stuff coming from? It bothered me so much that I kept a record of everything I saw in two weeks:

nylon rope
a bottle of suntan lotion
at least fifty plastic bags
an orange life preserver
two Pepsi cans, one 7-Up
a hairbrush
a brown bottle
a large, plastic-coated cardboard box
a vegetable oil bottle
a beer can, barnacled but refusing to sink
a yard-long plastic tube
drinking straws
a red, Styrofoam float from a fishing net

For every one thing that I listed, there were three or four that I couldn't identify. Too far away from the ship for me to see, or too broken down by water and wind for me to recognize, ugly lumps of anonymous garbage drifted by every half hour or so. My favorite debris was a beach ball, streaming seaweed, its lower half covered with barnacles. Its garish orange plastic had been faded by the sun, and the long trails of green and brown seaweed slowed it down, making it seem graceful in the water, bobbing along, almost alive. In fact it was alive, encrusted with living barnacles. In time, I supposed, more weeds and more shellfish would attach themselves to it. Maybe a bird or two would light on top, leaving guano, and eventually dust and seeds might blow on, and plants begin to grow. That beach ball might become a floating island.

Or, more likely, it might sink, along with the other tons of trash.

I wondered about what debris lined the ocean bottom. I imagined the Chinese beer bottles, filling and then floating gently down, past the fishes, into the dark, settling into the uneven sands at the bottom, a mile or two below us. I wondered how the ocean bed looked: used tires among the coral reefs, lengths of chain entangled in long strands of kelp. Barry told me that any food the cook threw out probably went down to the bottom, where the crabs could eat it, before the sharks even got near. If it was true that food reached the bottom, I thought, how much more true for glass and metal. At depths of thousands of feet, there were red cigarette lighters and broken combs.

I became convinced that people could do this—hurl garbage into clean water—because the opacity of the ocean hid the trash. No one likes to see garbage, especially not Westerners. Americans package waste in deodorizing bags, in cans with tight lids, while it is on our own property. In most city landfills, waste is buried—out of sight, out of mind. If the ocean were a deep desert, would we cheerfully charter planes to dump barges-worth of rubbish on it? I think not— the sight of teeming, ugly piles would prevent it.

But obviously, burying trash, under earth or under water, doesn't make it disappear. The ocean hides but doesn't solve the problem. I remembered one of my college teachers talking about emotional issues, comparing them to household dirt. "Any bachelor will tell you, if you sweep something under the rug, it doesn't go away. It gets worse. It finds other stuff and bonds with it."

It bothered me that the garbage I saw suggested the presence of even more: I was just one observer, outside only an hour or so a day, seeing only the stuff that happened to float by on one side of one tiny ship on one minute strip of ocean on part of one short journey. And we were weeks away from land, days from the major shipping lanes. To reckon up all the garbage in the ocean you'd have to multiply what I saw times all the hours I wasn't looking, by all the angles I wasn't watching, by every other latitudinal line, by forever.

When I talked to my shipmates about my observations, they seemed unconcerned. "The ocean is vast," said the translator, as if the ocean were infinite, as if something large could not be ruined. These men knew the ocean, knew its hugeness better than I did, yet I thought it was romantic at best to think that humanity couldn't ruin an ocean, when already we had ruined so many large lakes and powerful rivers. I was frustrated that they would not take my concerns and Olaf's directives seriously.

The only small comfort was that the trash tossed off the *Tan Suo Zhe* was probably less harmful than average American waste, in that the Chinese goods didn't have as much packaging and plastic. The cooks stored rice in huge bags, pickles in earthenware urns. The meat in the freezer wasn't packaged at all—it lay, covered with frost, in big pink-and-white piles on the bare metal shelves.

Also, the crew used every old glass jar as a teacup. In the galley was a huge jar of Nescafé that Barry and I sometimes used; every day the men would check to see if it was empty yet. One day I noticed that they were drinking out of *American* jars, containers for spaghetti sauce and peanut butter, labeled in English. I asked the translator how the men got these jars in China.

"They did not get in China," he said. "This ship was in the United States five years ago. The jars have been on it ever since."

I was impressed at such resourcefulness, but it seemed odd to me that, despite hundreds of washings, many of the jars still bore their original labels, the brand names and logos bright and intact. Why did the glue have to be so strong? Did American manufacturers really have to use adherents and inks that could not be dissolved?

Still, drinking tea from jars was eminently practical. The lid could serve as a top, keeping the heat in, or as an ashtray. The lid also kept the tea from sloshing when the ship rocked. Also, you could see through the glass and tell when the green tea leaves were exhausted. They, too, were recycled—each crew member usually started the morning with fresh leaves, and renewed the drink throughout the day by pouring boiling water on the same leaves five or six times. This method produced a strongly caffeinated drink in the morning, and a mild, almost tasteless brew at night, as the tea leaves got weaker and weaker.

However, as admirable as some of their habits were, the men were still hurling too much stuff overboard. I tried telling Barry about the problem, showing him a memo that Olaf had given me. "Olaf said we're not supposed to throw trash overboard."

Barry laughed. "In American waters, sure, they can't do that. But here in the middle of the Pacific, you're not gonna stop them."

NIMBY. Not in My (American) Backyard. But the Pacific, being no one in particular's back yard, was fair game. "If they get in the habit now," I argued, "they'll do it in the Gulf, too."

"Look," Barry said. "I'm not crazy about throwing plastic into the ocean either. But what do you think the cities do with it? When the landfills get full, they just take the stuff offshore and dump it, too."

That stopped me from arguing with him. But still, I preferred burning and recycling to dumping, so I continued hoarding the bulk of my garbage. On the other hand, some things even I would discard: orange peels from when we had fresh fruit, then pumpkin-seed shells, and later, soda.

When my period finally came, I faced a garbage dilemma. Tossing Tampax overboard meant adding nylon string and possibly bleach and other nasty chemicals to the ocean. But even I wasn't willing to hoard used tampons in my room for four weeks. And so every few hours I sneaked out on the deck, looking over my shoulder to make sure that no one was around, and tossed little red packages overboard. I hoped they'd never reach the bottom: maybe my blood would end up as shark snacks.

The first day of my period came after an awful night, one in which I couldn't fall asleep for a long time. I hadn't been able to get really warm because of the air conditioning, and I'd lain awake thinking about the state of the earth, the state of this ocean, the state of this ship, and the state I lived in. My political differences with Barry were typical, I thought, of my differences with Texans in general: I wanted to go somewhere where environmental consciousness wasn't considered a big joke or a fanciful mistake. I noticed myself thinking more and more in terms of living in Iowa in the fall; without my having to make it, the decision seemed to be made. When I thought of going back to Houston, I felt dread. When I thought of the little town in the hills in Iowa that I had visited, and the people I'd met there and the lovely graduate program I'd been accepted to, I felt eagerness.

The jetlag and thoughts of moving house—so much to do in the two months when I got home!—kept me awake till dawn. When I did, finally, doze, I immediately woke back up to a horrible clacking noise. It sounded like a broomstick or a billiard ball rolling across the deck. I flopped over to face the other way, and pulled a blanket over my ear, but the noise was too loud to muffle. I got up, dressed, and went through all the cabinets in the passageway, looking for something rolling. No luck. It seemed to be coming from the space between my bed and the next stateroom, but it was too early to wake up Cui, who slept next door. I gave up and went back to bed, where I lay, annoyed and awake, for another hour.

Apart from the clacking noise and the rocking of the ship, I had cramps. It was impossible to get comfortable in such a small bed, confined by a wooden rail. Also I had several thick blankets on to keep out the draughts, and they were bulky and heavy. After a lot of tossing and frustrated stretching, I got up again and pulled my mattress down to the floor. The ship's movements slowed a little, and we weren't rocking much, so the billiard-ball effect stopped. I was able to sleep for a few minutes, but the noise began again when we reached some waves. I was so angry I woke up squeezing the pillow.

Finally, around eight in the morning, I gave up trying to sleep. Exhausted, feeling worse than when I'd gone to bed, I got up and went to toss a tampon. I watched it sink and then stood gloomily staring down at the sea spinning out from under us. The water was greenish gray and unexciting; the sky was muddy. No sun had emerged yet, and I was cold as well as sleepy and cross.

It was both strange and soothing not to see any airplanes. I'd never realized before how much a part of the sky's scenery they formed. Only when I had seen virtually no aircraft for weeks did I realize that they'd always been present everywhere I'd lived or traveled before.

As I looked at the reflections of the clouds, a shadow rose through the water—a dolphin leaping—then two dolphins, splashing out and back into the water, then more, all around us. Swimming right next to the ship, they were moving in swift lines just below the surface, skimming up and down and then leaping up to breathe. When they rose to the surface, I could see their breathing holes clearly, and I realized for the first time how clear the water was. It always looked dark because of the great depth, but now that there was something a few yards under the surface, I could see that the water was crystalline.

They weren't the big "Flipper" dolphins I'd been expecting, but small ones, about four or five feet long, and colored like two-toned cars: brown on top, creamy underneath. I clapped and called, encouraging them to jump. Suddenly there were dozens of them, maybe a hundred, diving under the ship, swimming away, coming back. Several caught up to the bow and stayed there, skimming inches ahead of us, weaving and streaming and surfing the bow wave. They kept even with the bow, using almost no movements—only their tails moved, lightly waving. We were doing nearly eleven knots, yet the dolphins had no trouble swimming and playing alongside. They could easily have outdistanced us.

I watched in great joy, thanking God for all the circumstances—the restless night, the rolling noise, my cramps—that had led to my being on deck at that moment. I watched one dolphin head away from the side of the ship and then down—when I looked back, they had all vanished. There was no sign that they'd been there. Still, it was good to look out at the sea and know they could be anywhere, and that they *were* there somewhere, spinning and swimming and playing and diving.

Feeling happier than I had in a few days, I took my morning stroll around the ship. As I'd predicted, no one had cleaned up any of the paint spill. However, it was a week or so old and mostly dry. I could walk over the spattered Abstract Expressionist surface. In a few spots, despite the days of sunshine, the paint remained tacky, so I had to avoid those areas or wind up with orange-soled shoes.

Heading aft, I saw something new nestled in the piles of painted lines. It was a brown, woven basket, inside of which lay a bunch of very dead eels. There were about six of them, faded to a dry brown, skinny, each a foot or so long. They looked evil and a little frightening. I didn't know whether someone had somehow trapped the eels—we were moving too fast for fishing—or whether they'd just come out of the freezer, to be left outside in some Chinese variation on curing. Either way, there would be eels for dinner that night.

In the afternoon, I headed to the galley to forage before the eel meal was cooked. In the dayroom, Ding sat next to a table, propping his feet on a bench. He was working at an enormous bowl of green beans, stripping the tiny threads of each bean, and cutting off the ends. Seeing me, he started to get up, but then winced. "Foot no good-ah," he explained.

Sure enough, his right foot was swollen as big as a melon, and wrapped messily in white gauze. "What's wrong?"

Mr. Ding looked down at his beans, shrugging. "No English. Foot bad."

I sat down with him and started trimming the beans. "No, no," he said, but I could tell he was glad for the help. After a while of companionable silence he tried again. "No walk-ah. Foot bad."

"Did you cut it?" I put the knife blade against my own foot, to show him what I meant.

He squealed, "No, no!" and made me put the knife down.

"Did you burn it?" I pointed towards the stove, although he couldn't see it from where he sat. "Hot water?" I said. "Fire?"

Mr. Ding squinted a little, but obviously didn't get what I was saying. "Bad foot."

I thought he was complaining of his foot again. "Yes, your foot looks bad," I sympathized. "It must hurt a lot."

"No foot!" He giggled weakly. "Food. Bad. Bad food. I no eat-ah pohk, beef-ah. Just fish, rice."

Sure, I thought. Another Chinese cure: he's going to try to heal his burn by fasting. "Maybe Barry has medicine," I said. "Remember, you took medicine for seasickness? Maybe Barry has something for your foot." I was just thinking out loud, but Ding evidently picked up on a few of my words that he knew.

"Med-sin," Ding mused. "Good-ah."

It became dolphin day. When I got to my afternoon class, Zhao had a comment ready for me. "Today I see—I saw teacher on boat deck. I saw you laugh."

I hoped I wasn't blushing. My favorite student had seen me not only cheering the dolphins, but also, perhaps, tossing away bloodied

Tampax. Still, although he seemed young to me, he was older than I, married, and no doubt acquainted with the necessities of feminine hygiene. So, focusing on the positive, I said, "Yes! I love the dolphins!"

The class didn't know the word, so I drew a picture, partly to teach them and partly for my own amusement. I made it especially large and elaborate, even adding a little shading.

When they saw what I was talking about, they looked perplexed. After conferring with the others, Zhao phrased a careful question: "Why do you love dolphin?"

It was such a charming question that I both spoke and wrote my answer on the board. "Because they are beautiful and intelligent."

The class seemed to understand, if not to share my enthusiasm. To warm them up for the day's lessons, I went around the room, asking each person to say what he had done that morning. I began with Gu, the electrician, a round, mild-eyed man, who gave the impression of knowing a great deal, although he rarely talked. He came to both the lower- and upper-level classes, shining in the first, struggling in the second. He could read somewhat and answer by rote, but improvised dialog was not his forte.

"What did you do today?" I said, slowly.

Poor Gu looked at me anxiously—he hated answering first. If someone else went before him, he could usually catch on to what was happening, but it was tough for him to understand me with no other cues. To reassure him, I smiled and repeated the question, and wrote it on the board. "What did you do today?" I gave him some examples of answers. "Today I made my bed. I saw dolphins. I prepared the lessons. I ate lunch. What did you do today?"

Gu nodded that he understood, then waited a minute, thinking. Slowly, he got the sentence out: "Today I get up. I make my bed. I repair clock."

"Very good!" I said. "You repaired a clock today?"

Gu nodded solemnly. "I repair clock for captain."

"Wonderful!" I said. I was so proud of him. "Captain, what did you do today?"

"Today I—ah—today captain—" he stammered.

I sighed, wishing again that he were taking the beginner-level class. Quickly, in the space underneath the dolphin I'd drawn earlier, I put on the board a mix-and-match set of columns:

Today	I	worked
Yesterday	you	ate
Last week	he/she	rested
Last month	we	sailed
Last year	they	studied

I had used this model with success a few times before, especially in the beginner's class. It allowed them to get used to the structures of simple English sentences (which were similar to Chinese) and express a variety of ideas. Most of the upper class students could change the tenses by altering the verb endings and the time markers. Keeping it simple for the captain, I pointed to the top line and read the first word, prompting him to make a sentence. "Today—" I said.

"Today—" he tried but then got confused. "Today I you—captain I—ah work bridge on twelve go me."

Sighing silently, I pointed again to the first word. The chief engineer whispered a sentence, and the captain copied it. At least it sounded like English.

"Very good," I lied. "Try again?"

The captain did not look where I was pointing. Instead, he was squinting at the big, bold drawing I had used to illustrate our conversation about the dolphins. "Fish!" he blurted out.

"Yes!" I said. This was spontaneous English usage; I didn't need to correct him and say that they were really mammals. "Big fish.

Dolphin." Someone handed him my Chinese-English dictionary opened to the translation. He squinted down at it briefly but then waved it away. Suddenly an idea hit me. I erased the picture and wrote the word "dolphin" in huge capital letters, many times the size of my usual writing.

"Duh-ol-pin," the captain read, quickly. And then I realized it wasn't that the captain couldn't read English letters, it was that he couldn't read anything small.

"Captain, do you wear glasses?" I pointed to the heavy lenses on Gu's face. "Glasses. Gu has glasses." I shook my head and pointed to my own eyes. "I *don't* have glasses. Do *you* have glasses?"

The captain made his hands into tubes and put them to his eyes. "I—uh—glass—" He conferred briefly with the chief engineer, then tried again. "I—you—" Then he lapsed into Chinese.

The chief engineer raised an eyebrow, offering to translate what the captain was trying to say. The captain nodded at him with relief. "Captain not have glasses," the chief engineer explained. "Ocean have glasses."

"You mean they fell overboard?" I made our usual sign for "overboard," pointing out the porthole.

The chief engineer nodded. Turning to the board, I erased what was on it and wrote in very large, dark letters. When the class saw it and figured it out, they laughed and looked admiringly at the captain. The captain looked up and read it, for once without squinting. Then he held up a hand, volunteering to try it out loud, and he read almost perfectly what I had written: "The captain is smart, but today he cannot read. The ocean ate his glasses."

How to Remember

Confucius, discussing student-teacher relations, said that the student must be insatiable in learning, the teacher indefatigable in teaching. Fatigue came easily to me on that ship, but my students, especially the older ones, seemed endlessly hungry for knowledge. They gobbled up vocabulary words like sweets, and they seemed to like many of our lessons.

Particularly successful was one about prepositions. We collected a variety of objects from the classroom—a few pens, some cigarettes, exercise books, jars of tea, and a jacket or two—and heaped them into a complex pile on, under, and around one of the chairs. The students took turns telling me where things were—"tea is top chair!"—and varying the arrangement and describing it. This activity was so successful that it lasted longer than I'd planned. When I told the class we should finish because it was past time for them to go to dinner, several of them said, "Finish?" with what seemed like disappointment. It was most gratifying.

In the second or third week of classes, I brought the morning class a tape player and a recording I had made of a storybook. The people who could read would be able to listen to the tape while following the words, and so improve their pronunciation and listening comprehension. I didn't know how effective a teaching aid this might be, but it might provide amusement and it couldn't hurt.

Xiu, the tall, skinny mechanic who had no background in English, claimed the tape player first, and took it away to his room even before he went to dinner. After the meal, I saw him in the bar, sitting hunched over the book, listening to the headset.

I had bought half a dozen small cassette players and what I thought would be enough blank tapes. But pretty soon all the machines were lent out, and I had filled all the tapes, recording just about every book I had. I also taped thousands of vocabulary words, everything from inventories of tools to the names of the parts of the ship. For Lin, I recorded a series of questions and answers pertaining to his job as a steward—things he might want to say to future guests on the ship. For Mr. Ding I taped the English names of all the meals he prepared, as well as some common expressions about food. "This is stewed chicken feet," I repeated, slowly, into my tape recorder. "Would you care for some sow's ears?"

The only problem with all the tape activity was that the batteries required recharging. I'd had enough foresight to bring along a small recharger, but I couldn't find anywhere to plug it in. When I explained the problem to Wang, he took me downstairs and showed me a part of the ship I'd never seen before. Below the dayroom and the bar was the main deck, which included the crew's quarters, the washing machines, some showers, and, further aft, the huge tool shop. On that level the air felt suffocating and greasy, as if the fumes from the engine room, one deck down, were rising.

I'd never explored much down on that level, because it was the crew's living area and I didn't want to surprise anyone in the sleeping cabins or the bathroom. Once, however, when I was doing laundry and everyone else was upstairs, I had glanced into the men's shower room. Water lay in cold puddles on the gray floor, and the shower stalls were rusted and rotten looking. I saw no soap anywhere. A few limp rags, probably used as washcloths, lay like dead rats in corners of the stalls. In a rusty holder on the wall, several battered tooth-brushes hung, the bristles mashed flat with years of use.

But on the day he was helping me with my battery quest, Wang led me through a hatch that I had never opened. Cold air chilled us as we walked into a large, brightly lit room, which looked far more modern than any other part of the ship. Long fluorescent bulbs illuminated every corner with solid white light, and the linoleum gleamed. Neat wooden counters lined the sides of the room, sur-rounding a huge computer flanked by control panels, video termi-nals, and printers. Lights blinked and flashed and the video screen showed a black-and-white view of the rear deck: Barry was moving around out there.

"Wang," I said. "Are we still on the same ship?"

"This is instrument room," he said. "This equipment just in-stalled before we left Shanghai."

"Is this all the seismic stuff? Is this how they measure the ocean bed or whatever?"

"Well, I think so. Zhao works here. I think that he could explain it well."

The room had outlets every three feet, so I plugged my little machine into one of them happily and left it to charge.

From then on I visited the instrument room every day, remov-ing good batteries from the recharger and replacing them with worn-out ones. Sometimes Zhao was there, tinkering with a printer or studying his English notes. When the weather was hot, the blue-white light and the air conditioning felt good; occasionally I brought my books down there to prepare for the classes.

However, I quickly tired of running up and down ladders carrying armloads of batteries. Every few minutes, it seemed, at dinner, on the bridge, even on the weather deck, someone would be handing me four or eight spent batteries, saying, "Please fix."

I had to dedicate precious shelf space in my cabin to two boxes, for charged and uncharged batteries. Often I made the mistake of handing out flat batteries and got them back and had to start again. I disliked the chore and wished I could pass it off on someone else, but the tapes had been my idea, and everyone else was busier than I. Besides, I was rewarded when I saw the men walking around wearing earphones, diligently repeating English phrases.

One night I was out in the passageway, trying to find some doors that were clacking open and closed as the ship rolled. This was a constant problem: I couldn't sleep with doors banging, and I always had to get up and latch things that had been left open during the day. Naturally, once I'd dressed and gotten out of bed, the ship hit a calm patch and the noises stopped. But as I listened, hoping for a telltale click that would lead me to whatever was unlatched, I heard a weird moaning sound.

It sounded like a Chinese ghost. Frightened, I tiptoed to the base of the ladder, where the sound was coming from. Was someone on the bridge in pain? I knew that the chief mate worked the late watch alone; if he hurt himself, no one would be there to help him.

I ran up to the bridge, trying to remember what I knew of first aid. The chief mate, all alone, was lying back in the captain's armchair. Both feet rested on the control panel, and his head lolled on a pillow. A tape recorder lay in his lap, and earphones hugged his head. As I watched, he hummed a little, then burst out in another moan of Chinese song.

One day while trying to prepare the lessons, I couldn't find two books I needed: a picture dictionary and a storybook. I knew I'd had them in class the day before, so I went downstairs to look for them.

It was after lunch, so most of the Chinese crew members were having *xiu xi,* the important afternoon nap, but steward Lin and several others were sitting in the dayroom, their heads together as they bent over something. Hearing me come in, they looked up. Lin quickly closed my book—the one I was looking for—and put aside some papers. Next to my dictionary, he had his notebook out, in which he had diligently been copying down English words. The others had been writing on napkins. Lin ducked his head awkwardly, his eyes lowered, as he handed me my book. "I am sorry."

"No reason to be sorry!" I said. "You are very good students!"

Lin shook his head, his straight, blue-black hair falling across his eyes. "Very bad student," he said. "Very stupid."

"No! You're very smart." We could have gone on like that all day, but Cui cleared his throat, preparing something to say.

Second Captain Cui was a remarkably pleasant man, with a square face and square, strong hands. At forty-five, he was older than most of the others and more experienced at sea. En route to Galveston, he was working as a general seaman, helping Ma paint and make repairs, but when Captain Tan left the ship in six months, Cui would take over. Although his status at the time was technically lower than theirs, the others treated him with deference. He was one of the most earnest of students, always carefully constructing an idea in words before trying to get it out.

He swallowed, then began: "It is your book." He was holding the other book I'd left in the dayroom, a large, illustrated children's book, called *Little Pig and the Blue-Green Sea.* It was open to the page on which the pig, having been taken onto a ship, topples overboard. When Cui spoke English, he raised his eyebrows and lifted his chin, like a schoolboy reciting a poem. "Little Pig fall in ocean?" he asked, motioning out the window.

"Yes," I said. "But it's okay. He can swim."

Cui's smile flashed as he bent over the book, eager to continue. "It is very interesting."

I told Cui he could keep the book, and we were exchanging cheery, all-communicative nods, when the chief mate came barging in. As always, the atmosphere changed with his presence. He hadn't had tutorials since the first week, and I rarely saw him, but when I did, his hoarse, loud voice grated on my nerves. I thought that he tended to shout because he was a little deaf, so I couldn't blame him, but it was still hard on my ears. Barry, who often went up on the bridge during the chief mate's watch, claimed that he wasn't so bad after a few drinks, but I had little desire to get to know him better.

The chief mate plopped down as close to me as he could get—it wasn't quite an arm's distance—waving a burning cigarette and exclaiming, "Book-ah! Good-ah! I read English book-ah!" He snatched the dictionary and started flipping through the pages, excited but not focused. As gently as I could, I turned to some words that might interest him: it was an illustrated dictionary, meant for children, and one page showed a variety of sea animals. He jabbed a yellowed finger at the dolphin. "Teacher like fish," he said. "I eat."

If he ate dolphins, I didn't want to hear about it. I pointed to the shark. "Shark," I said. "Shark eats people."

Second Captain Cui slipped away, holding the children's storybook under his arm, carrying his jar of ginger and water. I imagined he was going to spend the time before class studying in his stateroom, in peace.

The chief mate said something that made the other Chinese men respond rapidly; it sounded as if they were arguing, but then, it very often sounded that way to me when they were just chatting. I wanted to leave, but I needed the book, which the chief mate was gripping with both hands.

"Well," I began, "I should go and prepare—"

"How can call this?" The chief mate was jabbing at one of the sea animals.

"That's a turtle."

He laughed strangely. "In China," he said, "can call husband turtle."

"Oh yeah?" I tried to take the book, but he hung onto it, saying, "Husband is turtle—husband is cuckold."

Where had he gotten *that* word? I wondered. Then I remembered his ancient grammar book—he probably had an equally outdated dictionary somewhere. "A turtle is a cuckold?" I asked, vaguely. I guess my reaction wasn't shocked enough, because he hunched forward, studying me. The other students watched.

"In America," he said, loudly, "husband, boyfriend, what is difference?"

"One is married," I said. Though I could see where this conversation was headed, I tried to keep my voice neutral. "Husband and wife are married; boyfriend and girlfriend are going on dates."

"But make sex without marriage, okay? In America is okay." He crinkled his eyes.

"No," I said quickly. "It's not okay for everybody—"

"Yes," he insisted. "Bally say is okay. Also, wife and husband make love okay other people okay."

"No, no, *no.* Not okay." I tried to change the subject. "But in America, a lot of people get divorces—"

"Yes," he said, raising his voice to a yell. "Boyfriend girlfriend say 'I love you,' is okay, make love." He gave me a lewd, sideways glance, and I felt like smacking him. His English had never been so clear. He must have been picking up some choice constructions from his late-night conversations with Barry.

"America has 250 million people," I said. "There's no one rule for everyone."

Unimpressed, he regarded me with doubt, but he was quiet. To discourage any lascivious ideas he might be having, I lied. "I have a boyfriend," I said, "but I don't sleep with him."

Suddenly everyone at the table was extremely interested. "So virgin," the chief mate said, breathless.

In my mind, I cursed Barry for filling the chief's head with such questions. I should have slapped the chief mate long ago, but it was too late. And losing my composure would have damned me more than anything. So in answer to his question I looked faintly shocked, and nodded, as if too embarrassed to speak.

He leaned back in his chair, all the wind gone out of him. He spoke almost gently. "So boyfriend is just sweetheart, huh?"

The next time I ran into Barry I had plenty to say. We were standing on the aft deck, watching the sunset behind us through the veil of diesel smoke. When the wind lifted the gray film, the clouds glowed, silver and orange.

"Shit," Barry said when I accused him of corrupting the Chinese. "All these guys ask me about sex all the time. Every single one of 'em who can communicate, that's all they want to talk about."

Below us, the water churned, waves frothing white on black. I felt sick. "Even the translator?" I asked, sounding more plaintive than I'd meant to.

"No, not him. But all the others." Barry shifted and reached in his pocket for chew. He pulled a wad of brown fuzz from the can and stuffed it into his cheek. "It's pretty interesting. They've never heard of oral sex before. They can't figure out why American women would want to do it."

I stared down at the water, feeling betrayed. My shipmates—all of them except Wang!—were discussing "American women" like a bunch of horny teenagers. "Why do you have to encourage this?" I said. "Don't you realize that it makes it awkward for me?"

Barry spat a stream of black juice over the side. "Why?" he said. "You should just be honest with them. They even asked me if I'd been to your cabin."

"What?"

"Yeah! They think, 'American woman, American man, why not?'"

"Jesus."

"I told them it don't work that way."

"Thanks," I said.

"No problem." Barry shrugged. "Listen, I don't initiate this stuff. I just answer their questions."

I bet. I could just see him swaggering around the bridge with the chief mate, rolling out every dirty story he'd ever heard, drawing pictures on the backs of charts and using his hands to illustrate. "Look," I said. "If you've got to talk about sex with them, just leave my name out of it, would you?"

"Like I said, no problem." There was a hostile pause. Barry moved his chew from one side of his mouth to the other. "I don't see what you're getting so upset about. None of them believed you were a virgin, anyway."

I got mad. "My virginity should not even be an *issue* here, okay? I'm their teacher." After struggling a minute, I found words for what I wanted to say. "There was no good answer for me to give the chief yesterday. I said, 'Yes, I'm a virgin,' so I'm a liar. If I had said, 'No, I'm not a virgin,' that would make them think I'm a whore, see? I don't exactly feel like explaining my personal life in great detail, you know? There's a double standard here. If you talk to them, it's okay, but if I talk to them, I'm encouraging the whole thing."

Barry sucked his cheeks in, working the tobacco. "I guess you're right," he said slowly. "There was no good answer. I'll try to get them to lighten up."

All the talk of sex and marriage and stirred up my private thoughts on the matter. I had a dream in which my friend Margie was asking me, about Martin, "Do you want to get married?"

Not wanting to answer the question, I joked, "Is that a proposal?"

In waking life, too, I couldn't decide if I wanted to marry Martin—or anyone else—or not. I was thirty, about the age my mother and sister had been when they got married, and certainly my relationship with Martin could lead to engagement. For Margie and for many of my women friends, the answer had been simple—yes, they wanted to get married. But for me there was something in the question, or the answer, I couldn't understand.

After my candid chat with Barry, I was brooding in my stateroom when the phone rang. It was used so little that I almost didn't recognize the sound, but I picked up the receiver. Before I even got it to my ear, I could hear someone yelling "Fish! Fish!" down the line. It was one of the Chinese men, but I didn't know which one. I couldn't imagine what he was talking about and he couldn't hear my questions, but just kept shouting the same word, louder and louder: *"Fish!"*

Was he telling me the dinner menu? Was it a joke? I held the phone away from my ear, wondering what to do. Then someone else came on the line and said, "Uh, dol-phin."

"Oh!" I ran outside to look over the rail, but I caught only a glimpse of a few disappearing flukes. Still, I was pleased that someone had thought to notify me about my favorite visitors.

I went into the galley looking for dinner, but a burnt haze of bad-smelling smoke hung in the air. Wang, the interpreter, wearing a big stained apron, hovered over a stewpot, stirring furiously. Zen, the assistant cook, was rushing between the sink and the stove, carrying a steaming pot.

"Dinner is not ready," said the interpreter. "We are sorry. Few minutes more."

"Where's Mr. Ding?"

"He is sick. He is in his bed."

"His foot?" I said.

Wang nodded, angling the spoon to scrape the bottom of the pot. Whatever was in there seemed to be sticking. "Cannot walk. So I am assistant cook today. Zen is chief cook now."

Zen looked harassed. He was one of the younger crew members, maybe thirty-one, but he looked and seemed even younger than that. Quiet and hardworking, he spoke no English at all, and since he worked in the galley morning and evening, he couldn't come to classes. To cheer him up, I tried some of my pidgin Chinese on him—I pointed to the big pot and raised my eyebrows, and asked what was inside.

Zen smiled tiredly. His cheeks were pale, and the skin under his eyes hung in dark circles; he'd been cooking for twenty people all day. But my interest pleased him: he answered me in Chinese, spooning some of the food up from the pot.

"Stomach," the interpreter said. "Zen is sorry, but he did not have time to cook for you tonight."

It *looked* like stomachs. Gray, floppy, bulging, and soft. From what animal they had come, I couldn't imagine. Chicken feet were one thing, but stewed internal organs were just too exotic for my palate. "That's okay," I said. "I am very full from lunch."

After a dinner of rice and chili sauce, Barry and I went up to see the chief cook in the room he shared with the assistant cook and two other men. Ding was lying in his rack, the sheet and blankets tucked under his armpits. His bad foot stuck out, elevated on a tangle of clothes and towels. "Hello Bally! Hello Teach-ah! Chief cook-ah no good!" he screeched, waving toward the gouty foot.

"How are you?" I said. I poured him some Sprite I'd brought.

"Foot hurt bad," he said. "Too much-ah pohk." The translator had explained to us that they thought the gout in his foot was caused by rich foods. They were hoping that if he rested and ate lightly, the inflammation would go down.

"Here," Barry said. "I've got these pills for my arthritis." He held out a sample from a little plastic bottle.

"Aren't those prescription drugs?" I said.

"Nah. Well, yeah, they are, but I give these to everybody. The last ship I was on, I was the hospital, man. They were taking this for everything from headaches to—here, man, take this." He put two white tablets into Mr. Ding's limp hand. "Eat. Eat-ah."

"Pill," observed Ding.

"Yes," I said. "Western medicine." That was what he called my anti-seasickness medication, which he loved. He had several times asked me for more when we'd had rough weather.

"Ah," said Ding. He sat up, took a mouthful of Sprite, put his hand to his lips, and pretended to take the pills. He made a show of swallowing. "Sank-you," he said, slipping the palmed tablets under the covers.

Barry and I looked at each other. "How much do those cost?" I said.

"Too much to waste." Barry pulled back the blanket, opened Ding's hand, and took back his medicine. Ding looked apologetic.

"What's wrong?" Barry asked. "Why didn't you take it, man?"

"Foot no good," explained Ding. "No seasick."

After the first few weeks of the cruise, the nightly card games dissolved. Occasional rounds of Pig or Twenty-four still went on, but they were desultory, limited to two or three people at a time, watched only by another four or five. Other games took place behind closed doors—the captain played cards almost every night with some of the crew, but he hardly ever stayed in the dayroom in the evenings. Sometimes I was invited to join in the games, but I rarely accepted since the smoke bothered my eyes and, more importantly, I slowed the games down so much. The old man we called "Mr. Chess" still played, all night, but I'd given up on learning Chinese chess after the chief mate had tried to explain it to me by screaming the rules over and over.

One evening I came in from viewing the sunset to find nearly everyone in the dayroom, gathered around Zhao and Gu, the electrician. Gu was sprawled in a chair, with a towel wrapped around his neck. Zhao stood behind him, brandishing a comb and a pair of rusty scissors.

When Gu noticed me, he started squirming, kicking his legs and trying to reach behind to unclip the towel. He giggled, embarrassed, as if getting a haircut were somehow indecent. Waving at him to sit back down, I joined in the audience.

I sat next to Second Captain Cui, who pointed to his own neck. The hair was trimmed almost up to his ears, and little black cuttings lay all over his collar. Carefully, he pointed out, "My hair is little."

His description was charming, and I smiled to show that I appreciated the spontaneous English, but I felt compelled to use the moment to teach vocabulary. *"Short,"* I said. "You have short hair now." I held up a strand of my own shoulder-length hair and said, "My hair is long."

Zhao made a few more sweeps over Gu's hair with his scissors, then removed the towel and shook it out. Gu shot out of the chair, untucking his collar from his shirt and buttoning it up tight, with sideways glances at me.

"Very nice," I said.

"Would you like it?" Zhao waved the scissors near my head. I shrieked and pretended to recoil in horror, holding my hair away from him. Everyone laughed. Zhao whisked the towel around the chief engineer's shoulders and started combing his short gray hair.

From the kitchen, Barry gave a wolf howl. "Look out, Galveston women." He swaggered into the dayroom. "Wang, tell them that the chief is going to break girls' hearts."

Wang stared at Barry, his eyebrows pulled together over confused eyes. As good a translator as he was, he apparently was confused by the idea of broken organs.

"I mean girls will like him, because he has a *good body*." Barry flexed and pointed to indicate the chief engineer's wide shoulders and large muscles.

Wang translated, and the chief engineer looked embarrassed, but everyone else laughed, teasing him.

I felt awkward. I had never noticed the chief engineer's body, and if asked I would have characterized him as teddy-bear shaped, but he did look pretty strong. I almost never noticed men's bodies, and I wasn't sure I liked Barry's assumption that "Galveston women" would be looking primarily at a man's physique. On the other hand, this was a way for us all to kid around together and to give some compliments. So, trying to sound objective, I said, "Galveston women might like Zhao too. He has high cheekbones, like a movie star."

Wang translated my comments, and everyone looked hard at Zhao's bone structure. Laughing, Zhao covered his face and pointed to Zen, the assistant cook. I saw that he, too, had round, prominent cheekbones. What was it then, that made Zhao look so different, markedly more attractive than all the others? As I studied Zhao's face, he told me that he, too, needed a haircut. "No one can cut it," he said.

"Why not?"

"Well, only Zhao knows how to cut hair," the interpreter explained. "If one of us does it, it will look unusual. I think you say 'weird.'"

"Keep it long," I counseled Zhao. "It looks good that way." For me, this compliment was pretty daring, and I hoped I wasn't embarrassing him.

Zhao nodded, and the translator told the others what I had said. They fell silent, too puzzled—or something—to joke about it.

I didn't know what to do. It was too late to retract the compliment, so I went further, trying to sound objective. "Zhao is very handsome," I said, casually.

"Everyone looks better when you've been at sea a long time," said Barry. "I'm starting to see mermaids."

Fortunately no one understood his meaning, and the tension diffused. I was glad, since I tried to keep to myself that I was utterly charmed by Zhao. Not only was he the best student and the best-looking man on the ship, but he was, I noticed that night, the only Chinese person I had seen with curly hair. It was thick and shiny, and he combed it back off his face. He was always smiling, and he had cute little crow's feet at the sides of his smile. The others all parted their hair on the side, or, more commonly, let it fall into their eyes in long straight bangs. Zhao's face seemed clearer and his eyes brighter because his hair was swept back.

"Wang," I said. "Can you ask Zhao why it is that his hair is curly? Is he—from a different part of China or something?" I wondered if he might have an unusual ethnic background, but I didn't know if it would be polite to ask.

Wang translated the question and got an answer. "He says he is from Shanghai, like all the others. His father has the same hair, but no one knows why. It is a mystery. He combs it back so that no one will notice it."

"Tell Zhao," I said, "that in the United States people pay a lot of money to curl their hair like that. Maybe fifty or seventy-five dollars, for a permanent."

"No! Is it true?"

After I convinced him, Wang translated, and I could tell he had some trouble making the others believe it. They all looked from me to Zhao's hair, incredulous.

Zhao said something, picking up scissors to work on Lin's bangs. The interpreter leaned toward me. "Zhao says he will not cut his hair, then, if Americans like it this way." He spoke low, as if he were confiding something intimate. Zhao went on working, but over Lin's head, he gave me a beautiful smile.

In the upper-level class I was trying to get the students to have real conversations. Each day the lesson included a short lecture or demonstration on a grammar or vocabulary point, but then I prompted the students to use the new constructions in telling me about the ship or themselves.

One afternoon, when the captain didn't come to class, Lin explained his absence. "Last night, Captain working hard. He is tired."

"Very good," I said. To check for understanding I turned to Gu. "Gu, why is the captain tired?"

"Because working!" Gu's face lit up.

"Right! And how are you feeling today?"

"I am not tired." His face was shining. "I am happy today."

"Why?"

"Because today—" he broke off and consulted in Chinese with the other class members. Zhao opened his Chinese dictionary to a page and pointed to a word for me.

I read the English translation. "'Birthday!' Wow! Today is your birthday, Gu? How old are you?"

He looked confused. "Today—birthday—daughter. Chen."

"Oh." All my enthusiasm drained away as I realized that he couldn't share the day with his daughter. "Did you call her on the telephone?"

Gu shook his head.

That was dumb, I thought. Probably the crew members weren't allowed to use the ship's phone for personal calls, and I had just reminded him of that. Feeling sick and stupid, but still trying to put a good face on it for him, I asked, "Did you write her a letter?"

"No—" Gu tried to answer me in Chinese, then stopped himself.

"Letter is no good," explained Zhao. "We cannot put out the letters . . ."

". . . until we get to Galveston," I finished. That was still several weeks away.

Zhao nodded. "I am writing to my family."

"You write, even though you cannot mail the letters?"

Softly, he said, "I write very much letters."

His answer, on top of what Gu had said about his daughter, made my eyes prickle with tears. Turning away and pointing to the large map on the wall, I asked the students to show me where their families lived. About half of them said that their wives were in Shanghai, but several pointed to Nanjing or Hangzhou instead.

I pointed to the United States and said, "My parents are here," showing them New Jersey. "And my relatives are here," I said, pointing to England. "But I live here, where you are going." I showed them the coast of Texas. "Sometimes, I get homesick."

I wrote the word "homesick" on the board, underlining each syllable separately. "'Home' is where you live," I said. They didn't seem to be following this, so I had someone look it up in the dictionary. Then we translated "sick," and they all nodded, understanding the connection.

"Sick for home," Zhao said. "It is like 'unhappy'?"

"Yes. It's when you are unhappy about being away from home." I wrote a sentence on the board for them: "I feel homesick when I think of my children."

"Maybe this is how you feel," I said, uncertainly. I wasn't at all sure of what I was doing, but I thought giving them the English to express their feelings would be helpful. Also it seemed better to acknowledge their emotions than to ignore them.

Zhao nodded, but nobody spoke; all of them were writing the sentence down in their books.

It was too sad. A little depression had come over the class, and I thought I'd stirred up unpleasant feelings. Confused about how to proceed, I let the class out early.

I sat by myself at dinner, brooding. I didn't know whether I should drop the whole homesickness issue or attempt to ease their loneliness by encouraging them to talk about what they missed. I thought about myself—living in England, Egypt, and Germany, and traveling on Navy ships, I'd been homesick often. One thing that had always comforted me were my photographs of my home, and I enjoyed showing them to people I met there.

After dinner I asked Wang, the interpreter, to put the word out. "Please tell the students to bring their photographs to class tomorrow."

"Ah—pardon me?"

"For English class tomorrow," I said. "Please tell everyone to bring their pictures. Photographs of their family, friends, whatever. I would like to see them."

"Well, I will try," said Wang.

The next day, looking forward to the advanced class, I made up a vocabulary list of relations. I knew that the Chinese words for relatives were very complicated, compared to ours—they had special names for the daughter of an oldest brother as opposed to the daughter of a younger brother, and so on. Even every kind of cousin had a special name. It would be relatively easy, I thought, for them to learn the English words.

I went into the bar feeling jubilant. "Today," I announced, "no grammar. Just pictures!" I got out my own collection of photo-graphs, which I'd edited for their appraisal. After soul-searching, I'd decided to leave out the pictures of Martin and of the apartment complex in which we lived together.

We pulled the chairs into a little circle, and I began with a group shot of my immediate family. "This is me." They laughed at how I looked with very long, straight hair. "This is my mother, my father, my sister, my brother." I put the words on the board, but the students didn't bother writing them down. In fact they hardly looked up, they were so busy staring at the picture. Everyone complimented my parents, saying they looked healthy and kind. Then I passed around a photo of my best friend, Ti.

"She is Chinese!" said Zhao. All the men crowded over the photo, curious.

"No, Japanese. Her mother is Japanese, her father is American."

"Ah, Japanese. She is nice person?"

"Yes," I said. "And here is my cat! Also very nice!" This struck everyone as hilarious. They looked at the Persian in the picture and laughed at it and at me; they made yowling sounds and scratching motions.

"In America," I said, "our pets are our friends."

"Yes?" Zhao looked mischievous. "Cat is like baby, right?" He made a motion of holding an infant in his arms, cooing over it.

"Well, sometimes," I said. "I like to hold my cat on my lap, like this." I pantomimed how the cat curled on my knees and how I petted her. "She's very pretty," I said. "Very friendly."

"Cat sleep in the house?" Zhao looked shocked.

"Sure! Why not? She is clean."

Zhao translated this to the others, who exclaimed over it and looked at me curiously. Gu said something urgent to Zhao, who translated it to me. "Is true that sometimes dog and cat sleep on bed?"

I paused. Since most Chinese people still slept on thin mats, and a Western bed was considered a luxury, it must seem odd, maybe even unfair or decadent to them, that animals in the United States slept on mattresses. But I didn't want to lie to them. "Well, yes, it's true. But they don't have their *own* beds. Well, some of them have their own beds, but they're just baskets and blankets—" It was getting worse and worse, I could see. "Sometimes," I said, "they sleep on our beds. My cat sleeps on my bed sometimes."

Zhao smiled with a closed mouth, obviously thinking I was insane.

"Well, that's enough of my family." I got the photos back from the men, who gave them up reluctantly. Lin, in particular, seemed fascinated. Before he would give the photo back I had to again tell him everyone's relation to me, and their names. "Colin, my older brother," I repeated. "Valerie," I said. "My older sister."

"Who is eldest?"

"Colin, my brother."

"Very good. Big family!"

"No, not really, for a Western family," I said. "In America, most people have two or three children. Some have five or six children. A few even have twelve or thirteen!"

This caused incredulous giggling. When they had laughed enough and talked this over in Chinese, I tried to turn the lesson back to English. "So, let me see your pictures," I said. No one moved.

I spoke more slowly. "Yesterday, Wang told you to bring photographs. Your family. I want to see your families."

I knew they understood me, but no one responded. Some stared down, others looked ahead with blank expressions. Maybe they were shy about going first. "Lin," I said. "May I see your photographs?"

"Ah—do not have."

"You didn't bring them to class? Didn't Wang ask you to?"

"Yes, he ask."

I was mystified. Was there some protocol I was ignoring? Should I have asked to see the chief engineer's family first, since he was the oldest? "Anyone," I said. "Who will show me his photographs? I would like to see them."

Zhao spoke up softly. "We do not have." Several of the others nodded, seeming relieved.

Horrified, I realized that my having photos of my family might be seen as a great luxury. And once again I was reminding them of something they did not have. I was confused. "Why not?" I said as gently as I could. "Are photographs unusual in China?" I had seen at least one person on board with a camera, so I couldn't believe that none of them had one at home.

"No," Zhao said. "Maybe have a few . . ." He trailed off, unable or unwilling to explain.

"How can you remember your families?" It was an inconsiderate question, coming out of my confusion and sudden anxiety.

But the chief engineer understood my question enough to answer it. He looked at me intently, as if wondering how I could ask such a question. After a pause, he said, "How can forget?"

The following day, I came downstairs during the silent hour of *xiu xi* to get a glass of water. To my surprise, Zhao was in the dayroom, sitting with Cui, the future captain. "Hi!" I said. "Not resting today?"

Zhao beckoned me with a mysterious look. "I have a few photograph." He handed over a small photograph album, the kind that held about ten pictures.

"Oh, good." I wasn't even going to ask why he hadn't brought it to class the day before. Maybe, knowing the others wouldn't have any, he hadn't wanted to appear special. I opened to the first page and saw Zhao standing with three other Chinese men in some bright sunshine. "You're in a suit!" I said. "A tie and a suit! Were you working?"

"Ah—working, yes," he said. "In San Diego."

"What?"

"Go to conference in San Diego."

I knew he'd been to the United States before, but the reality of it had never struck me. Other photographs showed him—always in blue suits—in Houston, New Orleans, New York, and Tampa. "Computer conference," he said, of each one.

As I turned a page, a loose photograph fluttered onto the table. I caught a glimpse of two rows of men under a huge red banner of the hammer and sickle. Zhao quickly turned the photograph facedown and placed it to one side, away from me. He turned to a picture of New York. "Very nice town," he said.

I pretended to pay attention to the rest of the collection, but I could hardly wait until he closed the book to point to the facedown picture. "What was this one?" I tried to sound casual.

Zhao and Cui exchanged meaningful glances. With reluctance, Zhao turned the picture over. I saw that all of the men in the rows were wearing large red badges. Was this a Communist Party meeting? Closer inspection showed me that one of them was a face I knew. "Is this Lin?" I asked Zhao.

He nodded, seeming abashed. Then he confessed, "Also Gu."

I found Gu's round, cheerful face in the rows of other round, cheerful faces. Gu—the one student who came to both classes. Lin—the one man on board who had a key to my stateroom. I wanted to discuss the Communist Party meeting—if that was what it was—and to understand why Zhao and Cui were being so secretive about it. "What is this group?" I asked, trying to sound casual.

Both Cui and Zhao shrugged, but I didn't let them off the hook. I waited, and finally Cui said, "Workers."

"Workers discuss," said Zhao. He put the photograph away, firmly. The next time I saw the album, the picture was not in it.

The weather that night seemed surreal. A full moon glowed just off the port bow, and the pink, tropical sunset shone behind us. The warm evening air had drawn everyone out on deck; the men were smoking, talking quietly, or eating their "green pea" ice cream, looking over the side. Zhao and I drew together naturally as we were talking. After a few minutes I realized that we had been left alone by the others.

"Sometimes," he was telling me, "you—how can say?—remember me of my sister. She is very kind person."

We had wandered aft, to see the last of the sunset. The paint-stained red deck was glowing warm in the pink light; over the side, the waves were choppy, their caps pinkish-white, like mountaintops. For some reason we were standing away from the railing, in the middle of the deck, and when the ship rocked, I had nothing to hold onto. I began moving toward the railing, and Zhao followed. It made me nervous, his simple, silent agreement to go where I went; I wondered if he was lonely or simply being friendly to his teacher. I wondered if the others were leaving us alone on purpose.

In a few weeks, I would be seeing Martin and resuming my normal life. When the *Tan Suo Zhe* was just a memory for me, when I'd collected my paycheck and gone back to school, the ship would begin operations in the Gulf, and Zhao and the others would be just starting their contracts. This whole trip was merely a long commute to get them to the work site. Each of them would be away from their homes and families for six months. And while I did not want to flatter myself that Zhao might be interested in me as more than a teacher, I realized that the possibility existed that out of loneliness, he might begin to develop strong feelings. And for him to feel anything at all for me, especially after I'd gone back to Martin, was unthinkable. I had to put an end to flirting.

I said goodnight to Zhao and went back to my stateroom to brood about the difficulties of the day. I felt terrible that the men were lonely and didn't even have photographs for comfort. I knew they were earning good money and were glad to be on the trip, but that wouldn't mitigate their loneliness. There was little I could do to help except give them English lessons to think about, and provide some companionship—but not too much.

I wondered if I missed Martin as much as they missed their wives. Certainly I wasn't writing to him the way Zhao was to his family. In fact, my missing Martin was an abstract thing, something I assumed I would be feeling more than I actually did feel it. I missed having someone to chat easily with, someone who knew me well, but I was missing something else much more than my boyfriend— and the missing thing was women.

Zhao, the man I'd been the most drawn to, was by far the most feminine-looking man on the ship. He had soft eyes with long lashes and curly hair, and a sweetness to him that seemed feminine to me. The conversations with Barry and some of the men about sex had made me feel isolated and somewhat ostracized for my femaleness. Being around all men had made me feel more feminine, as my differences stood out. Showing the men the picture of Ti had made me miss her, too. I thought about my mother, my sister, and my girlfriends far more than I pined for Martin.

And sometimes, usually just when I was waking up from a dream or falling into one, I felt a slight, somber recognition of something else missing: something I didn't have a word for but that I had been missing for most of my life. It was that intimacy with women that I'd felt a few times in the past. Here on a foreign ship of all men, I was missing being with someone like myself. And missing all romance and sex, I found myself remembering and thinking about the few times I had been with women. As sweet and attractive as Zhao was, and as close as I felt to Martin, there was something that neither of them could fulfill, some longing that still wasn't going to be satisfied, even when I got back home to my boyfriend.

Unfit Company

It always made me feel better, on that small, slow vessel, to cross a time zone. No matter where we were, the ocean looked the same and endlessly changing, and the navigation charts showed edgeless water, no land within their margins. For all I knew, we could have been moving at nine knots an hour toward India. But each time we turned the clocks an hour forward, it showed that we were approaching the United States: home.

Just after the middle of July we reached the Pacific Time Zone. Although we couldn't see its coast, we were sharing California's hours. One day I saw a jet's vapor trail steaming across a corner of the sky. I waved cozily in the direction of my friends in San Francisco when we were on the right latitude, then, two days later, toward the people I knew in Los Angeles and San Diego. We had turned south along the California current; the wind grew even more humid, and the air conditioning in my stateroom no longer made the room too chilly. Being nearer to land, we saw more sea birds, and since we'd reached the major shipping lanes at last, we occasionally saw or heard from other vessels. These ships were usually far away, the largest of the freighters almost indistinguishable on the horizon, but I took comfort in their relative proximity.

Unfortunately, moving east disrupted my biorhythms even more. As most frequent flyers know, it's less wearing to travel west than east across time zones, because it's easier to stay up late than to force yourself to go to sleep earlier than you are inclined. After flying west to Shanghai, I had quickly adjusted to the ten-hour time difference. I woke up early, but not unduly so after the first few days. The problem came after we left China and started moving east: my body refused to change back to the rhythms of the United States.

Barry was out of sync, too: since he'd been in the East longer than I, he had adjusted to Chinese time even more than I had. It seemed that, having made one big change, our bodies refused to do so again. The others, the ones who'd come from China, had no trouble sleeping at night, but Barry and I often ran into each other at four or five in the morning, wandering around the quiet ship like ghosts.

One night I'd gone out to my "balcony," where it was pleasant at night, somehow warm and cool at the same time. My eyes adjusted slowly to the dark. There was no moon that night, so apart from one white bulb on the forward mast, we were in blackness: the stars were small but clear. I settled on my usual perch, my feet dangling down a ladder. From there I could hear and sometimes see the black-on-black ocean, but if I fell, it would be onto the main deck, straight below.

The engines hummed along, invisible waves splashed the side of the ship, and upstairs, on the bridge, I could hear the captain giving parting instructions to the chief mate. It was 4 a.m., and they were changing watch. I began singing to myself, a sentimental Jackson Browne song I hadn't been able to get out of my head.

"Unh?" In the darkness, someone moved. It was Barry, who had been lying full-length on the deck, his head not a yard away from me.

"Jeez," I said. "Sorry. I didn't know you were here."

"Neither did I." He sat up, yawning hugely. "Now why is it I can sleep out here just fine, but in my room—sheesh. I wish I had some sleeping pills or something."

"Me too." We were quiet for a while. I heard the captain close his stateroom door, and above us, his porthole filled with dim yellow light. Having woken Barry up, I felt somewhat responsible for his amusement. I asked, "Want to go play the video game?"

"I am so sick of that game. Besides, you know I'd whip your ass. I got a million points."

"Hmm."

Barry rolled onto his back, his arms under his head. "I tell you what Peter said on the phone?"

I hadn't thought about Peter, the dour operations manager, since leaving China. "Let me guess," I said. "We're getting flown off the ship with helicopters and taken to Mexico for a break?"

"Not quite. He said he's going to meet us in Panama. Wants to check out the repairs I've been doing. He may ride back to Texas with us."

I grimaced. "Oh, no."

"I knew you'd be happy." I heard the soft brush of a match, and then the little flame lit up Barry's face, his hands scrunched around a cigarette. "You and him get along like cat and dog. But I'll tell you something; he's not that bad a guy. I wouldn't mind having his company the rest of the trip. He'd get this tub shipshape pretty fast."

"Great," I muttered. Was Peter coming to check up on my performance, as well? "Where's he going to sleep, in the galley? There are no more staterooms on our deck, and I'm not moving below."

"That's a point." Barry blew smoke through his nose, thoughtfully. "I don't imagine he'd like to bunk down with the crew, and he can't throw the captain out. That means me or the radio officer would have to move downstairs. Probably me."

"Well, try to talk him out of it." I had a new burden now, something to worry about.

"Oh, relax. He may not even show."

"Well, why'd you bring it up then?" I had snapped at Barry before I could stop myself. "I'm sorry. I just don't like him." There was a little pause in which Barry did not dispute this. I added, "Or rather, I don't think he likes me."

"You want to know what it is that set Peter against you?"

"No," I said. "Don't tell me."

"It was that first day on the ship. He told you it was important to get to know the crew, but all you did was complain that you wanted to go back to the hotel."

"That's not true!" I remembered meeting the crew, how overwhelming it had been to be surrounded by smoking, jabbering strangers. I reminded Barry that I had hung around for several hours with nothing to do except make inane conversation. My voice had been giving out, I said.

"Don't blame me, I'm just telling you what Peter thought. He's got a thing about appearances. He thinks he knows everything about what the Chinese want to see happen, and he had it in his head that you were supposed to spend the day with them."

"Hell with him," I said. "He's not a teacher; he can't tell me my job. It's not like his job, where he had stuff to do all day. I didn't even have a book with me!"

Barry shrugged, flicking ash from his cigarette onto the deck. "Like I said, it's appearances. Don't get me wrong; Peter's okay."

The ship took a sudden lurch as Barry spoke, and I grabbed the railing. When we were steady again, I thought about what he'd said, and thanked him.

Barry didn't say any more, but I was grateful for the insight, because it meant that Peter's coldness to me wasn't really about me.

General concern for appearances was easier to accept than personal dislike.

"Also, there was one other thing about you," Barry said. He feigned a reluctant tone, but his words came out quickly and he was almost laughing. "You know that day, the day before we left, when you called him at 6:30 in the morning?"

I hadn't known Barry had heard about that. "Sure," I said. "I wanted to tell him about the food, because I thought he was mad about it."

"He wasn't sore about that. He couldn't care less what we ordered. You noticed they didn't get most of it anyway. No, what really set Peter against you was that you called him at that time in the morning, and he'd been on the phone to Olaf until four."

"Well, I didn't know that then! Anyway, I thought you guys went down to the ship every day at the crack of dawn."

Barry shook his head, grinning. "Not that morning. That was the one time we got to sleep in. And you woke him up while it was still dark, fussing about the grocery list. He must have told me about it five times."

"Generous guy," I said.

"Hey, I never claimed he was that."

While we had been talking on the deck, the sky ahead of us had whitened. We were moving into the dawn. "Hell's bells," he said. "Another night without sleep. Let's go up on the bridge and harass Chief."

I followed Barry slowly, thinking about what he'd said. It bothered me that he got along with Peter and I didn't, and I was frustrated by his acceptance of Peter's bad manners—such as at the farewell banquet—and his unpleasantness toward me.

Barry and I were so different. In college I'd never known a single football player, but I'd disliked them on principle. Barry was one of those guys—he'd been a quarterback at the University of Oklahoma—yet he was a good guy. He worked hard, he had plenty of common sense, and he was good company. I had to admit I liked him.

One of the reasons I liked him was that he was a good conversationalist. He asked questions and told me jokes and brought up ideas. He seemed more conversationally agreeable than many men I'd spent time with. Was he just a friendly guy, or was he talking more to me because he didn't have other men around who spoke English? I hoped it was the former.

Barry went ahead of me up the ladder, his wide back filling the narrow space. When he reached the bridge, I heard him curse. "Look at this!" he snapped. Again, the chief mate was stretched out in the captain's chair, his feet propped solidly on the control panel. I'd seen him like that before, but this time he was snoring.

"God *damn!*" Barry slapped the bare soles of the chief mate's feet, twice. "Wake up, man! This ain't your rack!"

The chief mate jumped awake, saying something in Chinese.

Barry leaned into his face. "You're on watch, guy! Wake up! What the hell you been drinking?"

The chief mate stared, his face gray and frightened in the dim light. "No ships—no ships, okay."

"No!" Barry spoke harshly, almost yelling. "Not okay! There were no ships around when we were way out, but there's plenty of ships here. You stay awake, you hear?"

Astonished, the chief mate stumbled to his feet. Swaying slightly, he stared out to sea. He glanced at the instruments and guiltily checked his watch.

Barry went outside on the bridge wing, grumbling that the chief was "damn irresponsible." I followed him out, though there wasn't much room on the wing—it was just a small observation platform. Barry spat over the railing. "That guy could have killed us. I swear."

I felt guilty for not mentioning that I'd seen the chief mate napping on watch earlier in the trip. "Well," I hedged. "This may not be the first time."

"It's going to be the last time. Wait till Olaf hears this. That guy will be history."

"Really?"

"Think about it! If another ship's coming toward us or cutting in front, what are they going to do? They'll try to radio him, and if he's sleeping . . . who knows? A big ship can't change course all that fast. Could plow right into us."

"Right over us, you mean?" Why hadn't I realized the danger?

"That's right. Then *we*'d be history." Barry lit another cigarette, then whipped the match out. "Guess I know where I'm spending my nights from now on."

Barry stayed angry for some days. He called Olaf the next day to expose the chief mate's transgressions, and messages were relayed from Olaf to the interpreter to the captain to the chief, and apparently the messages did not include sympathy for the chief mate's long hours. He went around looking hangdog and ashamed.

I was feeling irritable, too. It seemed to be taking an extraordinarily long time to move down the Mexican coastline. Panama looked close on the map, yet it was still ten days away. The winds were generally against us, and we were making less than nine knots an hour. Furthermore, since coming within a few hundred miles of land, we'd been invaded by hordes of flies. I was able to keep the population down in my stateroom by keeping the door shut, but the kitchen was constantly swarming.

I'd long before given up my resolve not to eat sugar. Out of boredom and for lack of any good munchies, I'd been eating ice cream and drinking Coke for some weeks. When the ice cream stores ran out, I found myself craving more sweets. I started hanging around the galley in the evenings, experimenting with making desserts. The place was pretty dirty: besides the piles of uneaten food, the unwashed pots, and the ubiquitous rice cooker and its steam, for a long time there was a piece of cooked ham hanging on a bit of greasy string above the sink. I didn't know what it was doing there, and I didn't ask, but the flies apparently found it delicious. The meat was usually blackened by swarming insects.

My first attempts at dessert-making were out-and-out failures. I tried to make tarts with some strawberry preserves and an ancient package of biscuit mix I found in the pantry. I think the mix had been there since the ship's last trip to the United States; it didn't rise very well. I ended up with soft, undercooked dough cases, puddled in the middle with low-quality jam.

We had plenty of butter on hand, however. Nearly all the other fresh food supplies were gone, but for some reason we still had dozens of pounds of butter. So I learned to make candy by melting a stick of butter in a heavy pot, then adding sugar and milk powder. The result, depending on how long I cooked and cooled it, was either a gooey caramel or a brittle toffee-like mixture. Proud of my creation, I offered caramel goo to everyone.

Most of the Chinese men tried it, murmured politely, then left most of it on their plates, where the flies congregated. Barry was more direct: "That stuff'll give you the runs for a week. Keep it away from me."

My only ally in dessert-eating was Tsu, the radio officer. Compared to his shipmates, he had quite a sweet tooth, and would come into the galley any time I was cooking and say, "Very good! Candy good!"

One night, feeling particularly grouchy, I tried making an apple pie to cheer myself up. Mr. Ding, still bedridden, had given me pidgin instructions on pie-making, and I was using some canned apples I'd found, despite the rust covering the can. At a tricky point in the pastry-making, the chief mate came thumping into the kitchen, taking one of his frequent breaks from the bridge. He leaned over me, disturbing a settlement of flies and fouling my food with cigarette ash. "What is this?" he shouted. "How can spell?"

I ignored him, because I felt like snapping. He moved closer in on me, as if I hadn't heard him, demanding, "How to spell?" and jabbing at my pastry.

"I don't know." To get away from the chief, I turned to my left, but Tsu was standing behind me, peering over my shoulder. A fly buzzed in my face. I said, "Excuse me please," but he didn't move. Feeling trapped, I pushed Tsu—I didn't mean to shove him, but to guide him out of my path since my English was not clear to him.

He jumped back as I touched him. "I just look," he said, pitifully.

I felt *terrible*. I wasn't even mad at Tsu, but at the chief. And even the chief hadn't really done anything wrong. I'd learned that he habitually shouted because he'd worked for many years in the engine room, and his hearing was impaired.

I apologized lamely to both of them and went to sit in the dayroom to calm down.

By the porthole, someone had left a pack of cards, which I dealt for a game of solitaire. I was hoping to be left alone, but Zhao came and sat next to me. In a minute he was telling me which cards to play. I hated it. When he touched my cards, I made a slapping motion at his hand lightly, as if I were joking. He gave me an odd look, but went on coaching, trying to help me win.

Feeling that I was not fit company, I started up to my stateroom to sulk, but then remembered the mess I'd left in the galley. When I went back to clean it up, Tsu was cheerfully washing my dishes.

"Tsu," I said, abashed. "Thank you, Tsu, but you don't have to do this. They're my dishes, I can do them." I spoke too quickly, but Tsu got the message.

"Is okay," he said. "No problem."

In fact he was just about done. "Thank you very much. I owe you one." I grabbed a rag—they were all equally filthy—and tried to wipe down the counter where I'd been working. The whole area was covered with grease. In remorse for my bad-temperedness, I decided to clean it off properly.

First I looked for soap, but couldn't see any. Then I searched under the sinks for scrubbers or steel wool: again, nothing. Finally I resorted to hot water on the greasy rag I was holding, but when I wiped down the counter, it just smeared. I gave up. When I tossed the rag back down on the counter, it startled a fly, which came buzzing toward me.

I picked up the rag again to do battle. I rolled it up and thwacked at the fly, and got a hit. It was very satisfying. If I could kill one, I thought, why not more? I went around with my cloth weapon and clubbed the counters where the flies were the thickest. They must have been logy from the tropical heat or from too much ham, because they barely moved when I attacked them. I moved around the kitchen, killing things.

Tsu watched me in amazement. "Why?" he kept saying.

"It's fun. Here." I could hardly believe myself; I was worse than Barry shooting things on the video game. I gave Tsu a towel. He waved it at a few flies, but he wasn't ambitious enough to kill them. He tottered over to the corner and came back with a battered fly-swatter, which he handed to me as one might give up a magic wand.

The swatter was an ancient plastic one, the rectangular surface torn, and the handle bent. I took it like a gift from God, and went after the insects faster and harder. I killed thirty-six flies that night, and went to bed smug.

"I'm a murderer," I told Barry the next day. I explained about my sortie with the insect world. I had never in my life enjoyed killing anything, but last night I'd rampaged.

"Some pacifist you turned out to be," he said. "Speaking of flies, have you noticed . . . ?"

"Have I noticed what?"

"These guys all go around with their pants unzipped?"

We were sitting in the bar, watching a few of the mechanics play the video game. None of them understood English well enough to follow what we were saying. I took a quick look. Sure enough, Barry was right. Since many of the guys wore their shirts out, pulled down over their hips, I'd never noticed, but they didn't zip up their pants. They were buttoned or hooked at the top, but not otherwise closed.

"They need to stop that before we get to Texas," I said. "I don't think the Norwegians will be able to handle it."

"It looks weird," Barry said. "I'm going to tell Wang to make them shape up. Hey! Get it? I'm going to tell Wang to make them keep their wangs in place."

Since he'd pointed it out, I paid more attention to every-one's appearance. I'd become so accustomed to being surrounded by Chinese men that I hadn't thought much about it. Most of them shuffled around in long, baggy pants, wearing plastic "slippers"— wide-banded thongs—over thick, dirty white socks. Also, almost everyone, almost all the time, carried a jar of cooling tea, with leaves and pieces of ginger floating in the rusty water. Their hair, often flattened by oil and dust, fell over their eyes, and whenever they sat down, they lit small, yellowish cigarettes that burned with a terrible odor.

Apparently Barry talked to Wang that night, and word got out after dinner. He told me later that Wang had thanked him. "He said they never think about it," he said. "Just like we leave our top buttons unbuttoned on shirts, they leave their flies open to be more comfort-able. Makes sense, I guess, except their shorts show."

We could have continued this interesting exploration of cultural differences except that Lin came charging up to us at that moment. "Ji Lian, Bally, if you please excuse me," he said. "But I wonder if you would care to have some fresh towel in your rooms?"

Barry's jaw dropped. He turned to me. "Did you teach him to say that?"

I shook my head. I had made Lin a tape of helpful expressions, but I hadn't been expecting him to start sounding like an English butler. "That was very good English," I told Lin. "But no, thank you, I have plenty of towels."

"Please let me know, if I can do anything else," Lin beamed, "to make more comfortable."

"Okay, thank you."

Lin left, all but bowing his way out. Barry turned to me. "Maybe those classes are paying off!"

The following day, all trousers were demurely zipped. At one point I was sitting with Zhao and Lin, struggling over my Chinese, when Cui walked in. He'd been working outside, and his hands and face were speckled with orange paint. As he walked up to us, he stopped and looked down, and then pulled up his zipper. As he did, he gave Zhao a smart, knowing look. They were obviously humor-ing us.

Many of the men had asked me to make specialized tapes for them after Lin's amazing progress with the "steward's phrases" tape. More and more often, I saw the men wearing the headphones to the portable tape players, their lips moving, eyebrows drawn in concen-tration. As we neared Panama, where we expected to encounter new people—shipping agents, pilots, and so on—the English lessons took on a new urgency. In class we studied lists of things we were ordering in Panama: fruits and vegetables, tools, engine parts, and more blank tapes.

One night at dinner, Wang asked me to make a tape for Ding, who was still sick in bed. "He would like to study while he cannot cook," said Wang. "He ask me to ask you to tape some of this book for him."

It was a small, worn, paperback phrasebook, its edges soft with handling. The title was in Chinese, and the quality of the ink and the paper indicated that it had been made in China some time ago. I took it up with interest, opening it to a random page. There I saw what Mao Tse-tung had wanted the Chinese to be able to say in English:

We study hard for the revolution.

Wow!" I let out a whoop, and showed the sentence to Wang. "Look at this!"

Wang did not laugh. He colored and tried to take the book from me. "It is old book," he said. "Chairman Mao—"

"I know," I said. "It's okay." On the next page I found a few more gems of English construction:

Our country is a dictatorship of the proletariat.
She has a firm proletarian stance; that's the most important thing.

"This is great!" I said. "Do you think Ding would sell me this book?"

"Well, I do not think he want you to record those item. Maybe more simple phrases."

"I will," I said. "I just think this is funny." Actually I thought it was fascinating: I hoped to get a better explanation of Mao and his ideology by talking about it with the Chinese. The translator obviously wasn't open to discussing it, but the next day I took the book with me to class, and put up on the board one of the best English sentences I had found:

As long as imperialism and socialist imperialism exist, there can be no peace.

As I finished writing it, the captain jumped to his feet. "No good-ah!" he said. "No good-ah!"

"It's okay—" I began.

Zhao interrupted me, translated something the captain was jabbering at him in Chinese. "The book is not correct. It is an old book. Our government—not feel this now."

Impressed by his expression of such a complex idea, I began to praise him. "That's good English, Zhao. You put that very well. But I am just interested in the history—"

The captain ran to the whiteboard, and, in the only breach of classroom etiquette in the whole trip, he erased what I had written.

As we moved southward and my cabin fever increased, something happened that crystallized my bad mood and gave me reason to feel even worse. It started on a Sunday phone call, usually one of the high points of my week. Usually I chattered away to Martin feeling lighthearted and closely connected across the miles. Typically we would talk for five minutes at three times the usual rate, covering everything from what he'd had for lunch to my worst teaching moments to plans for the future. The word "Iowa" had come up in several phone calls, but I'd let it sift to the bottom of the conversational pile. This time, though, Martin started the conversation by saying he had big news. His voice thick with import and pleasure, he said slowly, "How would you feel . . . if I were to say . . . that I will be coming with you to Iowa?"

Once before in my life, I had had a premonition. The feeling I had as Martin finished his question was physically the same: it felt as if a brick had been thrown into my stomach. No words came into my mind, only a blank feeling of dread and wrongness at something that was supposed to be right. The first time I'd had the feeling, it was when I was twenty-two, right out of college. I had gotten a call from Condé Nast's HR department to say I'd landed a job as an editorial assistant at *Mademoiselle,* a dream starter job for an English major. I'd intuited—I'd felt physically—that although it sounded great, it would turn out badly. This time the lump in my middle and the blockage in my throat kept me quiet for a minute.

I was so quiet that Martin thought the connection had been broken, and said, "Hello? Are you there?"

The innocence of his question, the nervousness in his voice that he might have lost me, even by phone, made me swallow away my feelings and say, as warmly as I could, "Great. That's good news."

It wasn't exactly a lie. It *was* good news, in theory. It was what I'd been hoping to hear until the moment I heard it. He was obviously expecting me to be relieved and delighted that our relationship would continue. I would have to sort out the other feelings later, alone. I finished the phone call with talk of U-Hauls and UPS boxes, but when I finished, I didn't go down to dinner as I normally did. I went up to my stateroom and tried to cry.

I couldn't exactly weep, for some reason, although I felt a strange tension. It came to me that I was going to have to disappoint one of us, either Martin or myself, very soon. I didn't think I could tell him, after all this angst, *not* to come to Iowa—and I wasn't sure that was what I wanted. Yet I felt that if he did come, I would feel more of this unease, more of the difficult sense that no matter how great Martin was, the relationship wasn't right for me. I didn't want to be without him—but my desire for him was the way I'd want to be with a brother, not a lover. Martin knew me well and was good company, but I didn't think that was all one should feel for a romantic partner. I didn't understand, and I didn't know what I wanted, but it was something . . . other than what I had.

Bridge of the Americas

On July 29 I saw land again. When I woke up, the view of an island filled my porthole, and I rushed out to the weather deck. A month had passed since we'd glimpsed the mountains of Japan, so it was exciting to see something on the water that stayed still. As we were nearing the Panama Canal, dozens of tiny green-gray islands dotted the water, drifting back to the horizon like clouds. I could see three ships, too. I felt happy to be once again within swimming distance of safety.

Below me, Barry moved across the work deck. "See?" I called down. "I told you it wouldn't take that long to get to Panama!"

"Make that Costa Rica," he said. "We won't hit Panama till tomorrow. Then God knows how long we'll have to anchor out before we can get through the canal."

"Anchor out!" I'd been counting on getting off the ship for a while, stretching my legs and looking around a little. Barry had been talking to the people in the Houston office, and he'd forwarded my request to leave the ship, by small boat if necessary, to explore Panama City.

Barry grunted. "I don't know. Peter isn't too hot on the idea of us getting off."

Peter. "Oh, God, he's not meeting us, is he?"

"Nah. I know you're disappointed, but he couldn't get here on time. He's in Houston; I talked to him this morning. He said to tell you this is not a sightseeing cruise."

That stung. Since there was going to be a lot of traffic to and from the ship anyway, I didn't see what difference it would make if I left for a few hours. "Well," I countered, "If you get off, I'm getting off."

"I don't know what's going to happen. Captain's saying we'll be going through on the thirty-first, and we won't get in to Galveston till the eighth."

I felt like screaming. The threat of two extra days at sea, without a port call to look forward to, sounded like purgatory. All the pleasure of spotting the islands gone, I returned to my dim little room.

Everyone seemed restless in the next days. The sight of land, the rumors and counter-rumors about when we'd be permitted to pass through the canal, and the prospect of visitors on board unsettled us. I sensed why the men were feeling apprehensive—until now we'd been a patently Chinese vessel, sailing in the nowhere of the ocean. What with the language, the food, and the faces, we might never have left the East China Sea. Now, however, we had reached foreign territory. Messages came over the radio in English, and Wang had to stay on the bridge much of the time, translating for the captain.

Barry, Ding, and I wrote up a long list of provisions we wanted— or more accurately, were demanding—from the shipping agent. Mainly we craved fresh fruits and vegetables, but Barry also insisted on several cartons of milk and enough steaks to eat every night for the rest of the trip. Whoever had garnered the provisions in China had failed to provide steak, and Barry practically drooled talking about Panamanian beef. "They have the best cattle in the world there, did you know that?"

I thought I knew more about it than he. "Isn't that one of the countries where Burger King is ruining the rain forests?"

"Don't get your panties in a wad about it. If those fanatic environmentalists would get a life, we could make those countries rich!" In large, solid letters, he wrote: "Rib eye steak—20 lbs."

The next day we received word on the radio that if we reached the bay by 6:45 p.m., we could go straight through the canal that night. The captain cancelled classes, and Mr. Ding abbreviated meals and meal times as we prepared. Cui, Lin, and Ma finally scraped up the spilled, dried paint from the storm and slapped a new coat of orange over everything. The chief engineer donned a life jacket and rigged a wood-and-rope platform over the stern. He balanced on it, with several people spotting him, and then painted out the ship's Chinese name, replacing it with the English version, "Explorer." On the forward mast, the chief mate raised a Panamanian flag, and I learned for the first time that the vessel was under Panamanian registry. To my delight, several dolphins followed us as we moved closer to the canal. They were large, mottled brown and gray, perhaps attracted by all the ships in the area.

By 6:30 almost everyone was on the forward deck, watching Ma lower the anchor. The breeze came off the land damp, warm, and fresh. A few miles off through the sultry evening lay the coast of Panama, looking flat and khaki-colored. Between us and the coast were many small, hilly islands, which looked like the most beautiful country I'd ever seen—maybe because of the five weeks at sea.

Other ships surrounded us. Walking around our decks, I counted fourteen vessels, everything from oil tankers to yachts. We set anchor at sunset, just as the ships were turning on their lights, the first yellow gleams brightening against the dusk. Ours was by far the smallest international vessel, dwarfed by the tankers and cargo ships.

Small watercraft buzzed around the area, carrying people and goods back and forth from the port. About as long as a car, those wooden boats looked shabby and worn, but they delivered food, supplies, mail, pilots, and news to every ship that passed through the canal.

At 6:45 p.m., just when the shipping agent had promised, one of the small motorboats came chopping toward our vessel. To watch it approach, most of us moved to the stern, forming a line as we leaned over the rail. Cui ran back carrying a jangling metal ladder. He attached its top to the gunwale and then let down the chain of steps to the water. The boat came closer, and we saw in the mast lights two or three figures moving around, preparing boxes to unload.

"Mangoes," said Barry. "I can taste 'em."

The boat came closer and closer, then puttered by us. I thought it might turn around to come up against the lee side, but it continued out to sea, going to meet a huge gray ship that had just arrived, which hadn't even had time to anchor. It looked like a Navy ship, and for a minute I felt a weird nostalgia.

Disappointed, the men drifted forward or inside. I stood alone on the aft deck, wondering why I should feel an empty, ringing feeling for the Navy, when my time on those ships had been, comparatively at least, so unhappy. Though it was odd, I felt far more accepted, more part of the crew, on board the *Tan Suo Zhe* with the Chinese men, than I ever had on the Navy tenders full of Americans my own age.

Suddenly our engines were turned down, and in the sudden quiet the waves sounded like a lullaby. I stood on the deck until the night was black and the land anonymous. The silver lights coming across the water could have been any lights anywhere.

When I went back inside, a lot of the crew were sitting in the dayroom, their chairs once again drawn away from the tables in a ragged semicircle. To my horror, they were staring at the TV. I glared at the screen. The characters—it was some kind of game show—were speaking English, not Spanish. "What is this?" I said.

"American TV!" Barry seemed jubilant. "We can watch *Saturday Night Live.*"

"It's Tuesday," I pointed out.

"A rebroadcast, maybe. I miss that show."

"So what's the deal?" I said. "In Mexico it isn't like this; they have Mexican shows."

"There's a base down here, ain't there? Navy, Army . . ."

Of course. The U.S. military couldn't set up so much as a tent in a country without dragging along the essential nonsense of our mass culture. I remembered seeing taped Johnny Carson shows on a Navy ship in the Gulf of Oman and hearing my students swap sitcom jokes in class in Germany. American television was nearly as insidious as Coca-Cola, infiltrating every corner of the world.

The Chinese studied the chattering American faces on the screen. Some of my students had pens and paper in hand, and some had dictionaries open. Zhao drummed his fingers. Wang was trying to translate, but even he was mystified by some of the jargon. "What is Ninja Turtles?" he asked, his eyes fixed on the TV. "What does mean, 'hyper'?"

I answered him, of course, but I was annoyed. I could have been off the ship exploring a new continent, but instead I had to lurk in my room or be subjected to Hollywood game shows. I got a pack of cards and settled down with it, dealing solitaire.

After a few minutes, Barry let out a whoop. "It's Hank Williams Jr.!" The Chinese men and I looked at him in equal ignorance.

"Is he some country singer?" I asked. I hated country music.

"It's a special!" Barry said, sounding particularly Oklahoman to me. "This guy is one of my all-time favorites. I can't believe it!"

I couldn't believe it either, but the difference was, I didn't care. Country music was as foreign a culture to me as Chinese—actually, more so by that point.

"I wish I had me some beer," Barry said. "American beer. Man, this is great. You know this song?" He started singing along. To my surprise, he had a good voice.

Several of the Chinese men were thrilled to hear Barry sing; they tried to join in although of course they didn't know the words. Altogether it was quite a men's chorus in there—Barry bawling the words to the love song, Lin rushing forward to raise the TV volume, Wang translating lyrics, and a dozen Chinese men humming up and down, trying to find the right note.

Ding pounded an upside-down broom on the floor, in time to the music. "Bally dance-ah!" he called. "Bally dance-ah Ji Lian!"

Immediately everyone else started telling us to dance, scraping the chairs out of the way and nodding their heads encouragingly. Ding eased himself up, and, leaning on the bristly broomhead, hobbled across to another seat. He was using the broom as a cane, trying to keep the weight off his bandaged foot. I didn't really want to dance to the TV, but I was willing to, in order to provide entertainment.

Barry was shaking his head. "No dance-ah. I have to be in the right mood for that. Whiskey helps."

"Dance-ah!" Ding insisted. Something in his voice made the proposal seem slightly daring. It reminded me that until recently the Chinese had considered dance a harmful exercise in Western corruption. Probably no one on the ship had ever seen two Americans move to music, and they thought that we'd be dying to indulge in such decadence at the slightest opportunity.

"We don't really want to," I said as gently as I could. Mr. Ding looked disappointed.

Appalled by the music, I went back outside to see if I could make out any sign of the pilot, for whom we had rushed to anchor and prepare. Because the canal was busy and required special navigation, the authorities sent out local experts, the pilots, to every ship. The pilot would work on the bridge, next to the captain, the whole time we were passing through.

It was after eight. Someone had rigged up two new lights, one on each side of the ship; the bulbs illuminated the dirty water to a depth of a foot or so. Thin, oily waste made rainbows on the top of the water; cigarette butts bobbed, nibbled at from underneath by minnows; insects of all sizes whizzed around the lamp. Every few seconds, one would come too close, and the bulb would fry it, hissing and sending up a thin column of smoke. A quick motion came from outside the pool of light, and I leaned over to look.

Slicing through the water was a shark fin, unmistakably slick and triangular. The gray body underneath was about five feet long, thin and supple. Just as it reached the ship it turned and curved around the lighted area, hunting in loose spirals. Despite my safety—I was looking down at the shark from at least ten feet up—I felt afraid. Either I'd been successfully conditioned by anti-shark factions, or else there really was something primal and instinctive in my reaction: I couldn't stop watching the beast circle around and around, submerged except for one glistening fin. I felt irrationally afraid that, hypnotized, I might fall over into the water. I held onto the guardrail.

After a minute, another, slightly smaller shark joined the first. With both fear and excitement I peered beyond the lighted area, trying to see if a whole school might be surrounding us. However, I saw only the two, and my fear turned to a desire for action. Why not feed them? It would be fascinating to see a shark lunging for bait.

Recalling the ham that had been hanging up over the sink forever, I headed back inside. I didn't know if a shark would eat ham, and I felt too foolish to ask, so I kept the sharks a secret, crossing between the men and the TV with a silent, waved apology. I had my back to the galley door as I hacked off a generous lump of stale, fly-blown ham.

Then I faced the problem of smuggling the meat back out through the dayroom without anyone's seeing. My making off with this hunk of food was sure to raise interested questions, and Ding would probably jump up on his gouty leg to start frying chicken. After deliberation, I wrapped the ham up in a few napkins, and held it down by my side with one hand as I crossed the room. Everyone was so engrossed in or confused by Hank Williams Jr. that they ignored me.

I went down the interior ladders to the lower deck, the work area that was just above the waterline. As I approached the sharks, I saw that they were somewhat bigger than they'd looked from ten feet above. I could have touched their fins from the lower deck. Conversely, either one of them could have bitten off my hand. My face felt cold, and I stayed well back from the edge. The last thing I wanted was for sharks' great leaps for dinner to result in their landing on board. I took care, when I threw the ham, to toss it away from the ship.

To my disappointment, the ham sank instantly. Both sharks continued their swift, uneven circling in the pool of light. Apparently they weren't quite as predatory as I'd expected. Well, I thought, on the bottom, some crabs would have a feast.

On the other side of the ship, a motorboat was approaching. I left my shark friends and went to investigate. Seeing me, the men on the boat began waving and shouting. My first impulse was to get the translator, but then I realized that they were not speaking Chinese: it was heavily accented English, lilting with island inflections. As the boat pulled up next to us and its engine shut off, the wake caught up to it and nearly washed it into our side. Someone fended off, and another man threw a rotten tire out to keep the hulls from scraping.

"Hello, darlin'!" The one white man on the motorboat was American. "You the captain's wife?" He was standing on the gunwale of the little, rocking boat.

"I'm the English teacher," I said. Too late, I realized that I could have claimed to be the captain. "We've come from China."

"That right?" Ignoring the ladder Cui had arranged, the white man tossed a brown leather bag at my feet, and clambered onto our ship by hauling himself on the rails. In a second he was standing next to me, hand extended. "Name's Dave," he said. "Where's the old man?"

I took Dave up to the bridge, where the captain, Barry, and Wang were waiting with some documents. Various dull formalities had to take place before we could pass through the canal.

"Hey!" Barry stood up to shake the pilot's hand. "Good to see another American male. Got any cigarettes?"

The pilot tapped the case he was carrying. "Marlboros okay? I brought a carton. Most people are ready to kill for them by the time they get here."

Everyone was obviously about to light up and fill the room with smoke, so I went back down, using exterior ladders and heading aft on the main deck. Below me, the two men who were left in the motorboat were looking up and talking to a group of Chinese men who had gathered on the waterline-level deck to meet them.

They didn't know I was there, and they didn't hear me approach on the deck above, but I could see the tops of the Chinese men's heads as they leaned over the water, chattering and peering into the little boat. Mr. Ding handed over a couple of cans of Coke, which the two men thanked him for and popped open. I heard Ding say, "Welcome," but his voice was lost in the mêlée of a dozen men speaking different languages, trying to communicate about their journeys and ships.

There was a lot of pointing and laughing going on. The Panamanians asked over and over for beers, but I knew that the Chinese didn't know that word: we'd been using the Chinese word for beer, *pijiu.* Why hadn't I thought to teach them that important vocabulary word? I leaned over, about to translate for Ding, but then as I did I saw that one of the Panamanians was handing a magazine across the water.

I caught a glimpse of a glossy female crotch. The magazine was no *Playboy,* which would have been bad enough, but ugly, hard-core porn. Apparently it was given as a gesture of friendship, perhaps a thank-you for the sodas. I groaned, thinking of the shock waves this rag would send through the ship. Was Western corruption inevitable? Then, to my delight, I saw Lin lean forward over the water and pass the magazine back.

Misunderstanding the rejection, one of the men disappeared into the tiny hold, and then came back with another magazine. This one, I could see by the cover, boasted black models. As the Panamanian held it across the water, the centerfold dropped open, exposing a busty woman with her legs spread.

Several of the Chinese shook their heads disapprovingly.

Lin said sternly, "No, not want." He dropped the magazine back into the motorboat.

Even the chief mate, who had hassled me about my boyfriend, had rejected the porno. I didn't know whether they found the magazines offensive, ugly, or simply uninteresting, but whatever their reasons, I was relieved and glad. I remembered Ding's mischievous interest in American dancing, how the crew had thrown the chairs back and urged us to perform, thinking probably that dancing was a scandal. Yet here, offered the dirty magazines, the essence of Western smut, they proudly refused. At that moment, I loved every one of the Chinese men.

After about an hour, the pilot went back to his boat, explaining that he had to complete some paperwork on shore before he could guide us through the canal. Just before he jumped down the metal ladder, he warned me to be careful of the locals: "You've got to watch these guys like a hawk. They'll take anything they can lay their hands on." The two Panamanians—arguably part of the "these guys" he referred to—ignored what he said. One revved the motor, and the other steadied the little boat while the pilot dropped in and settled himself. "Lock all the hatches before anyone else comes aboard," he called up, shouting over the noise. "Those guys delivering the food are absolute pirates. Don't let them rip you off."

"Thanks," I said, and the motorboat roared off into the darkness.

Barry, too, had issued a warning about the Panamanian canal workers. Through the interpreter, he had told the crew, "They're thieves, plain and simple. They know you don't know who they are, and you're not going to stick around and try to track them down. Don't just lock your stateroom, double lock it, and put away your money and everything where they can't find it if they break in."

Considering this advice, I went to my room and, for the first time, used the key that locked it. However, I wasn't terribly worried. My only valuables besides a few travelers' cheques were my Chinese rugs, which I didn't think would be very attractive to a ship-looter since they were too large to conceal. Still, I was concerned that the Chinese crew members, unused to taking precautions against crime, might get ripped off. I moved around the rest of the ship checking that the hatches were locked, and repeating what the pilot had said.

By the time the supply boat came, we were all but armed with defensive measures. Every hatch was locked except the one to the passageway that led to the freezer. That hall and the whole main deck were lined with nervous Chinese men. The captain, Barry, and Wang had moved down to the bar with their paperwork, so they could keep an eye on the proceedings while they filled in forms and checked information.

The small boat pulled up, riding low in the water with its boxes of goods. One of the men called up something long and cheerful, of which I understood only the first two words: "Hey, mon!" I assumed he was asking for the captain, but the captain was busy, as were Barry and the translator. That left me, as the only English speaker, to deal with these guys.

"Come on," I said. "We've got plenty of hands here." Swiftly, the heavy boxes were offloaded onto the ship. The two Panamanians were small but strong, and they hefted the cartons up the metal ladder with easy smiles. As soon as the goods reached the top, one or two of the Chinese men would grab them and make for the freezer. We had taken on about ten huge brown boxes in this manner when I realized that I had no idea what we were getting. "Wait!" I said. "Don't do anything."

I jogged into the bar and interrupted Barry. "Do we have an order sheet or anything for this food? They're unloading it already."

"Oh, right." He shuffled in a huge stack of notes and came up with a tattered copy of our grocery list. "Make sure we get what we paid for," he said. "And make sure it's not bad. These guys love to give you rotten fruit, stale bread, whatever they can get rid of."

Then I had to run down into the freezer room to find out what had already been stored. Since I was wearing only a short-sleeved blouse and jeans, the cold soon slowed me down. My fingers grew numb as I tried to pry open the cardboard crates. Seeing Mr. Ding looking down the ladder, I called for him to come help me. Meanwhile, feet shuffled above, and after Ding, several men came down the ladder, balancing heavy boxes.

The freezer space was long, about twenty feet, but very narrow. Only one person could fit between the shelves. Already the stuff was piling up, and soon we'd have just a mountain of food, with no way of excavating the stuff at the bottom.

"Wait!" I yelled at the first man. It happened to be the chief engineer, who could understand some of what I was saying. "Slow down! We don't have room to put all this stuff yet and we have to check it."

"Ding, what's in here?" I repeated it in pidgin Chinese, and showed him how to pry open the boxes. They were fastened with immense staples that we couldn't undo, so in order to look inside we had to rip the thick cardboard. He leaned his broom-cane against the freezer shelf, and sat down on a box.

"Oh, God, I'm sorry," I said. "I forgot about your foot. I wouldn't have asked you to come down if—"

"Wait-ah." Ding backed out of the freezer and thumped down a passageway to another storage area. The cane didn't slow him down at all. He returned with a couple of chopsticks and a big, blunt knife. While he attacked the boxes with his new tools, I began looking into the cartons that had ventilation holes. About ten were banana crates; undoubtedly they were teeming with tarantulas, but the fruit looked all right, so I crossed "10 bananas" off the order list.

Behind me, Ding wrestled another box open. "Salad," he announced.

"Salad?" I couldn't see past him, so to get out of the way he scrambled like a rock-climber up the mountain of boxes. He climbed with two hands and his good foot, holding his broom under one arm. When he reached the top of the pile he let out a little shriek—he was stuck between the crates and the ceiling. All I could see were his plump legs as he wriggled, trying to get down. Then something gave on the other side, the legs disappeared, and he tumbled down the other side, along with several boxes.

I couldn't see him over the pile. "Mr. Ding!" I yelled across the cartons, "Are you all right?" He answered me in cheerful Chinese, and I heard him shoving a few cartons back into place, so I figured he wasn't hurt. Still, I felt guilty—climbing wasn't in his job description, and he was already injured. On the other hand, food-checking wasn't in my job description, and I was freezing, but it had to be done.

Inside the carton Ding had called "salad" were dozens of heads of lettuce. It looked good, but it also looked like enough lettuce to feed a Navy tender. I consulted my list: sure enough, Barry and I had asked for fifty lettuces.

On the far side of the food mountain, someone else came down the ladder, puffing, and dropped another cardboard box at the base. "Salad!" called Ding. He'd barely had time to stow that box when another one appeared above his head. I was beginning to feel like the sorcerer's apprentice when the broom went mad, only, instead of water, we were being flooded with lettuce.

Zhao backed down the ladder, holding above his head a large plastic milk carton. At least I knew what was in there, but the freezer was getting very crowded. Also, my cheeks and mouth were getting so numb I could hardly speak.

Throwing cartons randomly right and left on the shelves, I rearranged the boxes so I could climb back through the freezer toward the ladder. I had a feeling we'd never again see some of this stuff I was stowing, but I had to clear the way before the cartons collapsed on me. Finally I decreased the pile enough that I could clamber into the tiny space left between the boxes and Ding and the ladder. I was breathing heavily and feeling warm despite the freezing air.

When Zhao reached the bottom rung, there wasn't room for him to turn around. "We have to start using the shelves," I said, pointing to the empty metal racks. "Put the milk here."

He did so, and he and Ding went back up the ladder. I was about to follow, thinking that I could check the incoming food at the top where it wasn't so cold, when I passed the milk, at eye level. Just above the word *"leche"* in bright red letters, a date was stamped: 23/7/91. The twenty-third of July had been six days ago, and the milk was supposed to last us another week.

Furious, I ran up the ladder. Tsu and Gu were there, bent under the weight of another carton of milk. "Take that back!" I bellowed. "No good-ah!"

They looked at me with wondering expressions—they didn't even drink milk, so they probably didn't understand why we were getting so much of it to begin with—but they followed my pointing finger out to the deck, returning the offending milk to the small boat.

I accosted a Panamanian who was carrying a drum of oil on board. "That milk is old!" I shouted. I felt furiously protective of Barry's request for milk and of Olaf's money. "We aren't going to pay for that!"

The Panamanian guy just looked at me, his eyebrows arched mildly. "Okay, mon. No problem."

After the food—and some fresh milk—was on board, the paperwork done, and all of us settled again, the pilot returned. This time he came in a larger, sturdier-looking boat, carrying six or seven men. One of them followed him aboard and, seeing me, muttered something lewd, which I chose to ignore. The other strange men were also boarding our vessel. To avoid them, I moved forward.

On the starboard side of the ship, I sat down on a chest, but two of the canal workers spotted me and oozed forward. One of them shoved a gold coin, nestled in a jewelry box, into my face. "You want to buy? Is very good coin, very valuable. Good price."

I wondered: was there nowhere on earth an American could go without being hassled to buy? Well, yes, there was—Shanghai. I hadn't been pressed to spend my American dollars there, but having stuff I didn't want shoved at me was very familiar from other countries. I didn't bother to answer, just shrugged and retired inside, where the workers weren't allowed. I went to the port side of the ship, where I could sit in the shadows and see but not be seen.

From the bridge, the pilot shouted to his men to hurry up. Agile as gymnasts, the Panamanian crew swarmed everywhere on the *Tan Suo Zhe*. It was a little intimidating, how quickly they took over our vessel. Some Chinese men gathered to watch the Panamanians, offering to help but being brushed away.

Rebuffed, four or five of our crew members stood leaning against the bulkhead, their hands in their pockets, as the canal workers hustled around with lines and boat hooks. The Chinese men had probably never seen anyone working so fast.

Every now and then one of the Panamanians would stop work to ask one of the Chinese crew for something; I heard the words "Coke" and "soup." But the Chinese men either didn't understand or pretended not to. They shook their heads.

The two men who had hassled me to buy something came onto the forward deck. Spotting the group of Chinese men, the more aggressive Panamanian man strode across to them. He again produced the little blue box containing the coin, and offered it to Tsu and the others. I couldn't see what was happening, but someone said, "No sank you."

The other man joined the first one, and they moved close to the Chinese, backing them against the bulkhead only a few yards from me. The Panamanian voices grew louder, more insistent.

Ding came clumping across the deck on his upside-down broom. Eager to see what they were looking at, he leaned into the circle of men hunching over the coin. Everyone stopped talking. "No good-ah?" Ding sang, in a soft voice. I could tell he didn't mean it in a particularly negative way, but his inflection made it sound like a jeer, and the Panamanian holding the box clenched a fist. He rattled the blue box at Ding, arguing, "Is perfect! You buy!" Mr. Ding stared at him, his mouth loosely open and color rising in his soft cheeks. The man barked something and shoved Ding's shoulder.

Nervously, Mr. Ding laughed, and pushed back with an open hand. His movement looked boyish, like a high school kid playing around with a buddy. The Panamanian stepped back and swore through a tense jaw. He bent over; when he stood again he was holding a wrench overhead.

The Chinese crew pulled away, turned their backs, and herded into the passageway. They weren't running, because there wasn't room, but they hurried. Ding limped behind. The Panamanian swung the wrench up high; Ding squealed and turned, looking for something—he'd lost his cane. He stepped to the right and the bad foot twisted under him. He fell to his knees, yelping.

The Panamanian moved behind him, swinging the wrench up, almost hitting the next deck—the gray metal shone in the electric light, looking hot. Trapped, Ding hunched down and said something in Chinese.

Without making a final decision, I was on my feet, breath coming in cold to fire my lungs, and a voice in my mind said, "Don't let go," as I closed my hands on the back of the Panamanian's neck. His skin gave under my nails and I felt it rip, felt the slide of oily sweat under my palm. I dug in and held on. My nose jammed against his gritty cotton T-shirt, I smelled diesel and salt-human odor. Over his shoulder I saw another Panamanian man, staring, his mouth round and open.

The man I held was writhing, about to loosen my grip; then he'd turn on me with the wrench. Knowing the guardrail was to my right, I swung as hard as I could, trying to bash him against it. I caught him off balance, and he pivoted easily, swinging like a door. His ribs hit the rail and he folded. But the wrench was still in his hands, and I couldn't hold him for long.

I was screaming. Ding knelt up next to me, brushing my leg. Feet were flailing, and then Ding was lifting one of the legs off the ground. The man's other foot socked me in the jaw. My teeth crunched together; I tasted blood; there was a splash. We'd pushed him, or he'd jumped or fallen, over the side.

I held my sore jaw tenderly, watching the Panamanian gasping and swearing in the water. He looked like a wet dog, his hair slicked down and his shirt sticking to his collarbones. He looked small and angry as he splashed away to the small boat.

Ding was laughing or crying; he put a hand over my hand, patting my hurt face. "Teach-ah!" he said.

The men in the small boat were rocking their craft with frightened laughter. Still, when the man got there they hauled him up the side of their boat. With a rush of dripping water he scrambled in, less hurt than I was but embarrassed.

I carried Ding's cane and he leaned on me to limp into the galley. I sat down while he scraped together some freezer frost and wrapped it in a greasy cloth. He gave me the icepack, then joined me at the table with two cups of ginseng tea. I held the ice to my chin, drinking the warm tea over it. Between slurps we jabbered at each other in Chinglish.

"Did you see that?" I said. "He was going to hit you! No good-ah! Could have killed you! Dead! The wrench, the wrench-ah, did you see?"

"Teach-ah help me!" Ding announced. Several men were coming through the door, and Ding rattled off an excited explanation in Chinese. Lin and Cui came in, clucking over my bruised face, and Barry came behind them, saying, "Jesus, what happened down there? Did that guy fall overboard?"

Wang told Barry the story, and I tried touching my jaw. Despite the ice, the sensation was returning, and it was swollen. My teeth were solidly in place, but my tongue bore a nasty cut on the side.

"I guess you're the hero." Barry gave me half a hug, one arm around my shoulders. "And here I thought you were a pacifist."

The Chinese men, seeing that it was okay for Barry to touch me, crowded around, patting my shoulders and head. "Teach-ah good-ah!" They made the sounds they used for victory at the video game—"Poom! Paow! Teach-ah hit-ah!"

Ding had red-rimmed eyes, looking at me and making some sort of speech in Chinese. They were making me feel heroic but embarrassed.

"Okay, okay." It hurt me to get the words out. "No big deal. I couldn't let them hurt the guy who makes chicken feet."

We raised anchor late in the evening, and the pilot stayed on the bridge, directing the captain how to steer through the channel. As the bay narrowed and we came into the isthmus, the Bridge of the Americas rose into sight, its arch lit up all along the sides by tiny golden bulbs. High enough that any ship could pass under it, this thin strip of metal was the only solid link between the two land-masses. It reminded me of the connection between our ship and the small boat of Panamanians—the hands, reaching across the water with cans of soda and magazines, that had formed the first link between these Chinese men and this new country.

After we passed under the bridge, we joined a queue of ships waiting to move through the locks. The locks could hold several vessels of our size at once, but we had to wait until our turn. Since we were coming from the Pacific, the lower side of the canal, the locks would lift us up the twenty-six or so meters to lake near the continental divide. At the same time, we'd be moving about fifty miles north; the whole trip would take up much of the night. The locks and especially the lock gates were essential, complicated machinery, and it was important that the ships not damage them. Large, grim, black-and-white signs warned "Dead Slow" in several languages.

We waited about half an hour outside the towering, rust-colored gates of the first lock, which closed the canal off from view. Finally our turn came, and the huge doors eased open to admit us. Ahead of us, an even more gigantic metal door dammed up the canal. The door rose above us like a red-brown cliff. We couldn't see over the top.

To my disappointment, I also couldn't make out much beyond the embankments. On our right, huge white spotlights glared down, lighting railway lines that ran along the canal. Beyond them lay a thin, irregular line of small buildings, parking lots, and shacks. To our left, beyond the man-made island that ran down the middle of the locks, was a southeast-bound ship, going from the Gulf of Mexico to the Pacific. Running lights silhouetted the resting crew members of the oil freighter as they leaned on its guard rail, smoking cigarettes. Their low voices sounded across the water in a language I couldn't name. But beyond those sights I could see only blackness with occasional large shapes.

As we reached the head of the first lock, we were approached by a tiny rowboat, which two men were oaring rapidly across the water. One of the Panamanians on our deck coiled a bowline and hurled it to the rowers, who ferried it back to the concrete canal wall. There they attached the bowline to a loop of steel cable that dangled from a little trolley car on top of the embankment. Then the men on our bow hauled the rope back, bringing across the cable loop, which they attached to the bow. This was repeated four times, until the *Tan Suo Zhe* was tethered fore and aft to four small railcars, two on each side.

Meanwhile other vessels were filling in the lock. Several small yachts, sails reefed, motored in behind us, and after them came a cargo boat. Like us, they were waiting for the lock to open so we could be floated up to the next level of the canal.

The lock gate ahead of us slowly began to open, and water flooded in. The mass of liquid moved toward us, enormous white bubbles churning like a giant spring, and slowly lifted the ship. The movement was quieter than I'd expected. It wasn't like the crashing of a waterfall so much as the soothing rumble of a large, rocky river. The ship bobbed quietly, her engines off, the only sound the driving water and the hum of the railcars. Slowly rising, we waited.

After the ship had risen for several minutes, the trolley cars began to move, slowly tugging us forward. The cables went taut, glistening and dripping in the bright lights as the trolleys worked stolidly up a short incline. We were pulled along a plateau and placed in the next lock, and the cables slackened and dipped into the water when the trolleys stopped.

Inside the bridge, the pilot and the captain were silent. Unable to steer the ship, they watched the trolleys narrowly. Each was manned by two people; one sat inside the car and operated the controls, while another man, presumably the lookout, was buckled into a seat on the front of the engine, where he slept soundly. If a line broke or if our ship was pulled too close to the wall, the captain could start the side propellers to fend off, but he would have to move fast. Things were pretty tense.

On the bridge wing, it was so quiet I could hear jungle noises from the banks of the canal. Tropical insects sung, and the night birds warbled in high, eerie, back-of-the-throat sounds. Every now and then the air shook with an excited screeching that sounded like monkeys.

All night I sat on the wing, watching our slow, serious progress up the canal between the continents. Time seemed suspended, all motion slowed to a dream, as we were floated up and washed forward, over and over, through the night. It was hypnotic and fascinating. Every so often Barry would come outside to smoke; sometimes the pilot would step out to see that we were not too close to the island. But for the most part I sat alone, watching. And all night, the birds and monkeys and insects sang and screeched that we were passing through their jungle.

223

Just before dawn, we reached the lake in the middle of the canal, and the pilot told us to set anchor. We'd received permission to come only this far for now; he had to leave the ship there and another pilot would take us the rest of the way, perhaps the next evening. I was sorry that we would not see the locks in the daylight, but the pilot explained that the cruise ships got priority for sightseeing. The night had become cloudy and cold, so I went to bed.

I woke up early, missing the familiar rhythms and noise of forward movement. It seemed too quiet on board, making me feel as if I had to get dressed silently. Anxious to look around, I grabbed my camera and went up to the bridge wing.

Unfortunately, the clouds of the night before had not burned off. A low, gray sky covered everything, the mist closing the edges of the lake. Using binoculars, I peered at the few places where the haze thinned. Off to the south I spotted what looked like the world's hippest country club: a palm-roofed building with a waterside bar, some of the lake roped off for swimming, and a stretch of white beach. Tempting as it looked, the place was deserted. No one moved on the beach or inside the building.

Despite the gloom I took a few pictures. The chief mate came out of the bridge, his voice hoarse and eager. "You take-ah picture me?"

I hadn't planned on getting a photo of the chief mate, but he was grooming himself for it, tucking in his T-shirt and smoothing down his hair. "Sure," I said. "Let's get Captain, too." The chief mate ducked back inside, and I thought maybe I'd hurt his feelings. But he reappeared a minute later with a Chinese camera, shyly asking if I would pose.

I did so, first alone, and then side-by-side with the captain. We had quite a time trying to squeeze next to each other on the bridge wing without touching. We had to break the rule about keeping an arm's distance, and the captain kept clearing his throat as we waited for the chief mate to stop fiddling with his camera and snap the shutter. Both of us folded our arms, smiling stiffly at the lens.

"Sanks very much!" the chief mate boomed. "Sanks you!"

Then it was my turn, and they both posed with their backs to the lake and the swimming club. They put their arms around each other like brothers, and the chief mate tilted his head at me. "Good picture me?" he asked, so humbly that I had to reassure him. His excitement over the photographs softened me toward him. He seemed like a rambunctious boy, eager to impress the teacher. And he evidently *liked* me; that was hard to resist. When we were done I thanked him, and realized that I would be glad to remember him after all.

The Face of a Friend

fter weeks of enjoying the black, starlit nights as we rocked east and south over the waves, we'd finally come within a week of home, and the sight horrified me. Grim, industrial oil rigs broke up the horizon as we passed them during the day, and at night the Gulf of Mexico was lit up like a circus.

Barry was on the forward deck one evening when I came out after teaching. Skyscraper oil derricks towered above us, ruining the stars, ruining the air, and probably ruining the water. Barry must have heard me react, because he chuckled. "Pretty, ain't it?"

"It looks like Dante's Inferno. No, it's worse. It looks like the New Jersey Turnpike!" It smelled like it, too; underneath the salt was a stench of smoky fumes, worse than our own diesel.

"I'll tell you one thing, though," Barry said. "If you went overboard in this water, I bet you'd have as much as a fifty-fifty chance of survival."

"Yeah?" I looked down at the green wash. It was not inviting.

"Yeah, and I'll tell you why. For one thing, the water's warm. If you had a life jacket on you wouldn't lose all that much body heat real quick. For another thing, there's so many ships through here someone would have to see you and pick you up. And even if they didn't, there's so many of these oil platforms, if you were a good swimmer you could probably make it to one of them. I bet I could make it to that one." He pointed to the nearest black-and-silver monstrosity. Purple flames belched from a thousand-foot chimney-pipe; at the base, machines chugged and vehicles crawled around like slow, ungainly insects.

"This is awful. I'm going back where maybe I can't see them." I moved toward the rear of the ship, keeping my eyes down.

Barry called after me, "Don't eat your liberal heart out about it. This is why we got the cheapest gas in the world."

"We don't," I threw over my shoulder. "It's thirty cents a gallon in Saudi." I should have added that furthermore, who cared if we had cheap gas, that was why the air was so foul in L.A. Better to have petrol heavily taxed like in Europe, so people would bike or ride buses. But instead of returning forward to argue, I kept quiet and tried for a clear view of the ocean. Off to port was a decent sunset, a pale orange sun spreading out behind a column of gray clouds and rain.

As I climbed the steps to the helo deck, something on a storage cabinet fluttered. It was a tiny yellow bird, cradling its head under its wing, sleeping directly in the path of the diesel smoke. It wasn't a seabird—it looked like a pet canary. We were nowhere near the Canary Islands and many miles from any land. I wondered if the creature had escaped from a cruise ship, or if it had been blown out to sea by a storm. Either way, it looked exhausted and seemed likely to suffocate in the smoke.

Tsu, the radio officer, was also prowling around the back decks; he came over to investigate. When he saw the bird he laughed and reached out to grab it.

"Stop!" To indicate that the bird was sleeping, I rested my head on my hand and closed my eyes. "It's tired. Leave it alone."

Tsu slowed down, but he still put his hand out. To my surprise, the bird let him stroke its back. Then his fist closed on the legs; he picked the bird up and put it in his pocket, grinning.

"Don't!" I said. "Put it back!"

"Give to cook." He grinned at me, still holding the bird. "Eat-ah. Put in stew."

I scowled at him, not kidding. "Put it *back,*" I said. If the bird wasn't already dying, it would surely expire from fright in a minute. I felt like yelling at Tsu, but I tried to keep the annoyance out of my voice. "Come with me, help me get it some water."

Tsu removed the bird and then set it down like a book, on its side. "Eat-ah," he repeated, hoping I'd get the joke, but he followed me inside. In the galley, I made him hold a dish of water while I rummaged around and found some old white bread. It was stale, and not very good bread to begin with, but it was probably better for the bird than diesel fumes. "Okay, Tsu. Don't you have to go back to work now?"

"You give bird?" His face expanded in amusement, and he told Mr. Ding and Zen what I was doing. They all laughed heartily, and Tsu opened a steaming pot lid and pointed inside. "Here bird," he said.

"Ha ha ha." I took the water dish away from Tsu, hoping he'd leave, but he traipsed out after me, still chuckling.

The canary remained where we had left it, but its head was no longer under its wing. I put the bread in front of it, and the dish of water close by.

The bird cocked its head back and forth, blinking. The movement reminded me of a budgie my grandmother had kept when I was a little girl, called Binkie. "Binkie," I said. "Want to eat something?"

228

"Eat-ah!" Tsu grabbed the bird and stuck its head in the water.

"Damn it, Tsu! *Stop* it," I began, but the bird stirred, moved its beak in the water and then raised it to swallow. It dipped its beak again and drank some more.

Four or five times it took water, then rested. Each time I felt a little bit more hope that the bird might live and recover.

Tsu grabbed the bird again, this time making as if to throw it into the sky. "Don't do that!" I snapped. I didn't care anymore if he heard how angry I was. "Put it down! Not there, here." I showed him a spot in a corner, out of the path of the smoke and sheltered from the wind. Tsu did so, and I placed the water and bread next to the bird.

"Maybe it will sleep," I said.

"Die," said Tsu, definitively. "We eat-ah now."

"Shut up." Tears pricked in my throat, and I had to move away before Tsu saw me crying. Over my shoulder, I growled, "You leave that bird *alone*."

Without me there to provoke, Tsu lost interest in the bird. He sauntered away, hands in his pockets. I went up to my stateroom, and closed the door behind me. Looking out the porthole at all the smoky, electrified structures the oil companies had stuck in the ocean for the purposes of digging up more obnoxious, polluting sources of energy, I wondered how long the bird—or any of us— might survive.

On our second day in the Gulf, the captain called a meeting after dinner. All of us crowded into the room where the crew ate, some of the men still working on their big bottles of beer. The captain stood in front of the room, facing us from behind a table. Mr. Ding, who was recovered enough to cook again, had fried pork with onions that night, and the spicy, oily smell hung in the air. Everyone on board came to the meeting, though the chief mate slipped away after the first few minutes; presumably he had watch. The rest of us barely fit around the eight tables. For once the one-yard rule had to be suspended: Wang sat next to me on a small bench.

He whispered a few translations, but most of the time he sat with his head down, looking bored. No one seemed to be paying particular attention to the captain's speech. They didn't actually talk or move around, as I'd heard that Chinese audiences tended to do, but neither did anyone look at the speaker. Half the men sat with their backs turned.

The captain continued unfazed for quite some time. My back was aching from sitting on the bench. I rested my head on my hands as many of the men were doing.

In my ear, the translator said, "Captain is talking about Bally now. He says he has done a good job with supervising repairing many things that needed work. He says Bally is good to work with, that he hopes all the Americans will be so good to work."

"Great," I said sleepily.

"Now he is talking about you!"

I straightened and looked at the captain, who was smiling at me. "He says that you are not only a good teacher but also a good person. They have learn very much of English from you. And now he is saying—they have learn something else. That they thought it would be strange for you to be on the ship, they were expecting a man teacher. But he says they have learned from you, that a woman can be courageous and strong too, and he admires what you have done."

Suddenly I felt wide-awake, and willing to attend to anything else the captain had to say.

The last few days were confusing, like the ones before we had reached Panama. Every couple of hours I'd hear another version of when we might get in to port. Barry took charge of rumor control, as he was constantly talking on the phone to Olaf, giving and getting updates about our progress. Every time I ran into Barry he issued a new report. "Captain says we're running behind schedule; we won't be in till the eighth. Olaf can't get us a berth that day—the pier is booked. So we'll be hanging around till the ninth," he said on Saturday. That was August 3, so we'd be waiting almost another week.

Sunday morning his prognosis changed: "Olaf says we got to be there by the fifth, hell or high water. They're getting ready for the shakedown. I goosed the engines again, and we're making eleven knots."

Later that day, Barry held a conference on the bridge and came to dinner looking irritated. "The translator told me that the captain thinks we can only make it by the seventh, at night. I told Olaf to do whatever he could to get us a berth then."

Whatever happened, it looked as though we'd be home within a few more days. I began cleaning out my closet, packing my recycling into three large bags, separating the garbage and giving it to Lin to hold until we got to port. My classes were winding down, finishing with odd bits of grammar and vocabulary, but mostly focusing on free conversation.

On the fifth, I decided to make a final taping of my students' speech, as I had on the first week of the journey. I organized my notes of questions and gathered my much-used cassette recorder with fresh batteries and a final blank tape I'd been saving.

I took the recorder to where the men were, since most were too busy to come to me. I went first to the gun shack, knowing I'd find several of the mechanics and air gun operators there. I began with the one Barry called Fang, the leader of the air gun operators, the one who had worked so hard to help the others learn. At the beginning of the cruise he'd hardly been able to say his name. Now I was able, without the translator, to explain what we were doing.

"Like English class," I said. "Talk here."

"Okay!" He grinned at me and sat down, his tea-jar in his hand.

"What's your name?" I asked, and held the tape recorder up to his face.

He took the machine and spoke clearly into the microphone. "My name Chen Li Jie. American name Fang."

"What do you do?" I asked. "What is your job here?"

"I am air gun operator. I—" he paused, raising his eyebrows.

"Yes, go on."

"I control gun," he said proudly. "I raise gun, lower gun. Guns away!" He mimicked the orders he was expecting to hear during seismic operations.

"What are you holding?" I said. Fang shook his head, not understanding. I pointed to his jar. "What is this?"

"This tea."

"Good! And what is this?" I picked up a tool lying on the counter.

"This wrench-ah."

"Good. And can you tell me, what day is today?"

He shook his head, so I repeated the question. "What day is it? Monday, Tuesday, Wednesday?"

"Ah—today—Monday."

"Great. Thank you so much." So what if it was rote learning? It beat Chinese. I didn't know what would happen to my students once the new people came on board. With luck, some of the Americans would take the time to talk slowly, to use the simple words and phrases the Chinese had mastered, to try to understand the English through the Chinese accents. It would be hard for everyone to communicate, but I hoped more than anything that the newcomers would not be condescending or aloof. If the Americans and Norwegians refused to try to use English with the Chinese, if they relied on the translator, my students would get no further. They would stay in their own group, speaking Chinese, unable to communicate or make friends. Although I'd done my best, I couldn't control what would happen to them next.

After I'd taped the mechanics and the air gun operators I went upstairs to see who might be hanging around the dayroom. Barry was there, watching American TV and eating some pineapple. "Hey, Wang's looking for you," he said. "Better find him tonight; we're getting in tomorrow."

"Tomorrow!"

"Yeah, Captain was just making that up about the eighth. He just said that so it'd look good when he got us in on time. I guaran-damn-tee you that's what he did. Olaf's going crazy trying to get us a berth."

"What?" I couldn't even make a whole sentence. There was so much to do before we docked. I hadn't even begun packing.

"Oh, you know that old routine. I can't believe I fell for it. The boss asks you to do something and you overestimate how long it's going to take you. Always. Then, when you get it done, it looks like you busted your ass to get done in a hurry."

"No, I've never heard of that," I said. "It wouldn't work with teaching English."

"No, I guess it wouldn't. Anyway, if Olaf can't get us a berth we'll be anchored out of Galveston for a day or two. Don't that sound fun?"

"But we could get a small boat in, right?"

"Not necessarily. First customs has to come on board, and them guys take their sweet time. Ah—" he waved a hand, dismissing me. "Whatever happens happens. We still get paid."

I went up the ladder feeling shell-shocked. I had one night to finish classes, pack all my stuff into the case I'd brought it in, get the imports ready for the customs officials, and take inventory of the various books, tapes, and recorders that were strewn across the ship.

More disturbingly, I had less than twenty-four hours to get used to the idea of saying good-bye.

Outside my stateroom, Wang was waiting, leaning against the bulkhead with a huge cardboard box between his knees.

"What's this?" I asked. Did I have to haul some unwanted thing somewhere when I got off the ship?

"Well, Ding told me you want the—what is the word? 'Vase?' The thing where he keeps pickle?"

"The urn! The stoneware urn? He's giving it to me?"

"Well, I am afraid not. It is not empty, so—not convenient to give. If you come back after some time, we can give. But Captain wants you to have this."

"Goodness. What is it?" I turned sideways to maneuver the cardboard box through the hatch and into my room. The container was about three feet high, maybe a foot across, but light. "Can I open it?"

"Yes! It is yours. Only one thing—" Wang's face thinned a little as he pursed his lips. "Maybe not tell Bally. Because Captain have only one."

"I understand." Secretly I was thrilled that, whatever the present, they'd chosen to give it to me. I untied the thin ribbon that held the cardboard together and pulled out balls of tissue paper. Underneath was a gorgeous Chinese vase, its delicate white china worked with pink butterflies and stems of pomegranates. It was a perfect mate to the one I had bought for myself, identical in shape and size but a different design. "Oh, it's beautiful," I said. "Please tell the captain I will always keep it and think of him."

"Well . . ." Wang shyly held his hand out to me. "It is small present, for very good teacher." We shook hands a little awkwardly, me trying to pump the warmth and gratitude I felt into his palm, him trying, probably, to avoid embarrassment at my touch.

That was a late night; besides saying the first round of good-byes, I had to finish taping my students and pack my belongings. I gave away all the books that I had bought with my own money and made a list of those that belonged to the company. I put Wang in charge of the company's tape recorders and books, thinking that he'd make a good librarian.

The next morning I woke to the sound of the anchor chain clanking and rattling down the metal chute. This was it: the last stop, the last time I would hear the engines die down and the sound of the waves taking over. I looked out at the grimy, American port buildings, their metal roofs baking in the yellow sun. We had anchored out too far for me to make out any people, but a few cars were visible, and I squinted, trying to spot my blue Honda, which Martin would be driving.

The heat made me sweat as soon as I stepped outside. On the forward deck, I leaned over the rail and strained my eyes in the Texas sunshine, regretting that I'd already packed my sunglasses. For greeting Martin, I had put on my best pants—light pedal pushers—and a fuchsia shirt I'd been saving in its dry-cleaning bag ever since the Portman Hotel.

Someone whistled; I turned. Barry and Cui were walking up to where I stood, nudging each other and giggling. "So you do have a figure," Barry said. "All these weeks of sweatshirts and jeans, we didn't know."

"Shush up," I said. I poked his ribs, and he raised his fists and danced around, feinting at me. "So the second thing you're going to do with Martin is put down your luggage, right?"

"The first thing Martin and I are going to do is go to a restaurant, I hope."

"Chinese food?"

"Sure. Of course."

Cui laughed. He leaned forward, shyly touching one fingertip to the cuff of my blouse. "It is pretty." He was blushing, but he seemed to be laughing at himself for being embarrassed.

"Thank you, Cui. That's a nice compliment."

"That is nice shirt."

The three of us hung around the bow for an hour or so, waiting for the pilot who would guide the *Explorer* to her berth. It felt like around a hundred degrees, but a milder breeze cooled us, and we were so giddy with the prospect of hitting land we could have put up with anything.

"There's only one problem," Barry said. "I can't take these guys to the bars right away. They can't get off yet. Their damn visas have to be processed or something."

I felt sorry for the men, because I knew how weary they were of ship life. They were probably more anxious about getting off in Galveston than I had been in Panama. "They can't even leave the ship?" I said. "Go into town?"

"No way. Olaf says he has to take all their visas to the embassy or something. I don't know—there was some screw-up in Shanghai. You know," he shrugged. "China."

Cui nodded seriously. "China."

I wished I were coming back, working on board during the operations, helping accustom the men to the new country. "Well, when they do get off I hope you'll give them a great time," I told Barry.

"Oh yeah. We're going to paint the town Red."

Barry's gloomy prophesy—that we'd be anchored off the Texas coast for days—proved untrue. A spanking blue and white customs boat motored toward us right after we'd set anchor. Dreading the arrival of customs officials, I'd made a list of all the goods I'd bought in China, along with their estimated value.

"You don't want to lie too much," Barry had tipped me off. "If they see you putting down fifty bucks for one of them rugs, they'll slap a fine on top of the import tax. A hefty fine."

I worried over the figures. I still had receipts for the carpets, but not for the dozens of knickknacks I'd picked up for gifts—jade figures, silk shirts, lacquered boxes. They hadn't added up to more than two hundred dollars, and I had no clue what individual items had cost.

My resulting written estimate was a mess. I made up some prices for the smaller objects, guessing as best I could. Then I wrote down the rugs' true value, because after all I had the receipts, and if I hid the receipts, the inspectors might assess the rugs at more than I'd paid for them. I'd heard that import taxes varied from time to time and place to place, and could run as high as fifty percent, which in this case would mean I'd owe the government some three hundred dollars I didn't have. I was afraid the officials would confiscate my goods when I couldn't pay, and then there'd be weeks of hassles and probably more fines, but I'd have to get the rugs back—one was for my mother.

Finally I took out all the gifts and souvenirs except the rugs and arranged them modestly on my tightly made bed. Let the inspectors challenge their worth if they wanted. The rugs I left rolled up in their paper sleeves, and left them beneath the bench in the storage box. I was hoping that when I lifted the lid to show them to the inspectors, the rugs wouldn't look so beautiful, and maybe I'd get away with lower taxes.

I was setting the padded seat back on top of the storage box when an unfamiliar American voice said, "U.S. customs inspection, ma'am." Two rounded men—one white and old, the other black and middle-aged—stood in the doorway. They wore pale blue uniforms and had ultra-short haircuts, like policemen. The older one spoke again. "Ma'am? We need to get into the room."

"Well, I think you're in." I unfolded my list of goods, preparing to read it aloud.

The older man glanced at the clothes and trinkets spread on my bed. "This all you got."

"No—" I coughed. Nervousness was constricting my throat. "No, I—under here." I stood up and indicated the bench. "I've got—"

"Ma'am." He shook his head, the bill of his peaked cap sliding over his eyes. "That wasn't a question. That's *all* you got. Under three hundred's not dutiable. That's all you got, right?"

Was it a trap? I stared at him.

His partner winked at me. "Welcome home."

As the tugboat towed us toward the pier, I still couldn't spot my car. There was a pickup truck on the street that ran by the water, a couple of forklifts, and a van, but no blue Honda. I felt let down. I'd given Martin Olaf's phone number, and Olaf should have been able to tell him when and where we'd be docking. My fantasies of a pier-side reunion faded as the ship angled into her berth.

It seemed ironic that I was so excited about seeing Martin, given that I had realized how fraternal my feelings for him were, but I was excited nonetheless. The bad news was that I wasn't dying to jump into bed with him again, as Barry was with his wife, but the good news was that I did want to see him and catch up. I *did* love him, and I *had* missed him, I thought, adamantly. There were going to be some very difficult discussions in the next weeks, but for the meantime, today was for celebration—yet he hadn't shown up!

Soon the lines were tied, and the rickety wooden gangplank again set in place, insecurely connecting us to land. Barry and I shuffled our suitcases down to the main deck. In the main passageway we ran into Olaf, the first on board. He looked tanned and rested, and he was the blondest person I'd seen in seven weeks. I felt like embracing him, but I restricted myself to a warm handshake. "Olaf! We had a great trip! I have tapes for you of them speaking English!"

"Do you? Very good!"

Barry leaned over me, slapping Olaf's back. "Good to see you, man. Glad you got us a berth."

"It wasn't easy." Olaf's blue eyes crinkled as he looked at us. "You look as if you've lost weight. How was the food?"

Barry and I groaned in unison and started telling Olaf about the cook's excesses. Mr. Ding, hearing his name from the galley, hobbled out to be introduced. "I am Mr. Ding!" he announced to Olaf. "Chief cook-ah!"

"Are you? Well, good for you!" Olaf's eyebrows shot up as he shook Mr. Ding's hand. "What's the matter with your leg?"

"Foot no good-ah! No walk-ah!"

Olaf leaned over to examine the dirty, flapping bandage. "We'd better get you to a decent doctor," he murmured. He stood up again and faced me. "You've done a good job with his English."

I didn't feel like mentioning right at that moment that Mr. Ding hadn't taken my classes.

The horrible Peter appeared in the doorway to the bar, just as Olaf and Barry went into the dayroom to start some paperwork. Peter went to follow them but I stopped him, reaching out my hand. "Yes, we had a terrific trip, thank you for asking."

Peter laughed—the first time I could remember him doing so— and shook my hand. "Well, you lasted," he said. "I have to congratulate you. We thought you'd be screaming to be taken off the ship halfway across the ocean."

"Of course not!" I said. More people came crowding into the passageway: the Chinese crew, Americans, and a few Norwegians. It sounded like the tower of Babel, and I felt for a minute how confused my students were going to be. But Mr. Ding was smiling, already hobbling into the bar with cans of Coke and bottles of beer clutched in his free arm. Zen followed, bearing a platter of grilled chicken.

Cui stood politely by the captain and the translator, waiting to begin work with the new boss. Cui would take over as captain in a few days, when Captain Tan flew home to take charge of another ship. Tan, well rewarded for the journey, would take letters and messages to the men's families. It seemed as if everything might be all right.

Stepping onto land felt like slamming into a wall. I nearly fell over, but spun my arms, staggering, and caught myself. I stood straddle-legged for several seconds, trying to get my balance.

Giggling came from above and behind me, where some of the men were watching from the deck. Having been to sea many times before, they knew to expect the change on dry land. I waved at them, feeling foolish, and took a tentative step. I had to swing my legs widely, because it seemed that the earth was tilting away at sharp angles.

I lurched to the company van, where one of Olaf's staff slumped in the driver's seat. "Howdy," he said, apparently not surprised to see an American woman staggering from a Chinese ship. Working for Olaf, he'd probably seen it all.

I asked if he'd noticed a little blue Honda in the parking area. "Nah," he said. "Got your husband in it?"

"Boyfriend," I explained. "At least, he was my boyfriend when I left."

"There's a phone back at the port gate. You want me to run you up there?"

I jumped into the passenger seat, and we chugged across about a mile of broken asphalt. I had forgotten how horrible Galveston was. The heated, humid air smelled foul, and the potholed road passed between a graffiti-smeared concrete wall and endless mud-colored warehouses. We jerked over a few chipped speed bumps, and then the driver stopped in front of a wooden barrier. "Phone's right over there," he said. "I can't get you any closer."

"Where?" All I could see was a jumble of junky-looking forklifts.

"There," he pointed. "By that Honda."

The car he was pointing to was mine. Martin was leaning on the wheel, staring out to sea at a tiny fishing boat that was coming in.

As I ran toward the car, Martin heard my footsteps and looked around. He smiled hugely, fumbling out of his seatbelt and getting out the door while I jumped up and down. In a second he was hugging me and laughing. "What are you doing here? I thought you were on that boat!"

"Our ship was a *little* bigger than that one," I said. "And slightly newer. Hi!" I pulled myself away from the hug to look at his face. There was the face of my dear friend, his smile making him look boyish and excited. His eyes behind the little round glasses had never looked so happy or so blue.

I took Martin all over the *Tan Suo Zhe,* which I could not get used to thinking of as the *Explorer,* and showed off the bridge, my stateroom and balcony, and the bar/classroom with its map and whiteboard. Everywhere we went, the Chinese men wanted to meet him; they shook his hand very properly and told him their names. The men called him "Mahtin-ah!" and patted his back. Martin was excellent, trying everyone's name and making them laugh with his pronunciation.

It felt like a party. Strangers were milling around the vessel, and no one seemed to be working. Olaf distributed mail and packages from China. "And what do you have for me?" I said, acting coy.

"Oh, yes!" From the interior pocket of his jacket he withdrew a check. No envelope, no stub, just a simple check made out for nearly six thousand dollars—the largest single amount I'd ever received.

"I shouldn't take this from you," I said, taking it. "Now that it's too late, I'll tell you, I would've done it for free."

Wang ran up to Martin and me in a passageway and issued a special invitation. "Ji Lian, the cook says is Chinese custom. Today is special day, farewell feast. He knows you do not have much time, but he make small dish for you and Mr. Martin-ah. He would like very much if you taste."

"Oh, great!" I said. "That's wonderful. Martin, you'll get to eat what I've been eating! Maybe he made grilled chicken, or some shrimp. Did he make shrimp, Wang?"

Wang's eyes narrowed, and he shook his head mysteriously. "Well, you might take a look."

In the galley, Martin and I were seated at a table by ourselves, but Wang stood by to watch as Ding brought out the special dish. It was a big pot, covered with a tight lid, trailing steam as he carried it to our table. To carry it, he made the special effort of hobbling without his cane. "Chief cook-ah say good-bye, and sank you, Teach-ah." He lifted the lid with a flourish to reveal the contents. Inside was a tangle of steaming orange chicken feet.

"My God!" Martin's face froze, and then went into a terrible, fake smile. So Ding wouldn't notice, I clapped my hands, making a show of delight.

Wang smiled, inhaling the odor of the steam. "Chief cook tells me it is a special dish—you asked for it after you save him, in Panama."

"I did?" Had I said something about him being the best chicken-foot cook in town? "Well, tell him we are very pleased. And Martin, we get to have these all to ourselves."

Using my chopsticks, I scooped out a few claws for Martin and myself. Martin closed his eyes, then opened them again to watch me. I picked up a foot and bit into the fleshiest part. "Yum, yum," I said loudly. To the cook's credit, he had done something completely different with claws this time. The spices were less like tar, more like salt and vinegar. If I ignored the gristly, fatty textures underneath my tongue, and tried not to breathe through my nose, I could keep the nausea under control.

Mr. Ding hovered over us. "Good-ah? No good-ah?"

"Great," I said. In very fast English, I told Martin he should eat at least one for appearance's sake.

"Darling," he whispered. "I can't."

"Just pick it up," I muttered.

He took a claw into his right hand, and grimaced at it. He looked as if he might throw up.

"Mr. Ding!" I said. "Could we have some Cokes?"

"Yes, yes." He scuttled away into the galley. I glanced around—the only other men in the room were settling down to a card game, not looking at us. I opened the porthole. Then, pretending to fiddle with the latch, I dropped my chicken foot outside.

"No good-ah!" yelled Mr. Ding from the galley.

"Oh, darn." I tried to think of an explanation for my jettisoned food—I'd say it was an accident. Mr. Ding went hurtling by, practically vaulting on his broom-handle, and I was afraid he was going to lean over the side and try to retrieve the foot I'd dropped. But he hadn't noticed. "No Coke-ah!" he complained. "No Coke-ah in fridge . . ." He disappeared into the passageway, limping along on his cane as fast as he could go. He was headed down the ladder to the storeroom, so we had a few seconds. "Watch behind me!" I told Martin. "Make sure no one's looking."

Gazing over my shoulder, he muttered, "Coast's clear." I shoveled a handful of chicken feet out the window.

At the same time, somewhat distracted, Martin took a bite of one of the claws. He chewed it thoughtfully for a while. "I'm hungry," he said. "This isn't too bad."

"It's pretty hard to get used to," I said. "But made with love. Do you think you could eat a couple?"

Martin nodded. I hurled a few more feet through the porthole, praying that none would land on the walkway outside. As Ding came back in I clapped the lid back on the dish. "Very good!" I said, and Martin copied me. "Delicious!"

"Some more?" Mr. Ding set two cans of Coke on the table. "Make-ah more. Chick feet good-ah."

"That's okay!" I said. "Maybe some rice?"

Delighted, he hobbled back into the kitchen. Martin and I rinsed our mouths with Coke, and waited till Ding returned to hold the chicken feet up to our lips. "Great!" I said. "Thank you so much! Good cook!"

"Yes!" Martin said, nibbling a toe. "And now, maybe I need some chopsticks!"

"*Kui-zi,*" I translated. "Please may we have some?" Mr. Ding nodded, and again turned his back, looking through a drawer for chopsticks.

I felt bad about asking Ding to run around and wait on us, but while he wasn't looking, we got rid of two more feet out the porthole. By the time Mr. Ding had brought us more vinegar, garlic, and some vegetables, we'd got enough stuff to dilute the chicken. We actually consumed a couple of feet each, and then the bowl was pretty much empty. I groaned and patted my stomach, pretending to be terribly full. "No more!" I said.

"Little bit," said Ding, happily. Wang came through the doorway carrying his dictionary, and Mr. Ding stopped him to brag how much we'd eaten.

"Please tell him thank you, this is Martin's first real Chinese meal," I said. Wang translated and Mr. Ding nodded excitedly.

"Tell him," Martin said, "that it was a meal I will never forget."

244

Lin, the chief mate, Fang, and his mechanics all helped carry my luggage and boxes to the gangway, but beyond that they were forbidden by law to go. It felt odd and unfair that I was allowed to step off but they were not.

Martin had parked a little way off from the vessel. We stacked my cases in the trunk and stowed the two vases carefully on a blanket in the back seat. Leaving Martin in the car, I walked back to the ship to say a last good-bye. The men were all watching me prepare to go home. Excited as I was, I felt very sad.

The last picture I took of the *Tan Suo Zhe* was of the men hanging over the guardrail to wave. It was odd, I thought, how many times I had stood there with them, looking down at the Chinese going-away celebration, looking down at the dolphins and the trash, looking down at the canal, looking down and down at the endless swirling water as we passed over the biggest ocean in the world. Now they, the ones I was leaving, were looking down at me, too, as I passed out of their lives.

Not everyone was there—the captain, for instance, was busy inside, as was Wang, and I had said good-bye to them already. But most of the people I cared about had come to see me off. Cui was there, waving solemnly, probably already thinking about his new responsibilities as captain. Tsu stood and flapped his hand at me, his smile spreading across his cheeks, broadening his pug nose. He'd enjoyed meeting Martin, to whom he'd made all my telephone connections.

Mr. Ding looked a little blue, resting his bad foot on the railing, but he smiled when he called to me, something about bringing Martin back to eat again. "Chinese food!" he said. "Kung Pao chick-ah! Good-ah!" I knew Olaf would get Mr. Ding to a doctor soon, and I was grateful.

The chief mate leaned far forward on the rail, beaming down at me. I hoped Barry would take him out on the town, to see the bars and meet some other Americans. Perhaps, as Barry had predicted, he'd meet some women who would appreciate his fine figure.

Finally I looked for and found Zhao, his intelligent, beautiful face following me, smiling shyly as he waved good-bye. I thought of his wife, how she must miss him, as he did her and his daughter. I had seen him say good-bye to them when we left Shanghai, and now he was watching me prepare to leave with my boyfriend. I thought how I'd miss him, how our lives and worlds had touched for a while but now would move apart, inevitably. Across the water that divided us, I looked him full in the face for longer than I had ever done before, memorizing his features. His high cheekbones, his shapely smile, and the dark eyes no longer looked foreign to me; they looked, simply, like the face of a friend.